THE BOY FROM BARADINE

Craig Emerson is an eminent economist, and holds a doctorate from the Australian National University. He was economic and environmental adviser to prime minister Bob Hawke, and a minister in the Rudd and Gillard governments, where he held the portfolios of trade, tertiary education, competition policy, small business, and minister assisting the prime minister on Asian Century policy. Before entering parliament, he was director-general of the Queensland environment department, and, at the age of 23, the youngest economic analyst at the United Nations in Bangkok. He has published extensively in economic journals and on newspaper opinion pages, and is now the managing director of his own economic consultancy, Craig Emerson Economics.

THE BOY
FROM BARADINE

CRAIG EMERSON

SCRIBE

Melbourne • London

Scribe Publications
18–20 Edward St, Brunswick, Victoria 3056, Australia
2 John St, Clerkenwell, London, WC1N 2ES, United Kingdom

First published by Scribe 2018

Typeset in 11.5/15pt Adobe Caslon by the publishers

Printed and bound in Australia by Griffin Press

The paper this book is printed on is certified against the Forest Stewardship Council® Standards. Griffin Press holds FSC chain of custody certification SGS-COC-005088. FSC promotes environmentally responsible, socially beneficial and economically viable management
of the world's forests.

ISBN 9781925322590 (Australian edition)
ISBN 9781925548877 (e-book)

A CiP entry for this title is available from the National Library of Australia

scribepublications.com.au
scribepublications.co.uk

To Ben, Tom, and Laura, our three miracles

CONTENTS

1

Mother, rows, and refuges

'Pud! Pud!' My father's anxious cry reached through the rustling of the gum leaves into my dreams from the top of the far creek bank. As I lay on the underfelt we had used to make the second floor of our tree house homely, I was jarred from my sleep, knowing something terrible had happened to bring Dad three kilometres out of town in the dead of night.

'What?' I bellowed back, startled by the emergency, but angry at the reason I'd had to sleep away from our house, perched high in the sprawling gum tree. As dark clouds raced past the luminous moon, the tree house was a scary refuge for a 15-year-old, but safer than the torment of life at home.

'Mum's tried to knock herself off!' Dad shouted, the wind and the rustling of the leaves muffling his words. 'They've taken her to the hospital and they're pumping her stomach out. You'd better come.'

As a self-conscious adolescent, I had to contemplate, yet again, the prospect of my mother dying from an overdose of sleeping pills. My reservoir of concern for her wellbeing had long been depleted. I thought only of the embarrassment, in such a small country town as Baradine, of being a kid whose mother had killed herself. Servicing wheat farms and forestry operations in the Pilliga Scrub of north-west New South Wales, Baradine was a rumour mill, like any other small country town. Gossip spread faster than the summer bushfires.

Our little town, populated by 900 hardy people in 1970, derived its name from local Aboriginal people who had reportedly told the

European settlers who proclaimed it a village in 1865 that Baradine was their word for red wallaby. Near Coonabarabran, not too far from Narrabri, but a hefty 530 kilometres from Sydney, Baradine was dead flat, its streets criss-crossing the sandy soil favoured by the cypress-pine trees that offered so many of the townspeople a living.

Most houses were built of fibro, their corrugated-iron roofs searing hot in summer, but providing a wonderfully deafening receptacle for the unreliable rains when they intermittently relieved the anxieties of the local wheat and sheep farmers. We could smell the rains on their descent through the crackling heat, well before hearing them crash onto the roofs. In the depths of winter, the water pipes froze and our toes ached with the cold until we did a mid-morning gallop around the school grounds during play-lunch time.

In its heyday, Baradine was serviced by the Mudgee Mail passenger railway from Sydney, terminating at the even smaller town of Gwabegar in the heart of the Pilliga Scrub, which is the largest area of continuous forest west of the Great Dividing Range, and was once the location of a dozen sawmills that, like the rail service, are now closed.

Baradine had a doctor's surgery, a bank, two cafés, two general stores, two barbers, two butchers, two churches, and five licensed premises. As in most country towns, Baradine's spirit resided in the Memorial Hall, a place of gathering for school assemblies and award nights, dances, and, above all, remembrance of the town's residents and nearby farmers who had enlisted for war, one of whom was my father.

Along the town's edge flowed the Baradine Creek from time to time. Mostly it was a series of waterholes, sometimes a trickle, and occasionally a raging torrent when the storm clouds burst over the Warrumbungle Mountains. It was those torrents that carved a gully a couple of hundred metres wide, home to silky oaks and the occasional eucalypt.

Building the three-storey tree house on the banks of Baradine Creek had been a marvellous adventure. Three friends — Bryn 'Bimbo' Kelly, Russell 'Rusty' Patterson, and Stan 'The Man' Forrest — had the idea, walking along the creek way past the town in search of a suitable tree.

Near the long-closed aerodrome, they came upon a sprawling eucalyptus tree, its trunk dividing into three strong branches that formed a cradle into which a tree house could nestle.

Bryn excelled in woodwork at school and, a year older than us, had already begun growing facial hair. Dubbed 'The Bearded Carpenter', Bryn cut down nearby cypress-pine trees and, with Rusty, sawed them into beams that became the frame of the tree house. By the time they had invited me to join them, they had erected beams for the three storeys and begun adding cypress-pine walls and floors. They had also built the basic structure of a 50-metre bridge across the creek. My job was to finish the walls, add the footway of the bridge, and build a freestanding toilet.

We couldn't afford to buy the floorboards, so I salvaged the offcuts that were left out for burning at the sawmill operating midway between the tree house and the town. These I strapped onto my billy cart, which I pulled from the sawmill to the tree house.

After months of labouring, we had a completed tree house. On the first-floor landing at the top of the ladder from the ground, I installed a shower. Having added guttering around the third-floor corrugated-iron roof, as well as plumbing from a drum I brought from town to catch and store rainwater, we had an acceptable source of shower water.

A second ladder led through a trapdoor into the middle floor, which I covered with green underfelt that I had scrounged from a disused shop near the main street. On this second floor we had built a window, enabling a clear view of the opposite bank and the bridge across the creek. Extending from this floor was a balcony looking out along the creek. Stairs from the second floor led to the top floor, a large area in which I installed a kerosene stove I had purchased from the department store, Permewans, where Dad worked as hardware department manager.

The whole town had come to know of this great enterprise. Mates slept at the tree house with us. I shot and cooked a topknot pigeon on the kerosene stove. I learned the folly of crawling out along a branch with a broomstick to dislodge a wasps' nest; wasps fly much faster than boys crawl backwards.

Having completed the walls of the pit toilet, I brought over our Victa lawnmower to cut through the long grass. I listened on my new transistor radio to Neil Diamond singing 'Sweet Caroline', Ronnie Burns singing 'Smiley', which was about the Vietnam War to which some of the older boys in Baradine had been conscripted, to Blue Mink calling for racial harmony in a global 'Melting Pot', to the Hollies assuring us 'He Ain't Heavy, He's My Brother', and to a wild heavy-metal band called Led Zeppelin blasting out a 'Whole Lotta Love'. Simon and Garfunkel had built 'A Bridge Over Troubled Water', and so, it felt, had I—to escape the trouble in our fibro house.

DAD WAS CONSIDERED HANDSOME, his curly greying hair, kind facial lines, and well-proportioned build affording him a distinguished look. He may have been the originator of Dad jokes, though many were bawdy, for his smile lines dominated the sadder, defeated features of his face born of his frustration that he'd failed to realise his potential as a highly intelligent man. Dad had appeared on a radio quiz show, powering through the questions, until he was stumped when asked for the word describing the opposite of zenith. Grappling with Mum's mood swings, he would often have experienced his personal nadir.

For as long as I could remember, Dad called me 'Pud', 'Pudden', or 'Puddenhead', for I was a chubby baby. Later, as I grew into a skinny child, he added to his repertoire both 'Muscles' and 'Mussiguts', but more often reverted to 'Pud'.

When times were good and the house was peaceful, Dad and Mum sat with me as a nine-year-old in front of the television on Sunday evenings watching a quiz show called the Quiz Kids. As these bright young city kids rattled off the answers to rapid-fire questions, Dad and Mum joined in, competing with each other and encouraging me to contribute whenever I could.

On a memorable occasion, the compere had stumped the room with a question: 'Why is the Frigate Bird so named?' As the students hesitated, I confidently proffered the answer: 'Because it's a friggin' nuisance!' Mum and Dad collapsed in laughter, tears rolling down their cheeks, admonishing me never to use that word again. It was only then that I deduced what 'frig' meant.

Mum was a dark woman in many ways. Of Celtic heritage, she

retained her strong Welsh accent and temper. Photographs of her as a teenager and into her early twenties confirm she had been a stunningly beautiful young woman. But she adopted her mother's habit and became a chain smoker. Smoking took a heavy physical toll on Mum. Each morning she woke with a hacking cough, trying to bring up the phlegm that had settled overnight in her damaged lungs. Her face was heavily lined. Before we finished a meal, Mum resumed smoking at the dining table. In most rooms were full ashtrays, often bearing a burning cigarette. In her later years, Mum's body shrank to a fraction of its natural size as emphysema tightened its grip on her breathing. Her eyes were blackened with ill health.

Mum's father died when she was twelve years of age. He was a pharmacist and a disciplined Anglican churchman. Mum didn't know him very well. She was forced to view his body, his ashen face, his waxed moustache, as he lay in his coffin. This awful image in a darkened room became the subject of Mum's recurring nightmares. She spent her adult life halfway around the world, far from her mother and the green valleys of Wales, in the dry heat of Baradine.

Ours was a small, yellow-painted fibro house. Dad had planted roses along the garden path connecting the house and the front fence. On the nature strip grew four kurrajong trees, one large enough to conceal me when hiding from my brother, Lance, who was four years my elder. On the opposite side of the street was the local tennis court where, on warmer nights, we could hear from our bedroom the 'thock, thock, thock' of rallies under lights and the laughter of parents enjoying a social hit-out. Mum and Dad, both 100-yard sprint champions in their younger days, never joined them.

Alongside the tennis courts lay a well-trodden dirt path leading to the main street. Once every couple of years, the roar of a café or general store on fire, lighting up the night, terrified all the kids in the neighbourhood. 'An insurance job', a grown-up would pronounce. We didn't know what 'an insurance job' was, but we feared there was every chance that all the shops in the main street would catch fire. Parents hosed their houses to prevent embers lodging in the corrugated-iron roof guttering. Dogs barked and kids cried.

While our house was small, it was neat and well presented; the lawns were regularly mown and watered with town bore water, offering the struggling grass some resilience against the relentless summer heat. To the outside world, it was a modest and peaceful home; inside, it was the scene of random acts of violence.

OPNLY LATER IN LIFE could Lance and I speculate as to why Dad was so unwilling to intervene to protect us from Mum's violence. Lance blamed Dad, but I wasn't so sure. As a child, he had most of his self-confidence beaten out of him. Spending several years as a prisoner of war in Italy and Germany didn't help him regain it. Dad described his mother in a short note he wrote as 'a clever, beautiful woman, always neat and clean who showed me all the love she could through her eyes — for she was deaf and mute and highly emotional'. At five years of age, he could converse with her by signing with his fingers. He said his reading of sign language was very slow, but his 'lovely mother taught me to smile and think, to be cheerful and to wonder'. He wrote that she sheltered and protected him because she needed him so much.

Dad's father was a cruel man, a policeman at Cabramatta in Sydney's west. Dad was shy and introverted. His father reserved for him special punishment, hitting him with his belt, buckle-end first. Dad's father dispatched him to Yanco Agricultural College near Leeton in southern New South Wales where, as a boarder, he received a good education. But Dad was not welcome at home for Christmas. Those were the Depression years, and Dad's father could not provide for all four children. All his fellow boarders would return to their families, and Dad would be left to spend the holiday period with the curator at Yanco.

After gaining his leaving certificate, Dad found work after the Depression at Gwabegar as a timber cutter. At the outbreak of the Second World War, like so many timber workers and farmers around the Pilliga Scrub, Dad volunteered, joining the army's 2/3rd battalion. They fought the Italians in North Africa at Bardia and Tobruk before unsuccessfully attempting to halt the German advance in Greece. Dad and a small group of comrades were evacuated to Crete, where he was shot through his left calf but escaped capture. After days on the run, he had to cut his boot off his swollen foot, but was able to make it to a hospital, where the staff concealed him from the Germans for six months.

A Greek Cypriot hospital worker who learned of his true identity told the Germans, who captured him and transferred him to a prisoner-of-war camp in Italy. When Italy capitulated in September 1943, the Italian guards told the prisoners they were to be freed. Instead, they were guarded with machine guns until the Germans arrived, when they were loaded onto railway trucks and transported to Stalag VIIIC near the small town of Klettendorf, then in Germany but since returned to Poland.

Dad didn't complain about his treatment at the hands of the Germans. Most days, the Allied prisoners were taken to a local sugar-beet factory to work, and were permitted to walk freely around the town. Two Americans escaped from the camp, but gave themselves up after five days, succumbing to the cold and snow. The Allied prisoners of war were actually paid a meagre wage for their work, in accordance with an international convention. At one time, they even staged a strike in pursuit of a claim for higher wages. The true hardship would have been not knowing whether they would live to gain their freedom and return to family and friends in Australia.

Dad kept a diary, concealed in the lining of his great coat. In it, he recorded that he gave a Russian girl 'a piece of chocolate today, and, as I looked at her and her companions, I realised for what we are fighting. Many of them are without boots with feet cracked and bleeding but still forced to work.'

Dad described life in the camp as miserable:

In an adjoining room I saw an American who was suffering with the worst case of frostbite I have ever seen. Both feet, from the toes to the insteps were absolutely black, but normal in size. From the insteps to the shins they were swollen like legs of pickled mutton from which the puss and blood dripped slowly. The smell was horrible. The blackened parts of the feet were hanging off. I learned that such must be the case with frostbite. The affected part must be allowed to take its course and drop off naturally before any surgical operation can be attempted, otherwise the line of demarcation caused by the frost continues to rise above the amputation and the patient is no better off.

During Dad's time as a POW, he became a pen pal with a Welsh nurse, Margery Lloyd Griffiths, who was working in a London military hospital and who would become our mother. The British nurses wrote letters addressed 'Dear POW.' It was a matter of chance as to whom, if anyone, received the item of mail. Someone at Stalag VIIIC handed Australian prisoner Ernest Victor Emerson the Welsh nurse's letter. Dad soon began writing her poetry.

When a world war is over, there is no plan. Dad wrote:

None of us knew where to go in the mayhem that followed the war's official end. We met German soldiers nine days later and asked for food and directions. They gave us both. We walked into Czechoslovakia with Germans who were terrified of the Russians. The Russians had proved just as brutal as the SS were during the Russian occupation in the early years of war. Civilians were shot, throats of women and children were cut, the women suffering so after being raped. The Germans still did not want to leave us until we were further behind the Americans' lines.

Eventually, Dad and his comrades were transported to Nuremberg aerodrome. 'I was up in a plane for the first time. It was a grand feeling. We flew to Belgium and then onto Dunfold aerodrome in England where we received tea and cakes and one pound sterling.'

Three weeks after the war's end, the ex-POW and the Welsh nurse married in Wales. Dad set off ahead of Mum for Australia, aboard one of the returning troop ships. As they disembarked at Sydney Harbour to be reunited with ecstatic loved ones, the clerks called out their names. 'Emerson', they announced. Dad moved forward. 'Emerson, H', the clerk clarified. A Harry Emerson, unrelated to Dad, came forward, to be greeted by his wife, Barbara. The call of 'Emerson, E' never came.

Harry and Barbara invited Dad to stay at their house in the suburb of Strathfield. After six years at war, no one greeted Dad upon his return to Australia, not even his father from nearby Cabramatta. Dad's brother, Allan, spent most of his adult life in a mental asylum, and one of his two sisters took her own life. Dad's other sister, May, remarked to my cousin, Mary, how Dad's father reserved special punishment for him. 'Poor little Ernie, poor little bugger', May lamented.

After the war, Dad brought Mum to the tiny timber village of Milliwindi on the road between Baradine and Gwabegar, where he thought he was to become a part owner of the local sawmill. Instead, he was employed as a labourer. Mum gave birth to Lance in 1950, and, pregnant again in 1954, moved to Baradine with Dad and Lance to bring me into the world and become townspeople. Like the sawmill, the town of Milliwindi no longer exists.

One day, Dad's father turned up unannounced on the nature strip of our house, far from his own home in Sydney. Lance and I joined Dad, walking up the garden path to meet our grandfather for the first time. Dad introduced us to his father, George, and then told him to get off the lawn. Dad turned his back on George, and we never saw our grandfather again. Nor did Dad. Yet many years later, Dad wrote empathetically of his father: 'My old dad, with four kids to bring up on a public servant's salary, tried to solve his problem by putting me at Yanco Agricultural High School, which in those Depression days carried the smallest charges.'

Compared with the fathers of my classmates, Dad was older, his enlistment at age 24 and the passage of time during the war years deferring his fatherhood, in my case until he reached the age of 39. As such, Dad was never really one of the boys who typically went on fishing and drinking trips to the Namoi River to catch freshwater cod better known as yellow bellies.

As Lance, tears dripping from his nose, remarked to me many years later, Dad began dying in his 40s. Dad often said to us that he wouldn't be around for much longer. By now robbed of all self-confidence, this beautiful writer, a shy and intelligent man, was defeated and exhausted by the constant fights with Mum, coupled with his own sense of under-achievement.

ON THAT SHADOWY, FRIGHTENING NIGHT at the tree house, I scrambled down the ladder and groped my way across the creek bed to my sad, disconsolate father. We drove to Baradine District Hospital, where the nurses advised us that Mum had been transferred, unconscious, to Coonabarabran Base Hospital, 45 kilometres away.

Mum's overdose was the unsurprising culmination of a row that had been going on all weekend. As always, its cause was not obvious. Any minor event could have set it off. Whatever the spark for this latest blue, Mum had gone into the bedroom, advising me she was going to knock herself off. After a few hours of fretting, I prised open the sliding bedroom door, against whose edge she'd moved a dressing table, to find she wasn't there.

As usual, Mum had pulled the venetian blinds closed to block out the daylight, but the afternoon sun that seeped through, defying her efforts, provided enough light for me to scan the room. I could make out the polished wardrobe on the far side of the bed and, next to it, the mirrored dressing table adorned with the cut-glass ornaments we'd given Mum over the years for Mother's Day and her birthday. Having checked the small spaces between the furniture, I was flummoxed: Mum had locked the bedroom door from the inside, but she was gone.

As a final thought, I kneeled on the floor to check the only remaining space — under the bed. Mum laughed, embarrassed at my discovery, and I laughed, too, momentarily allowing myself the emotional relief that we might be able to end the weekend farce with shared humour. But before I could entertain that hope, Mum shouted: 'Get out! Get out! This time I'm going to knock myself off. I'll take the whole bottle of pills!'

Distraught that my distress would be ongoing, I screamed: 'Go on! Do it! I don't care any more', and headed tearfully for the sanity of the tree house, knowing I might never again see Mum alive.

There we were, in the middle of the night, being told to go home, get some sleep, and drive to Coonabarabran the next day when notified by the doctors. From this, I concluded that Mum had lived, her latest suicide attempt would be the talk of the town, and nothing would change. I was right; it never did.

2

Behind closed doors

In our early years, while the other kids were out playing, weekends for Lance and me consisted of buying the order of meat from the butchers on Saturday, building a fire under the copper in the laundry to boil the water by the time Mum got home from work after midday, doing the washing with her in the afternoon, and cleaning the house on Sunday morning after Mass. Usually, we finished the house cleaning around 2.00pm, leaving us a few hours on Sunday afternoon to play before returning to school on Monday morning. Many weekends, a row erupted and raged, leaving no time to play at all.

One day, for no obvious reason, Mum ordered Lance and me to the garden bed adjacent to the back of the house. Maybe she was unhappy with our housework. Maybe she found dust or dirt at the back of the lounge-room furniture. It wouldn't have been hard; Baradine is a dusty town, especially when the westerly winds blow in from the outback, which is most of the time. As much as we dusted and polished Mum's ceramic and cut-glass ornaments, and swept and vacuumed the floors, the dust just alighted and resettled when we were done. Mum instructed both of us to gather a handful of dirt and eat it. I started crying. Mum wouldn't relent. 'Eat it!' she shouted. So I put the handful of dirt in my mouth and ate it. Lance did the same. He didn't cry; he just got angrier. He was always angry.

When Mum went back inside, I ran into the next-door neighbours' yard, spitting out as much of the dirt as I could. Joy Meyers, mother to my best friend, Kimmy, rushed out of the house to find out what the hullabaloo was all about. Joy was a kind woman. She worked at the local pharmacy, better known as Dicky Burt's Chemist Shop. Joy's husband, Ken ('Creamy') Meyers, was a timber cutter who from time to time took Lance, Kimmy, and me camping into the Pilliga Scrub, where we watched the draught horses pull hewn Ironbark and cypress-pine trees, stripped of their branches, onto lorries for transportation to one of the local sawmills.

When I told Joy that Mum had made me eat dirt, she walked to the main street and bought me two musk sticks, a type of pink candy, to remove the taste of the dirt. It was a very kind gesture. Joy threatened Mum that she would 'put the welfare' onto her. 'The welfare' was the children services department, such as it was in country New South Wales in the mid-1960s. Mum immediately befriended Joy, explaining what terrible kids Lance and I were, and that she had been forced into harsh punishment because nothing else worked to bring us into line. Joy found Mum persuasive, often describing us as 'buggers of kids'. To this day, I do not know what prompted Mum to make us eat dirt. It was no big deal. It didn't taste too good, but nor did it make me sick. It just seemed strange punishment for unspecified misbehaviour.

THOUGH MUCH BIGGER AND OLDER than me, Lance was small and short for his age. Rugby league teams at school were graded according to weight rather than age, forcing Lance to play in teams full of much younger kids. He found this to be humiliating, so didn't play much footy, which was sufficient reason for him to be treated as something of an outsider. Learning piano through his school years hardly endeared him to the tough kids of his class, and he endured a fair bit of bullying.

Like Mum, he had a fiery temper, prone to rages if I didn't behave in accordance with his wishes. Lance, too, became a chronic smoker. In adulthood, his forehead was lined with worry and despondency. He married three times and entered into several serious relationships, but none lasted. The loss of his only son, Joshua, through cot death seemed to define in Lance's mind his destiny for unhappiness on earth. Lance candidly and courageously confided in me that if he'd had surviving children it was likely that he would have been a violent father, so incapable was he of controlling the rage within him from his childhood.

On a hot summer's Saturday, when I was ten years old, Lance and I decided to give Mum and Dad a treat, using the shopping money to buy some devon, corned beef, tomatoes, cucumber, and lettuce for a cold meat and salad lunch. Holding up one edge of the meat tray in the fridge on the back veranda was a can of beetroot in place of a small metal post that had long been lost. Excited about our careful arrangement of food on the plates, I removed the can of beetroot from the fridge and added a couple of slices to each plate to make the display even more colourful.

Mum and Dad arrived home from work, and we kids proudly took them into the kitchen to show them our surprise. Our cool lunch was ready for the family to sit down and enjoy. Dad complimented and thanked us. Mum looked at the arrangements, noted the beetroot, and asked where we got it. She went to the fridge to observe that the meat tray was hanging, unsupported, at one edge. Mum returned to the kitchen, raised each plate above her head, and smashed it to the floor. She ordered Lance and me to clean up the mess, and locked herself in the bedroom for the weekend.

IN BARADINE'S CENTENNIAL YEAR, 1965, Dad was a patient at the Concord Repatriation Hospital in Sydney, having surgery on his painful varicose veins. Before being admitted to hospital, Dad built a rickshaw for Kimmy Meyers and me to use in the Baradine Centenary Parade.

Kimmy was a stockily built, blonde-haired boy, my age but much bigger and stronger. He loved playing Cowboys and Indians. He must have watched every television episode of *Gunsmoke*, *Laramie*, *The Lone Ranger*, *Davey Crockett*, *Daniel Boone*, *Wagon Train*, *Rawhide*, and *Bonanza*, and every John Wayne western ever made.

We built campfires, learning from experience not to throw pieces of fibro onto them, for they would explode when they reached critical heat. We chopped off eucalyptus-tree branches with our tomahawks to fuel the campfires, and I ruefully acquiesced to Kimmy's unrelenting demands that we play 'tyin's up'. Kimmy had learned all the knots used by the frontiersmen and the cowboys who tied up the lucky Indians they had decided not to shoot as they attacked the wagon trains. He put them to good use. If he tied me to a chair, I was obliged to wait for him to free me, which could result in my complete immobilisation for up to two hours. It would have been longer had I not threatened never to play 'tyin's up' again. My pathetic return effort was a double knot from which Kimmy could free himself within a couple of minutes, probably seconds. Kimmy packed a devastating straight right, so we played 'tyin's up' many more times than I ever cared to do.

But on the occasion of Baradine's Centenary celebration, Kimmy was not a Cowboy and I was not an Indian. All the kids dressed up, parading around Baradine's football oval before their parents assembled in the grandstand. Kimmy was decked out as a Chinese coolie and I as a pipe-smoking English explorer beneath a safari hat. Kimmy and I won a prize. Mum didn't come to the parade. Lance and I went home to encourage her to come out. Instead, she closed the two sliding doors into our bedroom, pushed chests of drawers against the door ends so that we couldn't open them, and advised us that she had a full bottle of sleeping pills with her and was going to kill herself. We paced the house into the night, fearful that our mother might die while our father was in Sydney, as the music and laughter of the townspeople wafted through the air to our dismal ears.

Yet, at other times, Mum seemed to be in the most joyous of moods, in full voice singing Judy Garland's 'Somewhere over the rainbow blue birds fly … They fly over the rainbow, why then oh why can't I?' Perhaps this Welsh woman, stuck halfway around the world from her mother and her homeland in a small, hot Australian bush town, yearned to fly over the rainbow to return to a happier life.

LANCE COPPED IT WORSE than I did, but after he left for Hurlstone Agricultural College south-west of Sydney in 1967, when I was twelve years old, I endured the conflict in our house and Mum's suicide attempts alone. By that time, Lance had been lifted off the ground by his hair, ordered to shoot his cat, kept back from school so often that he failed arithmetic—the first class of the day—while topping all other subjects, and made to miss the school bus to the regional athletics carnivals for failing to whiten his sandshoes correctly.

For understandable reasons, Lance had become a very violent brother. He would unexpectedly punch me in the stomach, taking the wind out of me, and, as I struggled for air, hold me down, the palm of his hand across my mouth, and his thumb and index finger squeezing my nostrils to prevent me from breathing. If I cried when he eventually released his hand, he reapplied it until I panicked, struggling for breath, but did not cry. But I wouldn't accept a word of criticism about Lance from the other kids in the town. I knew what he'd been through at home.

After one of Mum's suicide attempts, we received good news from the doctors at Coonabarabran Hospital, where she had again been taken. They suggested that Mum's depression might be caused by her thyroid gland producing insufficient iodine, making her tired and irritable. Lance and I were overjoyed. It wasn't her fault after all, we thought. She loved us, but couldn't help being so angry. But if she was prescribed iodine tablets, she never took them; or, if she did, they didn't work. Mum's moodiness remained as before.

Mum hit me with a feather duster so often that it eventually split and splintered along the length of its cane handle. Finally, she realised she had a problem when, now a teenager, I walked past her in the kitchen. Nothing seemed awry. Mum wasn't even complaining about me. But she picked up the feather duster and laid into me, cutting and bruising my arms, and causing a large lump to form on my elbow as I tried to defend myself. 'What have I done wrong?' I demanded. 'Oh, Ern! I've just hit Pud for nothing!' she said in shock.

It hurt, but not as much as earlier attacks: while I was indignant about being struck without reason, I also felt vindicated. This incident was just the natural extension of countless episodes over many years. Mum had now abandoned any effort at a flimsy pretext, exposing her inclination to strike out at me with no provocation.

From that day, the physical violence against me stopped. But the emotional trauma continued. At the age of fifteen, I had been selected to play rugby league for the Baradine Juniors under-18s team. My unique running style earned me the nickname of Emu, from the recently released John Williamson song, 'Old Man Emu'. Kimmy Meyers still calls me Emu. As an Emu, my rightful place in the team was on the wing, notwithstanding that Williamson had observed of Old Man Emu that: 'He had a beak and feathers and things, but the poor old fella ain't got no wings.'

Game day was Sunday, and whether it was because Mum had determined that I hadn't polished my boots to her satisfaction, or that the housework hadn't been completed, she held me back from joining my teammates in the dressing sheds in preparation for the game. By the time she let me go, I was a bundle of nerves, my confidence shot. When our outside centre and best player, Tony Lane, threw me a pass as I ran down the sideline, I mostly dropped the ball. I could see the ball coming towards me. *Don't drop it*, I told myself. *You can't afford to drop it.* By the time the ball reached me, my teammates and the spectators looking on with anticipation, I snatched at the ball, fumbling the simplest of passes. As the ball spilled to the ground, I could hear the groans from the grandstand. The referee blew the whistle for a knock-on, and the forwards, bigger and older than me, trudged over for the toil of another scrum caused by my error. I was humiliated, having let my teammates down yet again.

Eventually, when one of our players, Davey Head, returned from injury, I was relegated to the reserves bench. The Baradine Magpies Juniors went on to make the semi-finals. One of our forwards got injured and was looking like coming from the field. Our coach turned to this skinny 15-year-old and said: 'Emu, I might have to put you on in the forwards.' He'd assumed I'd be frightened up against the older, bigger players, but I loved tackling, thanks to the tuition of the nuns at our convent school. As it happened, our injured forward struggled on, and I did not take the field again for the Baradine Juniors. When the black-and-white Baradine Magpies jerseys were handed out at the end of the season, we were one short, and there was none for me. In the team photo, I am seen hiding behind a larger teammate, only my head in the shot, to conceal my lack of a jersey.

TRAINING FOR THE JUNIORS was on Friday nights. Dad finished work at Permewans around 5.00pm. Mum was now working as a barmaid at one of the two pubs, finishing at 9.00pm. After work, Dad would walk from Permewans to the RSL Club to drink beer. I'd plead with him to be home ahead of Mum to avert a weekend-long brawl. At the end of training, around 8.00pm, as I walked back to our house, I prayed to God that Dad was home. He rarely was. When I arrived home, I peered from our front veranda to the laneway behind the RSL Club, straining to see the silhouette of Dad's head bobbing past the kurrajong trees. Sometimes I thought I could make out his figure returning home ahead of Mum, only for my joyous relief to be dashed as the shadows dancing through the trees played tricks on my searching eyes.

When Dad failed to get home before Mum, he insisted on stumbling around in the kitchen, boiling the kettle for a cup of tea, instead of going straight to bed. Mum would call out some abuse from her bedroom, he'd respond with phrases that included the words 'Pommy bitch!', and the row was on. They re-ran all the grievances of their married life until it got physical. Dad never pushed or hit Mum, but she pushed him.

I cowered in my bedroom, covering my ears from the thumping and thudding of their feet, the clanging of saucepans, and the opening and rattling of cutlery drawers. *One of these nights, she's going to stab him*, I fretted. The shouting, pushing, and shoving continued into the night until, exhausted, they collapsed into their separate beds, Mum's in her bedroom and Dad's on the back veranda, only for the abuse to resume in the morning.

On one Saturday, tired of the constant fighting and suicide threats, I just wanted to disappear. I stepped into the broom cupboard and pulled the door shut to stand in the isolated darkness. It clicked and locked from the outside. Though the solitude had effectively dulled Mum's ranting, I hadn't factored in the off-peak hot-water tank in the broom cupboard next to me. As the afternoon turned into dusk, the heating system switched into action. After an hour or so, the heat in the broom cupboard was suffocating, but I was determined not to suffer the indignity of calling out for Mum to release me.

Finally, close to losing consciousness, I banged against the inside of the door. Mum emerged from the adjacent bedroom, opened the door, and I fell out. Instead of attacking me as I'd expected, she opened the bedroom doors and windows to enable the flow of fresh air, and sat me in the cross breezes. I feigned incoherence, and she responded with care and sympathy. She even offered me a sleeping pill, which I declined.

Years later, Lance recounted to me his memories as an infant. Mum never cuddled him or me. One night, he fell out of his cot. Mum picked him up and cuddled him before returning him to bed. For the next few days, Lance deliberately fell out of his cot, hoping for a cuddle.

I WAS A VERY SKINNY KID, too embarrassed to go to the local pool, where I'd have to take my shirt off to be teased by other boys in front of the girls. Often we were hungry. When I read out the Saturday order at Frater's Butchers, 'A pound of rissoles, a pound of mince, a pound of sausages and two bob's worth of dog's meat for the cat', Kenny Frater regularly quipped: 'Eat it here or take it away, Wak?'

Wak was my other nickname, following my father, who was known universally as Wacker Emerson. Boy, I would have eaten it there if Kenny had cooked it for me. One pound of meat is less than half a kilogram, and, with boiled potatoes and a can of peas or beans, is not a big meal for two adults and two growing children. Kimmy Meyers described me as 'malnutrished'.

Each Saturday morning, the grocery order included one packet of Arnott's cream biscuits. Sometimes Lance and I had eaten them all by Saturday evening. If Mum noticed, she punished us by keeping us awake into the night, seated in the kitchen, shouting at us if we began to nod off, until we were utterly exhausted.

My life was a misery. I was powerless, hostage to Mum's violent moods. I had wanted to run away from home, but where does a little kid go? If I were caught, which I surely would be, I would be beaten.

One day, I drew the largest carving knife from the drawer, took off my shirt, and pressed its tip against my chest. I would need to shove it in hard to get it through my ribs and into my heart, which I knew was on my left side. I doubted I could succeed, so I felt with my fingers for a space between my ribs where I could insert the knife. But would I definitely get it through to my heart? Then it occurred to me that suicide was a mortal sin in the eyes of the Catholic Church. I would go to Hell. There was no escape, no relief. I collapsed onto the kitchen floor, sobbing so heavily, crying so loudly, until there were no more tears. Only despair.

3

Losing faith and family

St John's Convent School provided me with the refuge as a little kid that the tree house became in my adolescent years. I loved being at our tiny school during the week, and dreaded the looming weekends of work and distress. Mum was a non-practising Anglican, and Dad had converted to Catholicism but rarely attended church. Neither of them pushed me towards religion, but the Sisters of St Joseph did. I embraced my religion with all my heart, all my soul, all my strength, and all my mind.

Catholicism helped me make sense of Mum's volatile behaviour where there was no sense to be made of it. Christ suffered and died for us, the nuns told us, so that we might live. We, too, could be expected to suffer for our faith. We would be tested. We must forgive those who trespass against us. We must love our fathers and our mothers and our neighbours as ourselves.

Acceptance of my childhood life required for me the involvement of a supernatural being with a bigger, fairer plan. The nuns instructed us infants that His name was God; in fact, He was three gods in one—God the Father, God the Son, and God the Holy Ghost. These three gods sat up in the sky, with God the Son seated at the right hand of his Father. We didn't know where God the Holy Ghost sat, but he was definitely up there in Heaven with the other two gods. These were my firm beliefs, the articles of faith expected of a Catholic.

Heaven was a great place to get into, according to the nuns and priests. They explained that up in Heaven, we would be able to marvel at the divine light of God for eternity, which for a small child was an unimaginably long time. Just quietly, I never found sitting around forever admiring God's divine light all that enticing. But it was infinitely better than the alternative place for dead people—Hell—a dark, hot cavern somewhere down near the centre of the earth, even hotter than Baradine at the height of summer.

The trouble was that it was hard to get into Heaven, and easy to get into Hell. To get into Heaven, you needed to have the stain of Original Sin cleansed from your soul. That could be achieved only if you were baptised a Catholic: Protestants, Hindus, Buddhists, Muslims, and pagans couldn't get into Heaven. The best they could hope for, along with dogs and cats, was Limbo—a place where you could catch an occasional glimpse of God's divine light emanating from Heaven, but from which you could never reach up and join Him. I didn't think Limbo sounded too bad, but I was already a baptised Catholic, so I wasn't eligible anyway. I'd heard of a planet named Pluto, so I imagined Limbo might be somewhere out in space on the other side of it.

For the relatively few humans who were eligible for Heaven by virtue of being a Catholic, there were still many ways to stuff it up. Specifically, if you died with a mortal sin on your soul, you were buggered, bound for Hell. Mortal sins included not only killing people—fair enough—but taking the name of the Lord thy God in vain, eating meat on Friday, or missing Mass on Sunday through your own fault. If you did any of these, you'd need to get off to confession with a priest, seek forgiveness, gain absolution, and rush out and do your penance before you had a fatal accident for a fast track to Hell. When a classmate told you his penance was six Our Fathers, six Hail Marys, and six Glory Be to the Fathers, you could be pretty sure he'd committed a mortal sin. One boy told me he got twelve of each. I could barely imagine the evil he had done.

My sins were mainly lesser ones, called venial sins. If you died with these 'venials' on your soul, you went to another unpleasant place, Purgatory. It was almost as bad as Hell, but with an important difference—you could get out after serving time for your sins, and be lifted up into Heaven by the angels. Venial sins were typically white lies. Since we kids at St John's Convent School usually told a white lie or two every week, or said 'bloody' as most bush kids did, the best we could realistically hope for when dying was a stint in Purgatory—unless, of course, you were lucky enough for a priest to be in the neighbourhood to receive your last confession and give you absolution.

Generously, the Catholic Church offered an incentive system for reducing the time you were required to spend in Purgatory. It was called Indulgence. If you made the sign of the cross, you got 50 days off your time in Purgatory. If you did it with holy water, you got 100 days off. The only problem with this otherwise good deal was that the priests and nuns never told us how long we would be sentenced to Purgatory per venial sin in the first place. So I regularly went into the little church with Tony Purdy, my closest friend from our class of six in kindergarten days, and we dipped our fingers into the holy water at the door and made the sign of the cross dozens of times. Walking to and from school, I made the sign most of the way, but at half the value of those done with holy water. No matter, on a good day I could rack up several thousand days' Indulgence. I could get a block of them done walking around the house, or kneeling in front of my shrine in my bedroom comprising a large picture of the Virgin Mary and my broken plastic crucifix I'd glued back together with Araldite, where I prayed morning and night. My two main prayers were that I go to Heaven, and that Mum would get better and stop hitting me.

There was one other way of reducing your sentence in Purgatory. If you were down there, suffering away, and living people prayed for you, especially on All Souls' Day, you might get early release. So, we did a lot of praying at Mass for the souls in Purgatory in the hope that our thoughtfulness might be rewarded by other living people praying for us when we were dead and doing our time in Purgatory.

From my early days in kindergarten, I had accepted that enduring Mum's moodiness and violence was God's test of my faith. The priests and nuns taught us of Christ's suffering, of his incredible tolerance for pain as, whipped by Roman soldiers, he dragged a heavy cross up Mount Calvary, had nails driven into his hands, thorns pushed into his head, and a spear stuck into his side. 'Father forgive them; they know not what they do!' Jesus cried as he died out of love for us. The least I could do for Jesus was bear a little pain from my mother's behaviour and beatings.

THE NUNS WERE VERY KIND TO ME and encouraged my learning. Sweltering in the summer months beneath their heavy black robes and habits, they combined strict discipline with a nurturing of curiosity and creativity. In exams, I achieved 100 out of 100 for catechism, and was also awarded high 90s for English, arithmetic, and social studies.

Mum and Dad, too, encouraged my learning. When I brought home a report card, they celebrated my high marks and the nuns' comments praising my efforts. Both gifted and the beneficiaries of a good education, they instilled in me a love of learning, but mostly I sought those precious minutes of adulation as they sat together in a happy home, poring through my report card.

On Sundays, I went to Mass at the church that shared the grounds with the convent school, the nuns' residence, and the priests' rectory. It was a tiny building—choir at the back, altar at the front, holy water at the side doors, and congregation in the middle, sweating in the summer and freezing in the winter. Framed prints of the fourteen Stations of the Cross hung on the walls. A brass tabernacle with lace curtains housing the consecrated hosts of the Body of Christ adorned the altar. Celebrating the Mass was a priest who spoke in Latin, and two altar boys who, on behalf of the assembled congregation of townsfolk and farming families, responded also in Latin. Sparrows and an occasional swallow flitted through the open church beams. At Mass, I was either a choirboy or an altar boy, a valued member of the congregation.

St John's was a primary school only, but I remained an altar boy through most of my secondary schooling years at Baradine Central School. Perhaps showing symptoms of what was later diagnosed as epilepsy, I sometimes became disoriented during the Mass, having to retire to the sacristy. In summer, the altar boy vestments, three-hour fasts for Holy Communion, and searing heat made these episodes more frequent.

Early on, Mum learned of my aversion to mortal sin. She became aware that I might lie to protect Lance and myself from a hiding if it was only a venial sin, but that I considered lying while holding my plastic crucifix to be incontrovertibly a mortal sin. When Lance and I got up to some mischief, he instructed me to lie about it, otherwise he'd hit me. If I told the truth, Mum would hit both of us.

In what Mum called the breakfast room in our small house was a polished wooden display cabinet. Arranged on it were various ornaments, stored inside were some Golden Books, and at both ends were curved glass windows through which our best crockery set was on display. Every Sunday, I was required to polish the cabinet after removing the accumulated film of dust with a dry cloth. At one side of the cabinet, closest to the kitchen, was a wrought-iron table and seat supporting our telephone, on whose face was a handle for rotating to alert the telephonist at the local exchange. At the other side of the cabinet, adjacent to the front window, was the breakfast-room table used only on Christmas Day. Floral-patterned linoleum covered the floor that led to the front veranda and through it to the garden path. When we polished the linoleum with floor wax each weekend, it was unnervingly slippery beneath scampering feet.

For amusement, Lance chased me around the house, armed with a sandshoe, intent on throwing it at me. The longest uninterrupted stretch in the house was through the darkened lounge room and into the sunny breakfast room. Here I was most vulnerable to being hit in the back by a flying sandshoe. I was smaller and faster than Lance, so I'd sprint through the lounge room, conscious of the need to turn sharply without losing my footing on the linoleum as I reached the breakfast room. During one circuit of 'evade-the-sandshoe', I turned hard right at the breakfast room. Instead of whacking me in the back, the sandshoe continued on into the curved-glass window, shattering it into pieces.

Frantic, we picked out the remaining shards of glass, and meticulously cleaned up the fragments from the floor and out of the prized crockery set as we anxiously discussed how to conceal the disaster from Mum and Dad. I was in such a panic that I had to concentrate hard not to wet my pants. Maybe they wouldn't notice the glass was missing? Unlikely. So Lance invented a story that pinned the blame on a neighbourhood bull terrier named Boof who visited us from time to time, even venturing into the house to greet us. Boof had an incredibly strong tail, and when he was happy to see us, it slapped hard against our legs and the furniture. Boof was a happy-go-lucky sort of bull terrier, never suspecting he was about to be fitted up with playfully smashing the curved-glass window. Lance would do all the talking.

As soon as Mum and Dad arrived home after the morning's work that Saturday, they noticed the curved-glass window was missing, dashing our hopes for Plan A. Lance defaulted immediately to Plan B, explaining that Boof had paid us a visit, thumping his hard tail against the window and smashing it. Although this story had a semblance of plausibility, it didn't explain why we had cleaned up the glass, removing all evidence of the breakage, or my anxious face. Having allowed Lance to complete the embellishment, Mum turned to me.

'Is this what happened, Pud?'

'Yes', I replied, minimising the risk of error, and ensuring I had committed only a venial sin.

'Is that a promise?' Mum inquired.

'Yes', I said, skirting between venial and mortal sin, but not definitely into mortal territory.

'Go and get your crucifix!'

I trudged off to my bedroom, knowing the caper was up, returning with my hand gripped around the base of my fractured plastic cross.

'Is this what happened, Pud?'

'No!' I howled, proceeding to tell her the whole truth about the flying sandshoe.

True to form, Mum took to both of us with the handle-end of the feather duster. Then Lance marched me outside and punched the living daylights out of me. But I had avoided committing a mortal sin and taking on the risk of going to Hell. My venial sin could be cleansed by a visit to the confessional and by saying three Our Fathers, three Hail Marys, and three Glory Be to the Fathers.

LANCE DIDN'T ACCEPT THE RELIGIOUS INSTRUCTION of the nuns and priests that I had found so comforting, preferring instead to describe Mum as a bitch. When Mum concluded that a feather duster had proved inadequate in modifying our behaviour, she persuaded Dad to order a cane from Permewans. As we all four walked home past the tennis courts that Saturday lunchtime, Dad joked that the new cane he was carrying would bring us into line. Lance didn't see the funny side of it. After Mum used it on him several times, he took it down to the woodshed, chopped it into small pieces, and buried them in the chook house. Lance told me this only much later, when we were adults, fully aware that if I had known as a kid, Mum would have instructed me to go and get my crucifix and tell her what had happened to it.

Lance and I were easy targets in the house, so when Mum attacked us we ran outside where, as small kids, we had the advantage of manoeuvrability. Lower to the ground, we could turn faster, but on the straight stretches Mum gained on us. Around one corner, slightly off the one side, was a dripping tap in need of a new washer. When the chase became desperate, Lance deliberately led Mum through the wet patch on the grass. She would hit it, sliding, to use a term of hers, 'arse over tit'. Lance would make good his escape in the hope that Mum would eventually calm down.

So distressed had I become at Mum chasing me around the yard that, one day, well into my teens, I turned, stopped, faced her, and shouted: 'You're not my mother! You're not my mother!' Maybe that hurt her, but she didn't show it, saying only: 'I'll never forget you said that.' At least it made her stop chasing me that day, so it was worth it. But at no time did I feel Mum didn't love me. Many traumatised children come to the conclusion that their mothers wished they had never given birth to them. That must be devastating for their sense of self-worth. This, I never endured. Rather, my sense was that Mum couldn't control the anger within her; that it burst out without warning, over nothing at all.

Although I knew it to be futile, I spent most of my childhood making Mum's home life as comfortable as I could, bringing her a cup of tea in bed each morning, polishing ornaments and floors, chopping the wood, and hanging out the washing. Yet she flew into a rage at the tiniest transgression, real or perceived. Mum looked for and found traces of dust on the skirting board I had just cleaned. Or I had hung the towels in half on the clothesline, as she'd insisted the previous Saturday, only to find that she'd reverted to requiring me to hang them with just the top fraction of towel folded over the clothesline, as she had the week before.

Perhaps this experience gave me the endurance and attention to detail that helped me in my professional life. I can detect the most minor grammatical error or spelling mistake in a document, and cannot finish reading it without correcting it. Soon after being appointed to head the environment department in Queensland, I earned the nickname 'Doctor Grammar'. I have no trouble working and concentrating for long hours. But the legacies are not all positive. To this day, I feel anxious if I do not use the same coloured pegs to hang an item of washing on the clothesline.

MORE THAN ANY OTHER TIME OF THE YEAR, Christmas epitomised the moodiness in our house. Little kids are excited by the approach of Christmas Day. We were no different. But my excitement about the celebration of Midnight Mass and the impending visit of Santa Claus was tempered by our experience that the happiness of the season would be shattered by a row lasting several days, often peaking on Christmas Day itself. Usually, it started on the day that, as a family, we put up the Christmas decorations. Dad brought rolls of crepe paper from Permewans, and we cut them with scissors to make streamers. By twisting the streamers, we fashioned pretty decorations whose ends we attached with thumbtacks, allowing the streamers to drape across the ceiling. Twirling the streamers to the correct degree was no simple task. Invariably, Mum declared the exercise a failure, and the Christmas row began. How Lance and I longed for it to be over in time for Santa's visit.

At most Christmases, Dad resolved to leave home following the inevitable arguments, walking up the garden path, his suitcase in hand, two sobbing boys clinging to him, begging him to stay. On one Christmas Day, when Dad announced he would be leaving the family and our home on Boxing Day, Mum made peace with him, and we cooked the Christmas roast. Seated around the breakfast-room table, Dad looked out the window to the front lawn and said: 'I'd better mow that lawn tomorrow.' Then, remembering his pledge, he added: 'Before I leave.' Mum broke into laughter, Dad joined her, and we boys added our young voices to the merriment. I could just as easily have cried; for me, there wasn't much difference.

My bonds with the Catholic Church began breaking when, as a teenager, I took a dilemma into the confessional. On a Sunday, I had returned home from Mass and was well advanced with vacuuming the lounge-room floor. With a familiar look on her face and an accusatorial tone in her voice, Mum demanded to know whether I had finished. Only a little area was not yet completed, but I knew from experience that if I had truthfully told her the job was not fully done she would have headed off to the bedroom, enraged, with a bottle of sleeping pills in her hand. I told her I was finished, she accepted my word, and a crisis was averted. But I had lied.

Confession hearings were held late on Saturday afternoons ahead of Sunday Mass. That way, our parish priest, Father O'Mahoney, could travel from Coonabarabran, hear confessions, and say Mass the next day. Father O'Mahoney was a young, kind, and gentle Irish priest. As I prayed in the twilight, waiting for the other kids and parents to finish their confessions, I wrestled with my conscience, hoping for Father O'Mahoney's understanding.

'Bless me, Father, for I have sinned. It is two weeks since my last confession, and these are my sins', I said. Conversation in the confessional was most unusual. Normally, it was a matter of rattling off the nature and number of sins without offering any details, receiving your penance, gaining absolution, promising never to sin again, and saying the prayers required of you before leaving the church.

But my lie warranted an explanation. I recounted my exchange with Mum, confessing the sin, but explaining that I had averted the risk of Mum going into the bedroom with her sleeping pills and possibly committing suicide. I asked Father O'Mahoney to forgive my venial sin, and sought his guidance on what was expected of me if similar circumstances arose again, which they surely would. He did not equivocate. While understanding my predicament and my desire to avoid unnecessary harm to my mother and myself, Father O'Mahoney made it clear that my Catholic faith obliged me to tell the truth and accept any and all consequences.

This priest was much loved by the townspeople. In a sense, he had no choice but to give me that ruling; he could not condone lying, even by concealment and omission, no matter the circumstances. I was shattered. Through his kind parish priest, God was instructing me that, rather than conceal a minor truth from my mother, I should risk her committing suicide. And since a sin was not truly forgiven if the confessor failed to repent, I was under a holy obligation next time, in like circumstances, to let her kill herself.

After that experience, my mind became increasingly literal about sins. Failing to confess a sin, even by forgetting about it, annulled God's forgiveness and added a further stain on your soul. To avoid any possibility of forgetting a sin in the confessional, I adopted the practice of writing them down and taking my list in with me. Father Healy, who alternated visits to Baradine with Father O'Mahoney, was a cranky priest who insisted on a little less water and a little more wine in his chalice. At a confessional hearing, he heard the rustling of my paper through the dividing screen and asked why I had it. I explained the reason. He was most concerned with my obsessive behaviour to avoid any inadvertent failure to confess a sin. He asked me to meet him the next Thursday in the priest's rectory.

When I arrived, dripping with anxiety, he greeted me with a glass of lemonade. He told me that keeping a list was unnecessary. He pointed out that I was an adolescent and that adolescents were allowed to get up to some 'mischief'. Our cranky priest was advising me to lighten up and enjoy life. He also relieved me of the heavy weight of a responsibility I had for some time felt to join the priesthood. It was a terrible sin, the nuns had told us, to reject God's calling to the Holy Order. As one of only two remaining altar boys in Baradine, I felt God had been calling me. Father Healy advised me that if I wasn't certain, then God was not obliging me to join the priesthood. It was, to that time, the most liberating day of my life. I took Father Healy's directive seriously, and the instruction of the Church less literally.

WHEN I REFLECT ON IT NOW, Mum was profoundly depressed, and may have been addicted to the sleeping pills. She was constantly searching for a pretext to have an argument with me so that she could go to the bedroom with her pills. More than a decade later, after the family moved to Sydney, Lance was driving taxis. He had a fare that took him through our home suburb of Croydon Park, and decided to stop by and say hello to Mum. He found her unconscious, with her head slumped in the kitchen oven. The house was filled with gas. The paramedics advised Lance that, had he not come by, she definitely would have died.

From Mum's wild and unpredictable mood swings, I learned never to allow myself to become too happy. Happiness was vulnerability. The happier I allowed myself to be, the sharper was the descent into despair, as Mum flew into a rage and hit me or threatened to kill herself. By my early teens, the physical violence didn't really bother me, but the emotional trauma was devastating. All my romantic partnerships with women have suffered from my reflexive resolve to shield myself from the risks associated with true happiness. Several beautiful partners have declared their love for me, only for me to ask, in an unintentionally hurtful reply: 'What is love?'

Yet I now know unprotected happiness: the joy of being Dad, Pa, and Dadda to our three children, Ben, Tom, and Laura. Every day, I celebrate the miracle of their birth and the delight of their love for me and of mine for them. Every day when I wake up, I think, *It's my lucky day*. Every time I look around me at the astonishingly beautiful natural world, I am filled with joy and wonder. But the journey continues, and, when blessed with such happiness, my impulse remains to protect myself from a plunge into despair that so quickly followed it as a child.

In truth, we had many good times as a family and as kids playing with our mates. Mum and Dad were well liked by the people of Baradine. But the fond memories were pushed into the recesses of our minds by the bad times, the mood swings, and the violence of a suicidal mother. Yet through all their misery and anguish, despite the arguments, shouting, and abuse, Mum and Dad were dedicated to giving Lance and me the best possible education. We are both on the honour board as Dux of Baradine Central School. Our parents worked hard on their modest incomes to put us through school, and me through university. This was the gift of love to their two boys. I will never forget what they did for us. Sadly, all three—Mum, Dad, and Lance—died in their early sixties, their stressful, traumatic existence taking a heavy toll on their health and wellbeing.

4

Adventures in Baradine

Although I felt an overwhelming sense of sadness as a little boy, there were fun times, too. As a small town far from the big smoke, Baradine was a place where kids had to make their own fun. One of my earliest memories was of standing on the front veranda of our house at 10 Queen Street, admiring the gleaming 26-inch Malvern Star bicycle that Mum and Dad had just given Lance for Christmas. Little did I know that I would come to fear that bike, never learning to ride one myself until I was twelve years old.

For some inexplicable reason, Lance was obsessed with doubling me on the handlebars. We often had reason to go 'up the main street' to do the family shopping. Wellington Street was less than a 200-metre walk from our house along the dirt path past the tennis courts and the ruins of Steve Anna's burnt-down café. As soon as Lance declared we were going 'up the main street', I instinctively said: 'I'll run—see you there.' But Lance insisted: 'No, I'll double you.'

From there, the conversation took its predictable course.

'Aw, no thanks, Lance. It's quicker for me to run.'

'No. I'll double you.'

'But that's slower. I'll see you there.'

'No. I'll double you.'

'But ...'

'Get on the handle bars!'

Shaking, conscious of the inevitability of it all, I climbed onto the ram's horn handlebars while Lance struggled to keep them steady.

A heave, and we were away, wobbling along Queen Street's rough bitumen road until we needed to turn right into Darling Street, off which we would again turn right into Wellington Street. When the handlebars turned, I squirmed. Lance couldn't control the wobbling, and I would fall off. As I lay on the road, crumpled, grazed, and crying, Lance shouted: 'Get on the handle bars!'

I had two options: if I stayed on the ground, Lance would run over me, but if I climbed back onto the handle bars, I would wriggle, the handle bars would wobble, Lance would lose control, I would fall off, and we would do it all over again. Re-mounting the handlebars seemed a lesser risk than lying on the ground, aware that my brother was backing up his pushbike to get a run-up to ride over the top of me. The short journey along Darling Street offered brief respite until we were obliged to make the turn into Wellington Street, where the townsfolk witnessed the ritual of me again tumbling off the handlebars.

Having arrived at the main street on Lance's bike worse for wear, we did the shopping Mum had required of us, sometimes succumbing to the temptation of ripping a handful of hot bread from a freshly baked loaf we'd purchased at the bakery. We would worry later about how to conceal the hole from Mum. Then we'd ask Pop Hawkins at Permewans general store whether he had any free broken biscuits left over from the large Arnott's tins from which he supplied paying customers.

Next stop was Pop Pentes's café or Stan Tassell's milk bar where, if we had some money, we might be able to buy a milkshake. Lance usually had spent his pocket money within a day of receiving it, while I had put mine in a large, pink, plastic piggy bank that at one time was full of lollies. When Lance was short of money, he would raid my piggy bank and might generously shout me a milkshake from the money he'd taken. Lance could down a milkshake much faster than me. The coldness of the blob of ice cream in the milkshake induced a pain at the back of my throat with which all little kids are familiar.

As soon as Lance's empty milkshake canister hit the counter, he feigned a reason to return home immediately. If we didn't have to light the fire under the copper, or feed the chooks before Mum and Dad got home from work, or set the table, or water the garden, he would invent some other reason obliging us to rush off.

'Come on, Pud, we've got to go. If you can't finish your milkshake, give it to me!'

I resumed gulping until the pain in my head was unbearable and Lance's demands that I hand him the milkshake became irresistible. Defeated, I gave him the remainder of my milkshake. To this day, I involuntarily drink icy cold drinks fast and eat ice creams, rather than licking them.

After finishing the shopping and other chores, Lance and I, with Kimmy Meyers, would spend most of any free time we had playing in the horse and cow paddock at the back of our houses. We simply called it 'the block'. On Sunday afternoons, Kimmy would inquire across the chicken-wire fence between our yards: 'Can you two come out and play yet?'

For the three of us, 'play' on Sunday afternoon involved a regular game of manure fights. Each of us used a garbage-can lid as a shield and, as we strode out to the block, I insisted on 'No gangings up!' In deference to my stipulated condition of participation, Kimmy and Lance developed a practice of lobbing a token piece of manure in each other's general direction. Having performed this farcical ritual, they turned on me — one in front of my shield, and one to the side or back — peppering me with their ammunition pile of dried manure. When this recycled grass got down the back of my collar, it was unbearably itchy. Lighting the bathroom chip heater to wash horse manure from my back and out of my ears and hair was an unsatisfying way to finish the weekend.

By the middle of summer, the large tufts of grass that had grown through the spring had browned off. Country kids love lighting fires. Kimmy, Lance, and I each placed an empty plastic detergent bottle onto a stick, built a campfire like good cowboys, and from it lit the plastic bottles. As the bottles began melting, they dropped fiery blobs of burning plastic — 'blip, blip, blip' — making them a perfect fire-starting device. We ran from one tuft of dry grass to the next, setting them alight with the dripping hot plastic. Each of us had a wet wheat bag ready to begin beating out the fire when we judged it was verging on being out of control.

Kimmy was always the first to break. 'It's getting too big!' he nervously complained. 'Not yet. Not yet!' Lance insisted. Then, with half the block ablaze in the scorching summer heat, we took to the wheat bags and beat back the flames.

On at least one occasion, Lance's judgement was astray, and the fire got away. It jumped the dirt road bisecting the block and was heading towards the Baradine Bowls Club and various houses. A big gum tree caught fire beside the road leading to one of the local sawmills. The fire brigade arrived, brought the blaze under control, and prohibited us from lighting fires again—other than on bonfire night.

On the Queen's Birthday weekend in May, the kids of Baradine lit the bonfires they'd built with their parents' help. None was better than our neighbourhood's bonfire. Before beginning work on the bonfire, we had to wait for Kimmy's dad to cut down and haul in a cypress-pine tree to form the centre pole. Once he'd done that, we hurled onto the centre pole all the old tyres we'd been able to scavenge from around the town. Branches we'd cut from fallen gum trees followed next—their drying eucalyptus leaves burned especially well. Other bits of old wood, tufts of dried grass, anything combustible, we'd add to the bonfire.

But even a roaring bonfire was of no use without crackers. These fell into three categories: pretties, skyrockets, and bungers. Pretties included Catherine Wheels, Roman Candles, Flower Pots, and sparklers. Bungers were graded by size: threepenny bungers, double bungers, penny bungers, Po Ha's, and Tom Thumbs. We'd save up money all year by returning our collections of Reg Webber's soft-drink bottles for a one-penny refund for each returned bottle. By early May, we'd each have a school case full of penny bungers with a few packets of Po Ha's and several strings of Tom Thumbs. Threepennies could blow your hand off, so it was best not to mess with them; you lit the wick and ran. But for that reason they were not much fun, while costing orders of magnitude more than penny bungers. Pennies we could use in the weeks leading up to cracker nights, for playing wars out in the block. Po Ha's were safer, but boring.

Lance, Kimmy, and I, together with other neighbours interested in war games, dug holes out in the block, piling the dirt in front of them and laying on top of the mounds the rusting wire of tyres we'd burned in bonfires past. In lieu of hand grenades from World War II movies, we lobbed penny bungers into each other's foxholes. Testing our nerves, we held onto the penny bungers until the burning wicks fizzed to the entrance of the cracker. Mistiming was very painful, the exploding bunger leaving a charred, jarred aching hand.

Sometimes, instead of going to the RSL Club on Friday nights to drink beer while Mum worked at the pub, Dad went to the Bowls Club. It was diagonally across the block from our house. As I mounted my anxious vigil from my bedroom window, hoping to catch a glimpse of Dad's silhouetted form bobbing across the paddock, I could finally detect his outline against the bowling-club lights. Bob, bob, bob, and then he was gone! We hadn't told Dad about the foxholes we'd dug, and he fell straight into one. It seemed an eternity before he emerged from the hole — bob, bob, bob — fumbled through the back door, no doubt dusted himself off, and went to bed. We never spoke of it.

While most exchanges ahead of cracker night involved bungers, we found good uses for the occasional skyrocket, which were very expensive. In our woodshed, we kept a 44-gallon drum of wheat to feed the chooks. Mice found their way into the drum to feast on the readily available grain. If I felt around in the wheat, I could usually grab one. We tied a mouse to our skyrocket, and launched what we considered to be the first Mouse in Space. When the spent skyrocket fell back to earth, the mouse was gone, either escaping upon lift-off, or possibly still in orbit. We kids had little concept of animal cruelty, and I look back with horror at the way we treated unsuspecting creatures.

As the sun set for cracker night, all the neighbours and parents gathered around the bonfire. Ours burned fiercely and long. The kids from other neighbourhoods admired our work, as theirs expired more quickly than ours. We never told them that our secret fuel was the used tyres, for if we did we would no longer have monopolised access to them.

Cracker nights did not always go to plan. On two separate occasions, the Slade kids, who were bullies, torched our bonfire the night before, giving us no time to rebuild it. They liked to torment Lance and me at the pictures — now known as the cinema — kicking us from behind as we sat in the canvas seats, and beating up Lance as we made our way home. Mum eventually tired of this, and waited for them at the dark corner where they usually attacked us. As the Slade boys began taunting and pushing Lance, Mum emerged from the darkness and said: 'If you ever lay a hand on these boys again, I'll punch the shit out of you!' Perversely, this confrontation earned the Slade boys' admiration for Mum, and we became quite good friends.

Despite our communal effort in building the best bonfires, when the big night arrived some among us lacked honourable intentions towards others. All the other kids of the neighbourhood brought their arsenals of crackers to the bonfire in their school cases, or ports, as we called them, to prevent sparks or embers getting in. Inexplicably, one cracker night I brought my crackers, the product of half a year's savings and returned soft drink bottles, in a plastic bag. Kimmy, Lance, and assorted neighbours observed my folly, and conspired to drop a lit bunger into my bag while I wasn't looking. They had taken possession of the torches their parents had brought from the houses. My stash exploded, the crackers that had not ignited being blown across a sizeable area of the paddock. Lance, Kimmy, and friends used the torches to locate my unexploded ordnances, sharing them around and returning to me a token assembly of Po Ha's and a few strings of Tom Thumbs.

LIFE IN BARADINE was at its most dangerous when crackers and guns were combined. Of all people, Baradine's doctor, Rupert Catalano, for whom Mum worked as a qualified nurse until his death in a car accident, built a cracker gun for his only son, Ian, who was visiting with his mum from Sydney. While Dr Catalano's invention impressed Ian, it didn't have the same effect on his estranged wife. It comprised a length of pipe sealed at one end. A penny bunger's wick could be threaded through a small hole at the sealed end after unscrewing the stopper. The projectile of choice was a marble. Lance, Kimmy, and I tried it out a few times before Ian's arrival from Sydney. It readily blew a hole through a sheet of corrugated roofing iron.

Ian and his mother planned to stay a few weeks, and she thought it best that Ian attend our school rather than miss lessons altogether. Our school uniform comprised grey cotton shorts and acrylic short-sleeved shirts. Returning from school to Dr Catalano's surgery and house, Lance, Kimmy, and I suggested to Ian that we play wars with the cracker gun. Ian obliged. He pretended he was marching towards us over the top of his imaginary trench as we defended ourselves with the assistance of the cracker gun. Having observed the damage a marble could do to roofing iron, we prudently decided to use less harmful ammunition. Dr Catalano had arranged for a load of sheep manure to be delivered for use as garden fertiliser. We rammed dry sheep manure down the loaded cracker-gun barrel, as nineteenth-century soldiers would a musket.

We called on Ian to march towards us, which he dutifully did. We lit the fuse of the penny bunger and blasted him in the belly. Ian flinched, but to his credit did not fall to the ground, despite the edges of the hole in his acrylic school shirt burning and melting onto his skin. My lasting memory of brave Ian is of him lying on a table in the surgery with Dr Catalano using tweezers to pick out sheep manure from the hole in his stomach, and the doctor's wife admonishing him for the graphic reminder of why they'd separated in the first place.

At the end of our backyard garden path grew a huge Queensland wattle tree. I stood under it when Joy Meyers came running from her house, shouting that president Kennedy had been assassinated. Earlier still, when I was just four or five years of age, the branches of that wattle tree scratched across the corrugated-iron roof of the lavatory we used before the town was sewered. Beneath the seat was a tar-lined dunny can that, along with all the others, was heaved onto a council truck to take away its contents for disposal. Venomous redback spiders hid under the toilet seat and in the corners of the fibro-walled, tin-roofed toilet. Little boys could not hold their bladders through the night, and I dreaded walking down the garden path to the lavatory on my own. On each occasion, Mum instructed Lance to accompany me. He so resented this chore that he collected the flashlight from the laundry and shone it on his face from under his chin, making groaning noises straight out of a horror movie as we walked down the garden path. When I took my pants down, the wattle branches screeching across the tin roof, a dunny can half full, around me only darkness and redback spiders, Lance began in low tones:

> Old King Cole was a merry old soul
> A merry old soul was he
> He called for his pipe
> And called for his lamp
> And went to the lavatory.
> The night was dark and stormy
> The candle gave a flick

And old King Cole that merry old soul
Fell up to his ears in shit!'

I'd run screaming from the toilet, tortured by images of falling into the can of darkness to be bitten by the lurking redback spiders.

Eventually, after years of terror, Lance shared with me a moment of truth: he was almost as scared as I was trudging through the darkness to the screeching of the wattle tree on the toilet roof and the flickering shadows of its branches across its fibro walls.

BARADINE PEOPLE WERE TOUGH. Timber cutters lost limbs from circular saws flying out of control in the Pilliga Scrub. Labourers heaved logs onto tables at sawmills, and drove them through the vertical saw blades, day in and day out, through the stinking heat. Many years later, Warren Mundine, an Indigenous Labor Party president and aboriginal affairs adviser to prime minister Tony Abbott, recalled to me his time as mayor of Dubbo, a much larger centre halfway between Baradine and Sydney. 'We never liked playing teams from Baradine', he confessed. 'Those timber cutters were bloody hard bastards.'

Indeed, in 1969, the team from the bigger neighbouring town of Coonabarabran swept all before it, winning the prestigious Caltex Shield and being voted the best country New South Wales rugby league team. Captained and coached by dual international Ken Thornett, Coonabarabran needed only to knock over the Baradine Magpies in the Group 14 Grand Final to go through the season undefeated. Baradine hit the lead early and, with one player concealing a shattered jaw, tackled themselves to exhaustion, ultimately winning 10–9 in an epic display of bravery and sheer willpower.

As a town, Baradine never asked for much and was never given anything. It lost its doctor, lost its banks, lost its cinema, lost its aerodrome, lost its RSL Club, lost its railway line for transporting people and produce to Sydney, lost its football team, and lost all but one of its sawmills when the New South Wales Labor government gazetted most of the Pilliga Scrub—which did not exist before European settlement—as a national park. But the town has kept its convent school, kept its state school, kept its two pubs, kept its dignity, and kept its spirit. Baradine celebrated its 150th anniversary on 5 October 2015, half a century from when Kimmy Meyers and I paraded around the football oval in the rickshaw Dad had built for us. I still call him Kimmy, though he insists his name is Kim, and he still calls me Emu, which is just fine with me.

5

Nerds don't get girls

Although attracting girls was not among the motivations for building the tree house, if it offered that added advantage I wasn't going to decline the opportunity. My childhood sweetheart—though she didn't know it—was Anne Tassell, the most beautiful girl in town. Inconsiderately, she left me, without realising she was ever with me, to attend boarding school at Gunnedah, a town very far away for a 13-year-old boy.

Further into my adolescence, I became attracted to Wendy Edwards, a redheaded girl the year below me at school. Somehow I managed to persuade Wendy and her friend, Chocky Madden, now the most beautiful girl in town but beyond my modest reach, to join me for a walk along Baradine Creek to view the proudly completed tree house. That Wendy seemed so keen on making the journey gave me cause for cautious optimism. But all was lost when Wendy stopped in the damp sand of the creek bed to write in large letters with an equally large stick: 'I love Duck.' No, it wasn't an expression of her food preferences but of her affection for Ronnie 'Duck' Peel, a classmate of whom I immediately became envious.

This latest setback was just another in a long line of rejections for a boy who never quite made it into the cool group at Baradine. Without doubt, the worst of many names that a boy struggling for popularity in Baradine could be called was a 'brain'. Alternatively known as a 'square' or a 'drip', I was by default a member of a social grouping that, in more modern times, is commonly known as 'the nerds'. In my early teens I got on well with other brains, squares, and drips, but struggled for acceptance by the cool kids. In my mind, my classmates were very clever in so many ways. Our secondary school motto was *Non Scholae Sed Vitae*, which we were told meant 'not in learning but in life'. Though unintentional, the take-home message seemed to be that the purpose of school at Baradine was to give the boys a trade rather than to equip them for an academic career or a profession.

While this might have been realistic, given the financial circumstances of most parents in a struggling timber town located at the drought-prone edge of the wheat belt, I always thought most of my classmates were no less clever than me. Kids from the land had an earthy common sense and an uncanny sense of direction that I totally lacked. Some, including those who had conceived of, designed, and built the three-storey tree house, displayed a talent for practical tasks in woodwork. Others were quite brilliant at mathematics, but probably didn't fully appreciate the depth of their talent. I struggled to better some rivals in English and science. None of us, I assumed, would come within coo-ee of the vast number of smart kids in the big cities whose parents had the money to ensure that the best teachers taught them in well-equipped classrooms.

Baradine's best-looking girls were attracted to cool boys, not to brains or squares or drips. One way for a square to appeal to girls, I concluded, was to reveal my psychedelic side. It was, after all, the dawning of the Age of Aquarius. Jimi Hendrix wore freaky colours and jewellery, and Zoot performed in pink suits. I rummaged through Mum's drawers and found various pieces of jewellery that might heighten my appeal as a sensitive, new-age sort of guy. At a school dance, I wore a pendant and, yes, a necklace, over an orange knitted skivvy. I knew this behaviour risked the wrath of the cool boys, but I had nothing else going for me.

While my outfit attracted the interest of the girls, it also attracted the unwanted attention of the toughest guy in the entire district. Word had gotten around about a boy in Baradine dressing up as a girl, and it reached the ears of a thug from Coonabarabran named Terry Moyer. A friend tipped me off that the thug was asking about me, wanting to know my name and intending to bash the shit out of me if ever he saw me on Baradine's main street.

On a Friday night, I visited Pop Pentes's café for a milkshake. Pop had the canister of milk, flavouring, and ice cream whirring in the electric milk-shaker when in walked this hulk of a man. He looked about 25 years of age, while I was a skinny 15-year-old. He knew who I was, but, to put it mildly, he invaded my personal space and demanded: 'What's your name?'

I replied: 'Craig.'

'Craig who?'

'Craig Emerson.'

This was going to end badly, I predicted. So did Pop Pentes, who said in his inimitable Greco-Australian accent: 'Listen, if you boys are gonna fight, take it outside. I dunna wan' no fightin' in my café.'

Personally, I was happier to be inside the café and not out on the footpath, where fighting would be considered a more legitimate activity. But I knew that if I showed the thug from Coonabarabran any fear, I would be dead meat. Then came the killer question.

'Where do you live?'

For a boy who dressed as a girl, the answer I was to give would surely cause me to be beaten to a pulp by this monster.

With heart pounding and adrenaline pumping, I stoically replied: 'Queen Street.'

Fully expecting to be punched to the floor or dragged out onto the street, I looked straight into Moyer's eyes. After a short hesitation, he said: 'Hey, that's funny—I live in Queen Street, Coonabarabran', and walked out.

I gulped down my milkshake and ran home in case the thug changed his mind, learning a lifelong lesson that it's better to stand up to bullies than to cower before them.

THE MOST BEAUTIFUL GIRL IN TOWN—especially now that Anne Tassell had left for Gunnedah, Wendy Edwards had rejected me, and Chocky Madden had from the start been out of reach—was a curvaceous, sandy-haired 14-year-old stunner, Lorna Hotchkiss. Lorna didn't have a steady boyfriend, but I sensed her aspirations lay far above me. Adding to her loveliness, Lorna was one of the few girls with sufficient pity to agree to kiss me during a game of Spin the Bottle. When any of the other girls spun the bottle and it ended up pointing towards me, her friends gasped: 'Oh yuck!' This did nothing for my self-confidence.

For many years, Baradine's social magnet was the cinema, which we knew as the picture show. When Lance and I were little kids, and when there was peace at home, Mum and Dad sometimes took us to the Saturday-night pictures. I never lasted through the feature film, happy to have seen Mickey Mouse, Donald Duck, or Tom and Jerry. Dad lifted me onto his shoulders for the walk home, and I clung onto his wiry hair as the scent of Californian Poppy hair oil wafted into my nostrils.

I urged the coolest boy in town, Johnny Crawley, to ask Lorna whether she would sit with me at the pictures. To my astonishment, she said yes. For the rest of the week, I was excited in every possible way. On the big night, I arrived at the picture show early, in anticipation of a night of passion, or at least a kiss and a cuddle. The shorts started. Then the Elvis Presley feature began. No Lorna. Confused and disconsolate, I paced up and down the main street, as if that would make her appear. I concluded she was just trying to please my cool friend, whom all the girls wanted to please.

Half a lifetime later, when we were in our late 50s, I finally mustered the courage to ask Lorna why she had jilted me. She revealed she had never received any message from Johnny Crawley on my behalf. It didn't seem prudent to ask Lorna whether she would have sat with me if he or I had asked her.

During this unfolding personal teenage disaster, Graeme 'Hairs' Head informed me that another girl had approached him as an emissary to ask me whether I would sit with her. She was lovely, but I had my heart set on Lorna. So they sat together and had a wonderful time. I could smell the perfume on his denim jacket for weeks. Just to rub it in, he took the jacket from his wardrobe whenever we were at his house to wave it under my nose.

Hairs and I had started up what was to become a lucrative lawn-mowing business. We named ourselves the Rapid Annihilators, turning the grass around the houses of Baradine townsfolk into lawns with Dad's Victa. We Rapid Annihilators made enough money to finance a train trip to Sydney, where there were lots more beautiful girls.

Uncle Harold and Aunty Barbara, as Lance and I knew them, were generous not only to Dad at the war's end, but to Hairs and me, allowing us to stay at their house in Strathfield. We took along my slug gun with the most ignoble of intentions. Birds were very wary around Baradine, with every second kid owning some sort of rifle. But on a previous visit to Sydney I had noticed that the city birds, especially the pigeons, were tame. Around Baradine, topknot pigeons were prized quarry. They wisely stayed well clear of the shooting gallery in the skies above the town. If you were ever lucky enough to down a toppy, which on two occasions I was, you could cook it up and eat it, which I did.

Ostensibly in search of birds of a different feather, Hairs and I turned up at Strathfield, and on the first full day I shot an unwary pigeon at close range. But instead of obligingly falling dead in our yard, it flapped into the neighbour's backyard, flopping around in the garden. Aunty Barbara, hearing the commotion, came out to advise me that the next-door neighbour was a bird lover. I scaled the fence, retrieved the dying pigeon, ended its misery, and put my air rifle away for the rest of our city holiday.

The next morning, Hairs and I walked from Strathfield to the Westfield Shopping Centre in the neighbouring suburb of Burwood. Hairs wore his perfumed denim jacket, and I wore my orange skivvy. Testosterone was in the air. Girls were everywhere, hanging out at the balconies and at the tops of the escalators and just, well, hanging out of their tops. We eventually struck up a conversation with two of them. If Hairs' denim jacket didn't give away our country heritage, our slow drawls surely did. The girls promised to meet us again, and wrote down a phone number for me to ring that night to arrange a time and place.

I hadn't been so excited since Johnny Crawley told me Lorna Hotchkiss had agreed to sit with me at the pictures. The girls told us to phone after 8.00pm. Aunty Barbara could see I was edgy through dinner and as we watched TV in the lounge room. After what seemed an eternity, the grandfather clock literally struck 8.00pm, and I asked Aunty Barbara if I could use the phone.

In the privacy of the empty hallway, I eagerly—even friskily—dialled the numbers on the scrap of paper the girls had written out for me. There must have been some mistake. I got a recorded message. I dialled again, carefully, again and again. Each time, it was the same message: 'You have rung Dial-a-Prayer. Tonight, we have a prayer to Jesus from the New Testament ...' Unable to comprehend what had happened, I returned to the lounge room and described the situation to Aunty

Barbara and Uncle Harold. They were rolling in their lounge chairs, roaring with laughter. A 15-year-old country boy's humiliation was complete.

AS WE ENTERED OUR FINAL YEAR at Baradine Central, we needed to start thinking about which jobs and careers might appeal to us. A weeklong excursion to Sydney had been organised for the schools of north-west New South Wales. We all stayed at the Narrabeen Fitness Centre on the hinterland of Sydney's northern beaches. There I met a tall, blonde-haired girl from Narrabri. We sort of became boyfriend and girlfriend for a few days, though I had to endure a re-run of my experiences with Spin the Bottle. When my blonde sweetheart pointed me out to her school friends from a considerable distance, I could clearly hear them exclaiming: 'Ew, yuck!' By week's end, we were on separate trains back to Baradine and Narrabri and, although we corresponded regularly, it was difficult to sustain our love affair from a distance of 160 kilometres, with no driver's licences.

Back in Baradine, the jewellery and the orange skivvy finally worked, and my luck changed when one of the most beautiful girls in town, Jayne Underwood, suggested we start going out together. I was so thrilled that I used $14 of my income from lawn mowing to buy Jayne a friendship ring. But our romance never progressed beyond cuddling and awkward kisses. Jayne might have been fonder of the idea of owning a friendship ring than of having me as her boyfriend. Our enfeebled romance soon expired.

In my last weeks at Baradine, now almost 16 years old, I found true love at last. A lovely, sweet girl from the nearby village of Kenebri named Alison Burns combed my hair at the Baradine swimming pool. That was more than enough for us to become boyfriend and girlfriend. Alison asked me for a friendship ring. I explained that I'd spent all my savings on a friendship ring for Jayne, and that if Alison wanted a friendship ring, she would need to approach Jayne and try to persuade her to hand it over. Amazingly, Alison did exactly that and retrieved the ring. But just when the 'square' from Baradine had won a girl's heart and she his, events beyond our control were to conspire to cut short our romance.

6

Accidentally holy orders

Towards the end of 1970, we unexpectedly moved to Sydney after the state manager of Permewans invited Dad to meet him at Nyngan, 300 kilometres from Baradine, to inform him he'd been sacked. The Baradine district was in the grip of a severe drought. At the age of 54, Dad had no viable alternative employment. He tried returning to forestry work, but the only job he could get was swinging an axe, stripping the branches of cypress-pine and Ironbark trees that had been felled by timber cutters in the Pilliga Scrub. It nearly killed him. Dad's wartime commanding officer was the manager of John Lysaght's sheet-metal factory at Chullora in Sydney's west. In response to a plea for help, he offered Dad a clerk's position.

Mum and Dad moved to Sydney ahead of me, enabling me to complete my School Certificate exams at Baradine. By the time I joined them, Mum and Dad had taken up residence in a large, run-down house in the plush suburb of Strathfield, paying rent of just $40 per week. While that was equal to the entire weekly pay that Dad had been earning at Permewans, he was bringing in around $60 a week at John Lysaght's, and Mum had landed a clerical job at the Medical Benefits Fund in the city centre. On their combined incomes, they could just afford the rent and the other big-city living expenses. But they knew the rent on a house in such a fancy suburb would inevitably rise, so we would be moving again before too long. Bimbo Kelly and Rusty Patterson from our tree house days joined us as sub-tenants.

In the meantime, the next-door neighbours in Agnes Street

befriended Mum and Dad. Their son of my age was a student at nearby St Patrick's College, a non-government school. The government school system was based on a strict zoning system: students were obliged to attend the state school closest to their parents' place of residence, which for parents on the move could easily lead to a change of school.

Knowing we would be leaving Strathfield for another rented house, Mum and Dad looked up St Patrick's Strathfield in the telephone directory, and rang to see if they might accept me as a student.

I had begun work stacking shelves and mopping floors at Flemings Food Mart in Burwood about two kilometres' walking distance from our house, earning $24 a week. I played cards at lunchtime with the staff, met a checkout girl named Gail, and took a sickie to sit on the hill at the Sydney Cricket Ground, where I saw Graham McKenzie bowl in a cricket test match in the days before Dennis Lillee and Jeff Thomson. The store manager, Mr Yeadon, was talking of sending me to an in-house training course, which would lead to a promotion.

George Harrison had just released 'My Sweet Lord', the Kinks were going on about a transvestite named 'Lola', and David Cassidy was telling a girl 'I Think I Love You'. Just after Christmas, I attended my first open-air rock concert at the corner of Miller and Falcon Streets in North Sydney to hear Jeff St John and Copperwine, Alison Durbin, Doug Parkinson in Focus, and a host of other Aussie performers. I had all but decided against going back to school, enjoying work and in awe of this frightening but exciting new world of city living.

But Mum and Dad had persisted. They arranged to meet the Christian Brothers at St Pat's, having been told by phone that enrolments for Fifth Form (now Year 11) had long closed. Yet, at the meeting, to their surprise, they received an enthusiastic greeting.

'So, young Craig is keen to join us next year?'

'Oh yes', Mum assured them.

'And he was awarded dux of the school?'

'Yes, he did very well.'

'Has he got the vocation?'

'Oh yes', Dad replied.

'He's got the calling?'

'Oh yes …' That was when Mum and Dad realised something was amiss. Instead of turning left into St Patrick's College, they had turned right into St Patrick's Seminary. I was one misunderstanding away from being signed up as a novice for the priesthood.

When Mum and Dad correctly followed the Brothers' directions to St Patrick's College, the school administrators agreed to enrol me, accepting, in lieu of the usual fees, the $100 bursary I had been awarded by the state government as dux of Baradine Central School.

Perhaps the Labor premier, Jack Renshaw, who hailed from nearby Binnaway, had played a hand in awarding me the bursary, for he was keen to encourage high academic achievement by kids in small country towns. It was my first exposure to a Labor government, and I was grateful for the opportunity it gave me to complete high school at such an accomplished college.

MY FIRST WEEKS at St Pat's were truly terrifying. My cohort seemed full of boys studying first-level mathematics, science, and Latin. How would I compete? Amazingly, the school's headmaster, Brother Casey, took an interest in the endeavours of this shy boy from the country named Craig. He went to the trouble of ascertaining the marks I achieved in the School Certificate at Baradine. While I only made it into the fourth decile of students in the state in advanced woodwork, the fifth decile in advanced science, and had failed advanced mathematics, I did well in commerce, reaching the seventh decile, and stunned both Brother Casey and myself by scoring in the top 10 per cent of the state in advanced English and advanced social studies. 'You can succeed here', Brother Casey, advised me, 'if you play to your strengths.' He enrolled me in first-level English, commerce, and geography.

Making the transition from a class of fourteen students at Baradine Central to one of more than 100 at St Pat's was daunting enough. But the cultural change was the most difficult. To be accepted into the cool crowd was no easy task. They went surfing every weekend, most owning surfboards. We country kids had only seen surfboards on black-and-white television in *77 Sunset Strip* and *Adventures in Paradise,* or in Elvis movies at the picture show. My big chance for acceptance by the cool crowd arose with the correct answer to this question from one of its members: 'Which album do you like, *Cocker Happy* or *Hot August Night*?' Having listened to Neil Diamond's 'Sweet Caroline' at the tree house, I went with *Hot August Night*. Wrong. The St Pat's nerds liked Neil Diamond, while the cool kids were Joe Cocker fans.

Just when it looked like I was again destined for the nerds, the rugby season began. Based on the wildly embellished reports from an influential classmate, Greg 'Thommo' Thomas, of my exploits as a flying country winger, the Christian Brothers' coaches selected me in the First XV for a trial match against Homebush High School. Twice, the outside centre spun the ball out to me. Twice, I begged myself not to drop it. Twice, I dropped it. I was dropped to the Thirds, finishing the season in the Fourths.

Still, I ended up making good friends—none better than Kevin Whitton and Mark 'Faz' Farrell, who looked after me. As anticipated, our family had moved from the rented house in Strathfield to a duplex on the busy Georges River Road in the western suburb of Croydon Park. Kevin lived in the neighbouring suburb of Enfield, and we caught the same bus to school each day. Kevin, the Australian junior weightlifting champion in his weight class and Faz, a good footballer, formed a bridge between the cool crowd and the nerds. Along with Thommo, they taught me how to throw classmates over the balcony at the science block and, more importantly, how to break my fall when I was being thrown over.

My conversion from Neil Diamond to rock music was completed in February 1972 when Kevin and I went to a Led Zeppelin concert at the Sydney Showground. Standing in the enormous crowd, we had been restrained behind wire fencing at the edge of the stands way back from the stage. But when Led Zeppelin opened their performance with 'The Immigrant Song', we scaled the fence and poured onto the field, racing to within a few metres of the stage, adjacent to a huge bank of speakers. At first, the police tried to deter us, but quickly gave up. After a thumping performance of 'Whole Lotta Love', my hearing never recovered.

BEFORE THE START OF MY SECOND YEAR at St Pat's, I returned to Baradine for New Year's Eve. I was sitting on the bonnet of Dad's car at a campfire, zipped up in a sleeping bag, when two friends, threatening to throw me onto the fire, accidentally dropped me on my head. On

New Year's Day, I had planned to drive to Narrabri to see my blonde-haired girlfriend from the Narrabeen Fitness Camp, but early that morning, sleeping in the back of the car outside Tony Purdy's house, I had a series of fits, ending up in Baradine District Hospital. The nurses broke off the ends of the teeth next to my front teeth, trying to prise my mouth open to prevent me biting my tongue.

Back in Sydney, a Macquarie Street specialist conducted a brain scan and diagnosed me with epilepsy, prescribed Dilantin, and told me never to drink heavily or get overtired. At the beginning of the school year, we went on a religious retreat with girls from our sister college, Santa Sabina. So elated was I by the interest being shown in me by one girl that, unwisely, I stayed awake for 40 hours. As if to impress this girl from Santa Sabina, I repeated my *grand mal* performance at the retreat. To this day, I have no memory of it, only of waking to be comforted by her and one of the Christian Brothers.

We were to remain partners and later, husband and wife, until 1983, when we went our separate ways. A beautiful, generous, gifted woman with a golden heart, this young woman supported me emotionally when I desperately needed it. Sadly, I proved incapable of giving her the support she deserved. Although we still get on well, she long ago made a new life for herself with her partner, with whom she had children.

Despite the headmaster's personal support upon my arrival at St Pat's, we did not always see eye to eye. Long hair was all the rage in 1972. At several school assemblies, Brother Casey warned us to get our hair cut. Kevin Whitton and I were determined that, following the lyrics of the stage song 'Hair', ours would be 'shoulder length or longer; long beautiful hair, shining, gleaming, streaming, flaxen, waxen.' We went to great lengths, so to speak, to preserve our long hair, alighting from the school bus almost a kilometre from the school, and sneaking through a back gate to avoid the critical gaze of the Brothers standing at the front gate of the school as they greeted the busloads of boys each morning.

It had been six months since my last haircut when I received an instruction from Brother Casey to meet him in his office. This was the venue for meting out punishment via a cane, the likes of which I had not seen since Dad brought one home from Permewans. But upon arriving at the headmaster's office, I realised my punishment would be far more severe than six cuts with the cane. Standing behind a chair was Brother Casey, holding a towel and a pair of scissors. He invited me to take a seat, and wrapped the towel around my shoulders. 'Now, Emerson, are you going to get your hair cut, or shall I do it.' The local barber at Croydon Park's shops received an unexpected visitor that afternoon.

HAVING COMPLETED THE PREVIOUS YEAR's rugby season in the Fourths, I resolved never to play the game again, instead frequenting the Burwood Police Citizens Boys' Club with Kevin Whitton to build up my skinny body in the weightlifting room. That was until one of the coaches spotted in me an ability to tackle that I had acquired from my rugby league days. He asked me to join the Second XV in the forwards. Not once did I drop the ball. In the 1972 school magazine, our coach wrote: 'The forwards were the strength of the side and Craig Emerson, who was called up to the Firsts twice, was outstanding. He could always be depended on for a wholehearted effort and was never far from the ball.' Football, which had drained my confidence for two years, had for me become a wellspring of self-assurance.

As the rugby season ended, many of my classmates began athletics training. Those interested in selection for the St Patrick's College athletics team would be required to try out in various track and field events. I placed in each of the events I entered, winning the 400 metres, high jump, long jump, and shot put, which gave me enough points to be declared College athletics champion and captain of the St Pat's team. Having cleared five feet and two inches at Baradine, repeating the effort at the St Pat's try-outs was no problem. It was then that Brother Casey noticed my potential to do better. He supplied me with a pair of running spikes, which I had never worn before and, with his encouragement at the high-jump pit, I easily cleared five feet five inches.

At the inter-college athletics carnival held at St Leo's College, I started jumping when the bar was set at five feet two inches, and continued doing so past five feet five. As the bar was raised higher, most of my rivals missed their three attempts and dropped out. But the hot favourite for the event performed the Fosbury Flop, landing on his back on the piled foam matting available at elite schools, giving him a decided advantage over my old-style scissors technique, which had been necessitated by landing in the Baradine sawdust pits on our feet, legs, or arses.

The favourite had cleared six feet at his school championships. He began jumping at five feet and six inches while I had already been jumping for half an hour. Now I was in unchartered territory, achieving a new personal best, but knowing I would be no match for the Fosbury Flopper. The bar was raised to a height of five feet and seven inches. I missed at my first attempt, but, having only lightly touched the bar with my bum, I knew I could clear it. I did at my second go. My remaining rivals, other than the Fosbury Flopper, all bowed out. From now on, it was just the two of us. The Flopper faltered at his first attempt, too, but had no difficulty with his second. The officials raised the bar to five feet and eight inches, which was three inches higher than I had ever jumped in my life. The Flopper and I both missed twice, but I felt mine were good attempts. I needed to do just a little better at my third. To my astonishment, the Fosbury Flopping champion missed at his third attempt. He was out.

The inter-college record was five feet, seven and a half inches. If I cleared the bar on my third and last attempt, I would be inter-carnival champion and record holder. I spent what seemed like an eternity talking to myself as I prepared mentally for the jump. *You are going to fly, you are going to fly*, I said, over and over, until I was ready. The ground compere announced that I was attempting at the coming jump to win the event and break the record. A hush fell over the crowd of athletes and parents. So convinced was I that I was going to fly that I never contemplated missing. As I lifted my leading leg over the bar, I was smiling, and I cleared it easily. That's what happens when you're flying. At that instant, I learned a lesson I would carry through the rest of my life: no matter what the odds, no matter how superior your rival is, based on past performance, it is the moment that matters, and in the moment you can achieve the unbelievable. So, put yourself in the moment.

At the St Pat's speech night in the Sydney Town Hall, I was awarded trophies for college athletics champion and best athletics performance. The headmaster's speech was, however, not one of celebration of our year's achievement, but of admonition for our unacceptable behaviour.

One of our schoolmates had an uncle working at the local fruit-and-vegetable market. They were happy to be rid of boxes of fruit that had begun rotting, and we had a good use for them after our last day at school. On break-up day, we loaded boxes of rotting fruit into the back seat of Dad's 1964 Ford Falcon, which he'd bequeathed to me after giving up city driving. In the darkness at the corner of the St Pat's football fields, we waited on both sides of the road for an unsuspecting friend roaming Strathfield's streets to drive by. Faz obliged. With his windows down in the November heat, he copped oranges, apples, and grapefruit from both sides, pulling over to the kerb and staring blankly ahead as if concussed.

Next in line was an accomplished road-racing cyclist friend whom we visited at his parents' Burwood apartment. After smearing his mother's car with two crates of fruit and a can of shaving cream, we pressed the intercom buzzer, jumped into the Falcon, and sped away. As we drove off, we caught a glimpse of his mother turning the corner to witness our fruit-salad creation.

Revenge was swift. By the next evening, the Falcon was so splattered with fruit that many months later, when I took it to a garage for a service, the mechanics reported the undercarriage was caked with old fruit.

But we had one more mission before it was back to the books. Bethlehem Ladies College in Ashfield lies at the bottom of a hill. With our stores of fruit replenished following another early-morning visit to the markets, we agreed that I should drive while Thommo positioned himself on the back-seat windowsill, legs inside, body and arms outside. The greengrocer's cousin passed him mouldy grapefruit, which he tossed at the girls dressed in their purple uniforms as they waited for their buses to take them home. We made several successful runs, unloading most of our arsenal of rotting grapefruit.

'One more run and we're done', Thommo determined. Having reached the bottom of the hill, and having dispensed our last payload, I peered in my rear-vision mirror to see the face of a policeman in pursuit. Now he could see that I could see him and, with one curl of a finger, he beckoned to me.

'Oh, shit, there's a cop following us. What do I do?' I asked my partners in fruit.

'Keep driving', Thommo urged.

I reasoned that if I kept driving, slowly, the cop might lose interest and go past us. At least I had the good sense not to contemplate a car chase. I slowed the car to a crawl and kept driving, turning into a smaller street and then a lane. It was a dead end. The cop pulled up behind me, and instructed me to turn off the ignition and get out of the car.

Naturally, he asked me for my driver's licence and, unnaturally, after shuffling through my pockets, I could not produce it. The cop asked me for my full name and address. As he began writing it into his notebook on the police-car bonnet, I leaned down to assist him. 'Get your elbows off my car', he growled. He told me to expect a visit at my Croydon Park home during the next week to confiscate my licence. While I studied for my exams every night that week, I dreaded the promised visit from the cop. It never came. He'd done enough damage to my psychological health, and my lesson was learned.

At the Town Hall speech night, Brother Casey scolded the Sixth Form students for their fruit fights, but I was now a fully subscribed member of the cool crowd.

NOW OUT OF SCHOOL, we had not completely left the Christian Brothers behind us. Dominating the sprawling grounds of the seminary at Strathfield, which I had accidentally almost joined two years earlier, was a bell tower. We freshly minted St Pat's Old Boys formed the view that the bell was under-utilised. Following parties or a night out at a restaurant, we would routinely climb over the brick fence surrounding the training college grounds, sneak across the playing fields, climb the tower, and jump onto the rope connected to the bell.

For the Christian Brother seminarians, this was a bit of fun at first, but, as the bell began tolling on most Saturday nights, they started to lose their sense of humour. Eventually, fully agitated, they laid in wait. As we approached the bell tower, the seminarians gave chase, and one of them brought one of our mates down in a respectable rugby tackle. This wouldn't do, so a member of our raiding party drove his car through the gates and onto the fields, jumped from the car, and hit the seminarian over the head with a flashlight, causing him to release our designated bell-ringer. Seminarians and Old Boys were now running everywhere. Two seminarians were chasing our friend Mick 'Shirbie' Shirbin. We had already escaped over the brick fence to the safety of the suburban streets. As Shirbie lunged at the fence, we grabbed his arms, but the seminarians caught his legs. A Shirbie tug-of-war ensued, and we dragged him, scraped and bruised, to freedom. Sensibly for all concerned, the seminarians tied the bell rope into a loop knot, placing it out of reach and bringing evening peace to the streets of Strathfield.

Despite these pre-exam distractions, I did well enough in the Higher School Certificate to be accepted into university. But what course would I do? For some reason, I thought of dentistry, but soon realised I would struggle to get into the course with my lowly performance in science. While I contemplated the possibilities, Mum said I should do economics because I would earn lots of money. That sounded as good a reason as any; having done well in economics at school, I might be able to compete against the bright kids studying economics at Sydney University. My application was successful, and I was awarded a Commonwealth Scholarship, which would cover the cost of my university fees.

Eighteen days after the St Patrick's College speech night at the Sydney Town Hall, the Australian people elected Gough Whitlam as prime minister of Australia on a platform that included free university education. My friend Kevin Whitton didn't get a Commonwealth Scholarship. He was brighter than me, but, like me, his parents were working people who wouldn't be able to afford to put him through university. Before Whitlam's election, Kevin had made his decision: he wasn't going to university. I thought this was unfair; one or two marks in the Higher School Certificate would have separated us, yet one could go to university and the other couldn't. It was this injustice that led me in the direction of the Australian Labor Party. We working-class kids had to battle it out among us for the limited number of university places, while the rich kids would get into university courtesy of their parents' wealth.

7

Living in the seventies

In the holiday period before beginning my university studies, I got a job doing shift work at John Lysaght's Chullora, Dad's workplace. A standard shift was eight hours, but the overtime loadings made 12-hour shifts attractive, and 18-hour shifts, or 'doublers', highly lucrative. By the end of the holidays, I had saved $1,400—enough to buy a second-hand three-cylinder Fiat 850 sports car. It proved a reliable conveyance for several years, until I warped the aluminium cylinder head when confirming, on the freeway from Sydney to Newcastle, that it could travel at 100 miles an hour.

Holiday work at John Lysaght's had sustained me financially, if not spiritually. Relations between the workforce and management were fractious at best. One of my responsibilities was as a crane chaser. Overhead cranes, which were capable of moving along rails for the full length of the factory and across its expanse, were secured to the interior of the factory roof. Crane drivers aloft in their cabins communicated with crane chasers on the factory floor, who directed them to pallets of sheet metal to be picked up and taken to machines for fabrication and, when completed, to holding areas awaiting dispatch to customers. We crane chasers were equipped with tools enabling us to place and tighten metal straps around the sheets of metal and onto the wooden pallets.

Crane chasing was a hazardous business at any time, but far more so when the driver of the overhead crane was intoxicated; 10 tonnes of sheet metal swinging around your head could do a lot of damage. One day, when the crane driver for my night shift arrived drunk, the foreman sent him home on full pay. The union shop steward immediately called a stop-work meeting of the factory workers, and a motion for a strike was put. Only two of us voted against it. We were out for 12 hours in sympathy with the drunken crane driver for whom, as a crane chaser, I had no sympathy.

Management was no better. A new holiday recruit suggested that he and I try to break the shift record for the amount of iron channelling produced. The permanent workers were upset with us, since any new record established the benchmark against which their future performance would be judged while we were taking it easy at university. To their credit, however, the workers didn't object strongly and, after several attempts, we broke the record. For this achievement, worth a great deal of money to the company, we were to be paid a bonus of $3 each. It took six weeks of badgering the management before we received our meagre reward.

One of the workers, who'd stuck up for us while we were trying to break the record, opened the boot of his car after the day shift to display a collection of second-hand household goods, including vases and wooden ornaments. He invited the small gathering of workers to make offers on any items we wanted. As an 18-year-old, I was fascinated with this second-hand trade, and was about to inquire of the vendor where he got them. Another work colleague nudged me, and suggested it was probably best not to ask.

After two summer months working in the sheet-metal factory, it was a relief to be attending lectures at Sydney University. Within days, it became clear I was studying not for one degree, but two: economics and political economy. Two professors of orthodox economics, Warren Hogan and Colin Simkin, deployed calculus to bamboozle us about markets, competition, the 'invisible hand', and multipliers. Interspersed with these neo-classical lectures were those of Professor Ted Wheelwright and Dr Frank Stilwell on the evils of capitalism, the role of multinational corporations in usurping democracy, the manipulation of consumer desires through advertising, and the waste of resources intrinsic to built-in obsolescence.

Meanwhile, gay-rights activist Lex Watson tutored me in an elective subject simply called 'Government I', supervising my research project on the techniques used by media owners to impart their bias in the press, such as the judicious placement of stories, the use of unflattering photos, and the insertion of adverse editorial comment into news stories.

My case study was the coverage by *The Australian* and *The Sydney Morning Herald* of the Whitlam government's extraordinary raid on ASIO in March 1973. Without consulting the prime minister, attorney-general Lionel Murphy, accompanied by Commonwealth police officers, raided ASIO's Melbourne offices, suspecting the intelligence organisation of withholding information about fascist Croatian terrorist threats against Yugoslavia's communist prime minister, who was to visit shortly.

This didn't go down well with American security agencies or with Rupert Murdoch. *The Australian*'s editorial position was reflected in its coverage of the raids and their aftermath, whereas *The Sydney Morning Herald* reported it as a straight news story. When I became a cabinet minister in the Gillard Labor government 37 years later, I was already familiar with the techniques that some of the Murdoch newspapers, like *The Australian*, would use against us and in support of its adopted son, Tony Abbott.

As I journeyed through my early time at Sydney University, the student union's newspaper, *Honi Soit*, lauded the Marxist revolution in various central African countries, students protested against the Vietnam War, John Lennon asked us to imagine a world of peace, Don McLean lamented the day the music died, and Billy Thorpe and the Aztecs reckoned most people they knew thought they were crazy.

SPORT REMAINED AN IMPORTANT PART of my life in the seventies. To my delight, a group of rugby union players from the St Pat's Class of 1972 decided to enter a team into the Canterbury-Bankstown junior rugby league district competition. For the first few weeks, it was a struggle convincing the ex-union players to hold onto the ball when they were tackled, instead of placing it behind them into a non-existent ruck. To say the least, we were an unconventional rugby league side, scoring most of our tries from high kicks before the bomb was made fashionable in First Grade by a Parramatta five-eighth named Johnny Peard.

When I got home from playing rugby league on Sundays, I would climb into a warm bath to remove the grass, sweat, and blood. My first lecture on Monday mornings was in microeconomics at 9.00am. I never had the strength to get out of bed in time to make that class, passing only with the aid of the textbook and lecture notes.

These footballing friends and their girlfriends were to form the nucleus of our trips to the Griffith Wine Festival in central-west New South Wales. My friend Shirbie and I did the reconnaissance work, arriving a day ahead of the others and visiting the shops in the main street in search of anyone who might allow us to pitch a tent on their property. The local chemist obliged, and we soon packed 18 uni students into a tent a few kilometres out of town.

This was in the days before Griffith had gained notoriety as a production and distribution centre for marijuana. We should have been suspicious, since the wine was close to undrinkable. Yet after a few visits to the various wineries, the quality seemed to improve. At the end of the day, the wineries allowed us to take partially finished bottles to our campsite. There, the quality of the wine, especially the tawny port, continued to improve with every extra remnant consumed.

On a trip over the Easter weekend, having disposed of the balance of the day's wine haul, we retired to our cramped tent for much-needed sleep. As I slipped off into la-la land, the horn of my car, parked about 40 metres away, blasted through the still night. By the time I had unzipped my sleeping bag, opened the flap of the tent, and rushed to the car, I could find no sign of the intruder. Bemused, I returned to the tent, only for the episode to be repeated. Quicker off the mark this time, I could still see no shadowy figure escaping across the moonlit paddock. Next time I waited, poised, sleeping bag unzipped, tent flap open, and, sure enough, the car horn again pierced the night. So determined was I to catch the culprit that in sprinting towards the car I tripped on something and fell to the ground. Underneath me lay a rope, one end leading to the car horn and the other to the tent.

'You bastard!' I shouted towards the tent. It was never obvious to me how many campers in that tent were privy to Thommo's prank, but a lot of laughter emanated from it.

It had been a long night. But as good Catholic girls and boys, we attended Easter Sunday Mass the next day. Thommo, weary from his late-night pranks, fell asleep during the priest's sermon. When the sermon was over, we nudged Thommo and whispered for him to wake up. He broke into applause, probably the first time that priest's sermon had so ended.

Shirbie and I continued our university holiday adventures, camping on the front lawn of Parliament House adjacent to the Aboriginal Tent Embassy. If they could protest, we reasoned, so could we, doing our evening ablutions in the Parliament House washrooms. We drove to Baradine to mow the lawn of our house at 10 Queen Street in preparation for its sale, then immediately headed for the coast at Port Macquarie, 500 kilometres due east. It would have been one of the few times that the townspeople of Baradine had seen a car arriving in the middle of the bush with surfboards strapped to its roof racks.

AT CHRISTMAS 1974, following an economic slowdown, there was no holiday work at John Lysaght's. Fortunately, lawns and weeds continued to grow. During the year, I had gained a job gardening for the Isles family at Bellevue Hill in Sydney's affluent eastern suburbs. Mr and Mrs Isles headed for a day in Newcastle, asking me to move the sprinkler around the garden beds to ensure they were well watered. After they had departed, I noticed they had left a bedroom window open and that the sprinkler was spraying water onto the carpet. I slammed the bedroom window shut to keep the water out, which activated the entire alarm system in and around the substantial property.

In these dire circumstances, I did what any 20-year-old gardener from Sydney's western suburbs would do: I ran around the outside of the house three times in a blind panic. Then I remembered Mrs Isles had shown me where the alarm system's control panel was located in the house. So I broke in and silenced the alarm. Calm was restored, but only until the police cars arrived. The next-door neighbour had phoned the police to alert them to a break-in. Not every gardener gets dobbed in by a former prime minister—in my case, the Honourable Sir William McMahon.

Located at the back of the Isles' property was a large house, garden, and swimming pool owned by George and Jan Rockey. Mrs Rockey offered me $20 to garden for her once a week. This was good money, and I soon learned that her husband, George, was in business with Sir Peter Abeles. The Rockeys' butler brought me lunch and told me stories about the visits they received from a trade-union leader named Bob Hawke. Mrs Isles was very kind to me, and would not allow me to work if it got too hot. While doing her gardens, I was able to listen on my transistor radio to Lillee and Thomson steaming in against the Poms, regaining the Ashes for the first time in a decade.

My undergraduate university studies coincided perfectly with the Whitlam years. While I liked Whitlam's philosophy of helping the underprivileged, it was a shambolic government, always in trouble. Treasurer Jim Cairns was allegedly having an affair with his private secretary, Junie Morosi, precipitating what became an endless news story. Economics was not the government's strength: in a single year, inflation hit 17 per cent, wages rose by 33 per cent, and real government spending jumped by 20 per cent.

Then the government tried to enter into a massive Middle Eastern loans deal with a shady character called Khemlani, bypassing Treasury. It was an outrageous, half-arsed manoeuvre, precipitating a loss of confidence in the Whitlam government's economic management. The Fraser-led opposition blocked the supply of money needed to keep the machinery of government going, and the governor-general dismissed the Whitlam government four days before my 21st birthday.

Through this time, our friends' 21st birthday parties were in full swing. I left one such party on 13 December, despondent that only three among our group of friends had voted Labor in the rout of the Whitlam government. At every party, the band Skyhooks was singing 'Living in the Seventies'. That particular Saturday night was a horror movie right there on my TV, shocking me right out of my brain.

AS WELL AS MUM'S JOB as a clerk at the Medical Benefits Fund in Sydney's city centre, she took on the responsibility of union organiser for the Federated Clerk's Union. She was a firebrand, always fighting with management on behalf of her fellow union members. Yet Mum couldn't stand the Whitlam government, and voted Liberal.

Dad, too, was a union member. Much later, I learned that at both Permewans in Baradine and John Lysaght's in Chullora, Dad had the same union representative, the legendary Johnno Johnson. When I was elected as a Labor Member of Parliament, Johnno told me about his memories of my father. Although Dad was a union member, he was forever angry with unions that called strikes in holiday periods — especially beer strikes at Easter. Yet he was a Labor voter, as far as I could tell. We never talked about it much.

Having settled into Sydney life, Mum became less erratic and moody, but there wasn't a lot of happiness in the household. Huge rows erupted from time to time, and Mum would lock herself in the bedroom with her sleeping pills. I became so worried that I walked at night to the public phone at the Croydon Park Post office and rang the police. They told me that, since Mum had not committed a crime, there was nothing they could do.

Lance had married and moved with his wife, Patricia, into a rented semi-detached house in the suburb of Lidcombe in Sydney's west. Following the tragic cot death of their baby, Joshua, Dad wrote this verse:

Sweet innocent, you've left this earth
After just a few weeks' stay
The Lord above has called you, son
And taken you away.
With broken hearts, we miss you, mate
Your old Grandma and me
But we have solace with the thought
In heaven that you be.

By the end of 1975, the marriage between Lance and Pat had disintegrated. I had placed fourth in economics at Sydney University, and had accepted an offer to undertake an honours year. Knowing how unhappy I was at home, Mum and Dad suggested I move in with Lance to offer him some companionship.

I took their advice. However, Lance and I were so inattentive to grocery shopping that the entire contents of the fridge tended to comprise a half-eaten Easter egg and row upon row of Lance's bottled home-brewed beer. After consuming several dozen bottles over the first few weeks, I became accustomed to Lance's unique, chunky brew, preferring it to the far more expensive professionally brewed beer. Lance advised me that his brew should be poured slowly from a longneck bottle into a glass, leaving the sludge at the bottom of the bottle. But having learned that the sludge was rich in nutrients, I confess to having, from time to time, poured the entire contents of a bottle into a beer mug for want of any other form of breakfast.

Some of Lance's unpacked possessions, following his move with Pat to Lidcombe, remained in a pile on the back veranda. In the centre of the pile was a tin containing the remainder of their wedding cake. In the dead of night, we often heard the metal cake tin popping and twanging. I speculated that the cake had come alive and was trying to escape. We named this trapped creature 'Herbie'. 'Free Herbie!' became our cause célèbre.

Apart from Lance, Herbie, and me, the only living being at the Lidcombe house was Basil, a tabby cat. Basil had low expectations: 'Feed me, and I will hang around' was his value proposition. We fed Basil, and he hung around. To give Basil his much-needed exercise, Lance and I bowled him along the length of the large, linoleum-covered hallway. He didn't seem to mind. But he had a different attitude to a fierce thunderstorm that struck Lidcombe. So big were the hailstones that they smashed most of our windows and made a deafening noise as they crashed into the corrugated-iron roof. Terrified at the din, Basil ran from the house into our next-door neighbours' front yard. I ran out in pursuit, but after a couple of hailstones cracked me on the head, I retreated, soaked, into our house, resigned to Basil's death.

The next morning, the devastation from the hailstorm was clear. All of the roofs in the street, most of them made of corrugated asbestos cement, had been destroyed. Broken glass lay strewn along the sides of houses. Lance and I searched for Basil's body until we heard 'Meow, meow', spotting Basil striding towards us nonchalantly, as if nothing had happened.

AFTER FINISHING MY HONOURS YEAR at Sydney University, I began working over summer as a builder's labourer for Faz and Thommo, who by then had started their own business. They won a tender to renovate the interior of an old factory on Missenden Road near Sydney's Royal

Prince Alfred Hospital, and Faz and I got the job of lining the internal walls of the building with plasterboard.

We had slid a wooden plank between the tops of two tall stepladders, hauling up the sheets of plasterboard and nailing them to the beams. As we nailed at each end, I looked curiously at Faz, and he looked quizzically back at me. Without saying a word, it immediately became clear that we were sharing the same thought: *Why is the wall getting further away?* By the time we realised that the plank and two ladders were falling, there was nothing we could do but brace ourselves for the impact of hitting the ground. Down came the plank, the ladders, Faz, and I. As I looked over to see if Faz was okay, a further, worrying thought entered my mind. I had only just begun hammering the first nail into my end of the plasterboard. How many nails had Faz managed to hammer in? The answer was, apparently, none. As I looked up, the large sheet of unsecured plasterboard crashed onto us, smashing into pieces.

With an honours degree in economics on their resumés, my colleagues at Sydney University headed for the job market, two of them eventually becoming deputy governors at the Reserve Bank. But I still didn't know what I wanted to do for a career. During my childhood at St John's Convent School in Baradine, the nuns had told us of missionaries who caught leprosy trying to save starving children in poor countries. Placed on the desk at the front of the classroom was a cast-iron, curly-headed black boy into whose hand we would donate a spare penny. We pushed down a lever at his back, which raised his hand towards his mouth, and in slid the penny.

Somehow the missionary zeal never left me. When I explained to Professors Hogan and Simkin that I wanted to help poor people, they suggested I do another year of study, concentrating on economic development, which would convert my honours degree into an honours and masters degree in economics.

Working at an international-development agency appealed to me, but I didn't know where to start. At one point, I wrote a letter 'To Whom It May Concern' at the World Bank, expressing an interest in working there. Evidently, my letter concerned no one; I never got a reply.

Towards the end of my masters coursework and my thesis on the taxation of mining projects in developing countries, Professor Simkin, was approached by an Indonesian colleague, Benny Widyono, who had been working at the United Nations in Santiago, Chile. Several major multinational corporations had so vehemently opposed the democratically elected Marxist government led by president Salvador Allende that, in 1973, they financially supported a coup led by General Augusto Pinochet.

As this involvement of multinational corporations in the internal political affairs of foreign countries came to light, the United Nations established a Centre on Transnational Corporations in New York to monitor their activities and assess their economic impacts on developing countries. The UN then established offices in each of the regions, starting with Latin America. Benny was given the task of setting up the Asia-Pacific office to be based at the UN regional headquarters in Bangkok. The staffing contingent was to be four professional officers plus several locally engaged support staff. Benny asked Professor Simkin if he knew of a young economist who might be a suitable candidate for one of the positions.

Professor Simkin told Benny that it just so happened he was supervising an economist undertaking his masters degree, majoring in economic development. Benny visited Australia, interviewed me, and offered me the job. At the age of 23, I was moving with my young wife to Bangkok on a mission to save the world, or at least Asia and the Pacific.

8

Cows, conmen, and catastrophes

Before settling into work in Bangkok, we recently married ex-student adventurers booked a backpackers' holiday through India, Burma, Thailand, and Indonesia. Our first port of call was Calcutta. It was such a shock. Every imaginable noise and smell emanated from its crowded, frenzied streets. Foolishly, we had taken with us a large suitcase, as well as backpacks. As we struggled towards our hotel on foot, through the heat and grime, the heavy air thick with bus exhaust fumes, beggars thrust out disfigured arms in the hope of a coin, their faces scarred from smallpox or burns, some with only one eye, others with none. We were enveloped by teeming desperation.

Soon realising we couldn't walk the full distance through the crowds, we accepted one of the innumerable offers of a rickshaw, not bothering to bargain beyond the opening offer of five rupees—less than 50 cents. Suddenly the sea of humanity and cows parted, the two of us aloft in the carriage, our suitcase and backpacks wedged between our legs. Our small rickshaw puller wove between horn-blasting taxis, dilapidated cars, carts, and swarms of other rickshaw carriers, among whom there was clearly a level of mutual courtesy and respect.

Our rickshaw puller was sweating profusely under our weight, gaining momentum, only to be stopped in his tracks by a vehicle whose driver had neither the patience nor the inclination to wait for the poor man to pass. His tight, wiry muscles strained through his ragged shirt at the constant stopping and restarting until we arrived at our destination. Our tip of a further five rupees seemed to delight him, but did nothing to ease the injustice of two ex-students barely out of their teens already possessing more wealth than this poor man could imagine earning in a lifetime.

A remnant of the colonial era, the Great Eastern Hotel was amply staffed, with white-uniformed employees opening doors, manning elevators, cleaning floors, selling gifts, serving food, begging pardons, polishing wood, and tending gardens. Braving the streets again after checking in, we were instantly surrounded by hawkers, merchants, and their assistants, ushering us towards their stalls. I received countless offers to shine my shoes. No matter that I was wearing thongs: they could be shined, too, no problem. Beggars were everywhere. Deserted mothers carrying tiny babies pleaded for the smallest coin. It was traumatic and exhausting for us, but we couldn't imagine the pitiable existence of these poor, small humans; we were twice the size of the desperate people swarming around us.

At first, out of politeness, we responded to every approach.

'Rickshaw?'

'No, thanks.'

'Shoe shine?'

'No, thanks.'

'You want to see temple?'

'No, thanks.'

'Hotel?'

'Rickshaw?'

'Shoe shine?'

'Where you go?'

'No, thanks. No, thanks. No, thanks. No!' We had become rude.

So many impoverished Indians were confronting us that we quickly learned that engaging them, even if just to say no, only encouraged them to persist. After a couple of days, we began pushing past their approaches, remaining silent and avoiding eye contact. We felt awful: callous, uncaring. These poor, wretched people could only wonder at our affluence.

As evening closed in, the footpaths and alleys became places for the homeless to sleep. By dusk, the streets were littered with the day's waste — human, vegetable, manufactured-packaging, and plastic. Crushed husks of sugar cane lay strewn everywhere, and the available food was cooked on coal-fuelled fires, filling the night air with the smell of burning coal. We slept for 12 hours, waking at dawn to the caw-cawing of black birds perched on the roofs and windowsills of buildings, ready to pick through the waste that had accumulated through the day. Lowly paid street cleaners moved in, piling the rubbish into wicker baskets and dragging it away.

THOUGH WE HAD PRE-PURCHASED RAIL PASSES for second-class train travel throughout the country, the clerks at Howrath Railway Booking office advised us there were no available seats — not on any train out of Calcutta to anywhere — for at least a week. No matter whom we asked, we received the same answer from behind each window. It seemed implausible. But having queued for hours at different windows, we found a sign reading 'Tourists' and depicting a finger pointing around the corner like a ray of hope. Here we were issued our Indrail passes, which, when we eventually reached the front of one of the snaking booking queues, secured us two seats out of Calcutta that very evening.

Back at the Great Eastern Hotel, we collected our luggage from the concierge, having checked out earlier in the day. By now, my bethonged feet were filthy. I went to the washroom to sneak a quick foot wash. But in such a heavily staffed hotel, no sneaking was possible. With one foot in the washbasin, I heard the echoing command of the white-suited washroom attendant.

'Nooooo! Nooooo!' he insisted. 'Remove your foot from the wash basin.'

Thirty seconds longer, and I would have had the job done.

'Noooo! Noooo!' he repeated, as I struggled to complete the job. Had the washroom official allowed me to finish and dry off, I would have left no legacy.

Now feverishly scrubbing while bursting with embarrassment, I stammered: 'Just washing ... uh, nearly ...', but he insisted I leave immediately.

Of course, I left a grubby, wet trail across his freshly cleaned washroom floor with my dripping, dirty feet.

'Now you are dirty everywhere!' he shouted after me, alerting most of the staff and many guests to my disgusting behaviour as I trudged across the marble floor of the hotel lobby.

'C'mon, let's get out of here" I whispered to my 21-year-old wife, happy to return to the streets of Calcutta where, at least, my feet felt more at home.

At the railway station, after we'd struggled for hours through traffic and the crush of humanity, the platform erupted around us. People pushed and shoved and shouted in what seemed like a riot.

'What's happening?' I asked my wife fearfully.

'The train's here', she observed.

As the train backed along the platform, hundreds of frantic Indians swarmed the carriages. Death-defying headlong leaps through open windows were followed by bag after bag of luggage, merchandise, and farm animals, which were passed through by friends and relatives. Though the noise was deafening and order non-existent, there was no hostility or friction. Everyone appeared to recognise that they had an equal claim to the railway carriage; it was just that some were more agile than others. The slow, the very young, and the aged then joined their most athletic family member in the carriage like sardines in a tin.

India's caste system played out on our train journey to the north. Bejewelled women in fine silk saris and men in Western suits or the best traditional linen dress took their places in the spacious, sparsely occupied first-class sleeping cabins. Bodies of untouchables packed into and squeezed out of and onto the roofs of the succession of dilapidated, faded-red third-class carriages at the back end of the train. Jammed between these contrasting worlds on steel wheels were the green second-class carriages. While we had been allocated sleeping cabins, so had the hundreds of Indians who had seemingly purchased tickets for the same seats. On the first night, I slept on a luggage rack.

We stopped at Gaya and then Bodhgaya in Bihar state, where the Buddha is said to have attained enlightenment. As we continued our journey from Gaya to Varanasi in 42-degree heat, we gained ever more passengers. Over one four-hour stretch, I could find floor space for only one of my feet. If the luggage racks had given way, several of our Indian travelling companions below would surely have been killed, for the racks were laden with passengers who had boarded the train with no allocated seating.

Upon our arrival in Varanasi, exhausted, we asked a rickshaw driver to take us to a tourist bungalow. Instead, he peddled to the Mansarover Hotel, no doubt earning a commission from the hotel management. We were too tired to argue and, observing that meals were provided only via room service, we went to our room to eat and sleep. When something resembling what we had ordered arrived, delivered by a boy of around 14 years of age, I offered a tip equal to 10 per cent of the bill.

'Baksheesh!' he demanded, insisting on a larger tip. I was twice his size, yet I was frightened of him. His gaze was deep, determined, and menacing. I was relieved when he left the room.

Next evening, he brought our room service again. We offered him the same tip again, expecting him then to leave the room.

'Baksheesh!' he persisted. He did not move when I turned away.

To our demands to 'Go!' he responded: 'Baksheesh!'

I physically led him out through the doorway. We finished our meals, showered, and slept. I dreamed about the boy's staring, sunken eyes. 'Bang! Bang! Bang!' came a pounding on the door.

I'm dreaming, I thought.

'Bang! Bang! Bang!' Feeling in the dark for our alarm clock, I bumped into it, and it smashed on the floor. My wife woke with a start.

'What's happening?' she asked in a panic.

'There's someone at the door', I explained.

'Bang! Bang! Bang!' The thumping was louder this time. Shaking, I rose to my feet and picked up the broken clock. It was midnight. The banging continued. I unlocked the door, and the boy pushed his way into our room.

'Baksheesh! Baksheesh!' he demanded, his dark eyes peering through me.

I felt paralysed with fear, but managed to push him back through the doorway, his gaze still fixed upon me. Fastening every door catch, I stumbled back to bed and lay awake for the rest of the night.

VARANASI, on the banks of the mighty Ganges River, is a place of pilgrimage for Hindus. In the morning, we watched as recently deceased people were cremated and their ashes strewn into the river. A boy, clad in a singlet so heavily used that it would have disintegrated if he had attempted to remove it, rowed us up and down the river. As we passed by one set of steps leading into the river after another, we witnessed Hindus bathing, swimming, and beating wet garments on the rocks, while Brahmins performed their yogic salutes to the sun. Sounds of praying, chanting, talking, and the splat, splat of garments were soaked up in the vast expanse of water, the opposite riverbank barely visible to the naked eye.

As our river journey ended, our guide offered to show us the Golden Temple. To get there, we had to wind our way through the bowels of Varanasi. Tip-toeing past inches-deep dung mixed with animal urine, brushing past cows defecating in the narrow alleys, we tried to avoid the glances of the people living in these putrid slums. We were hopelessly lost, entirely at the mercy of our guide.

We were in tears, finding it hard to keep up with the guide's demanding pace, and daring to take a full breath only at the occasional place into which open air could enter. We both feared we would be robbed and beaten, but our indefatigable guide led us to a temple as promised. It was no Golden Temple, but a small, local one, close to which was a silk store — the guide's planned destination all along. We bargained hard, and bought the cheapest item in the house: a small silk scarf. Our guide reappeared and, within minutes, we were thrust back into sunlight. The bustle of animal carts, rickshaws, cars, and people, which had been a daunting experience for us in Calcutta just a few days earlier, was now a welcome encounter.

Ever conscious of contracting the dreaded 'Delhi belly', we drank only bottled Sprite and hot tea in earthen cups passed through the windows of train carriages. But these precautions were insufficient to prevent my wife coming down with a devastating bout of gastroenteritis. So weakened was she that we were obliged to stay in a cheap Delhi hotel for longer than we had planned. After a few days, she regained some of her strength and appetite, so we decided to splurge that evening on the backpacker luxury of curry containing meat at one of the many restaurants on Connaught Circus, a ring road in Delhi's central district. During the day, we checked out various places, comparing prices to help us decide on a suitable restaurant for our evening's special treat.

As we were leaving one restaurant following a menu inspection, we were pleasantly surprised by the friendliness of a departing customer for whom I had held open the door. His engaging manner was welcome, especially since we had not been on particularly friendly terms with the 100 million-or-so Indians we had met to date.

'Didn't you like the food there?' he inquired.

'Oh no', I explained, 'we were just checking prices for dinner tonight.'

'Are you from Australia?'

'Yes, we are.'

'My wife's sister married an Australian. Would you like to have a cup of coffee over there? I will buy. The new government says we should be courteous to foreigners.'

'No. Thanks anyway.'

'Are you sure? They make the best coffee in Delhi at that restaurant.'

As we had drunk only bottled Sprite and super-sweetened tea since arriving in India more than a week ago, his invitation for coffee sounded tempting.

'Okay', my wife said.

'Oh, I am very glad.'

We started walking towards the restaurant.

'My wife's sister lives in Melbourne. She likes Australia very much. They've been there for several years now.'

Sitting at an upstairs table, away from the clatter, we ordered three coffees.

'My wife and I live outside Delhi on an orchard. I work here in Delhi, and we have beautiful fruit, the mangoes especially. Are you a student?'

'No, I am an economist. Why did you think I was a student?'

'My wife's sister says that many Australian students have beards. You look like a student.'

'Well, I was one last year.'

'You see, she was right!'

We all laughed.

'Perhaps you would like to visit our orchard tomorrow? I could pick you up. My wife cooks good curries. Not like curries you get in restaurants. Real Indian curries. My wife's sister sends her Australian recipes, but she can't understand some parts. You could swap recipes. What do you think?'

'Sounds good to me', I said. 'We could go and be back in time to pick up our visas for Burma in the late afternoon.'

'Yes', said my wife cheerily, 'that'd be lovely.'

'Done. Oh, my wife will be so pleased', our host enthused.

The coffee arrived, and we moved into a conversation about India and Australia.

'You know, there's a regional celebration tonight in a hotel on the outskirts of Delhi. It is only for the state of Haryana, and there's traditional dancing and food as well. Would you be interested? We're going, and we could pick you up from your hotel.'

My wife, who'd danced since she was a little girl, was attracted to the suggestion, as we'd been talking about checking out options for a traditional dance performance. This was a perfect opportunity. We finalised details of when and where his wife would pick us up.

'The concert starts at 6.30pm, and my wife is meeting me in town. I'm afraid I don't have enough money on me to buy your tickets, and I don't have time to go home.'

'We understand. How much are they?' I asked.

'Fifty, 70, and 100 rupees', he said. 'We've got 70-rupee seats, and they're almost as good as the 100-rupee ones.'

'Okay, we'll take the 70-rupee seats, too', I said.

Seventy rupees were less than 10 Australian dollars, which was reasonable for a full night's entertainment and food. We'd certainly missed such luxuries, and were happy to give him the money.

With everything arranged, we changed the conversation to life in India. But we slowly became anxious about having given our host our money.

'We feel terrible', my wife said apologetically, 'but we've given you 140 rupees, and we don't even know your name.'

'Oh, I understand. Yes, I should have told you. My name is Shandra.'

'We've been cheated and lied to all over India', I added. 'So we've become very cautious. Then when someone like you comes along, we still don't …'

'Yes, yes, of course. You cannot trust anyone in India. Perhaps I should ring my wife and ask her to bring the money.'

'If you could, that would be better.'

Shandra got up to make the phone call downstairs. My wife accompanied him while I waited for the bill. When the bill arrived, I paid it quickly and hastened to join them. Shandra had to wait for another caller to finish, picking up the receiver just as I arrived. He dialled. There was no answer. He dialled again. Still no answer. But I had memorised the number he had dialled the second time.

'Try once more', I suggested.

He hesitantly dialled a third time. It was a different number.

'Okay, hand over our money!' I demanded.

Moving towards the door, he said: 'I'll get a taxi to my home and come back with the tickets.'

'No, hand over the money!'

My wife stepped in front of him, pushing her hand against the vest covering his ample stomach while I grabbed his arm. The three of us were shaking as he fumbled through his pocket and produced the banknotes we had foolishly given him. He ran out the door, and we learned a valuable lesson for the price of a cup of coffee. That night, the two of us spent some of the 140 recovered rupees on a delicious chicken curry, celebrating the attainment of a little bit of wisdom but not much enlightenment at Connaught Circus.

OUR CHEAP STUDENT AIRFARES from Australia to India required us to retrace the train tracks from Delhi to Calcutta, from where we flew over the Bay of Bengal to Burma's capital, Rangoon—since renamed Yangon. Descending over Rangoon was like flying into the nineteenth century: thatched roofs on wooden houses, a precinct of official buildings, Buddhist pagodas, and a striking absence of flashy neon signs and billboards, not even a Coca-Cola sign. Tourist visas were restricted to one week, and the tip from fellow student travellers was to bring in a bottle of Johnny Walker Black Label, which fetched sufficient Burmese kyats on the black market to fund the entire week's stay.

It didn't feel right for an appointed UN official to engage in such black-market racketeering. Judging by our taxi driver's astonishment and dismay, we must have been the only incoming tourists he had ever transported who had so refrained. Educated by having passed up this first high-finance opportunity, we hit the night markets, where we quickly learned that the competitive spirit was alive and well in the economy of the Socialist Republic of Burma. Although the official exchange rate was around seven kyats to the US dollar, we were being offered at least triple that rate. Soon we found ourselves bargaining with locals, their pockets stuffed full of kyats, eager to buy our US dollars. Following a dreamy, moonlit night at the stunningly beautiful Shwedagon Pagoda, we trekked the next morning to the Burma Airways office to buy tickets to Mandalay.

Different country, same story—no seats were available. But this was a genuine case of too many backpackers and too few flights. We were forced to spend another of our permissible seven days in Burma in Rangoon. The following day, we revisited Burma Airways, and were successful in securing two round-trip tickets to take us to the ancient capital of Pagan, onto Mandalay, and back to Rangoon.

We needed, however, to be up at 4.30am and to check in by 6.00am for a 7.00am flight. Chatting with the other tourists in a long queue to the checkout counter, we finally reached the desk, only to be informed apologetically that, though we had been told to be on this flight, it was destined for Mandalay and we were not on the passenger list. *Our* flight, we were told, was scheduled for a 10.30am departure. We personally perused the passenger manifest to confirm our names were not there. Since the airfare was the same regardless of whether we travelled to Mandalay and then Pagan or in reverse order, I asked the counter attendant whether we could board the 7.00am flight if two passengers failed to turn up. Obligingly, he said that yes, we could do so, and that we should wait nearby.

We waited until the queue of passengers and those still arriving at the airport had checked in. Hopeful that a couple might have slept in, we approached the attendant, to be told that, unfortunately for us, all 44 passengers had turned up.

Disappointed, we walked upstairs to the cafeteria, where we ordered tea and eggs on toast and began settling in for the wait for our 10.30am flight. It was a misty morning as we peered through the plate-glass windows to the runway. As I began eating my breakfast, I noticed an ambulance speed past, then a fire engine, and then another. We made inquiries, and were soon advised that the plane had crashed upon take-off. All 48 people aboard the 7.00am flight were killed.

We felt physically ill. We had been talking and laughing with fellow backpackers in the slowly moving queue just over an hour before. Now they were all dead. For two hours, our plane was checked and rechecked.

During this time, the cabin crew decided to leave the cockpit door open. The pilots' demeanour did not inspire confidence. Everyone was freaked out.

Pagan became our convalescence home. We abandoned any thought of taking a further flight to Mandalay, preferring to play Scrabble in the state guesthouse and to visit some of Pagan's four million pagodas. After a day in the century heat, we walked from our cabin to the waterline of the Irrawaddy River. Although the cabin was on the river's edge during the wet season, in this, the dry season, the water was 300 metres away. When we reached the river, we submerged ourselves up to our necks like a pair of water buffalo. So still was the evening that we could hear the laughter of an out-of-sight child splashing up-stream. Fishing vessels stole silently by as the sun threw its dying rays across the vast expanse of water. We were glad to be alive.

9

The city of angels and villains

On my first day as a professional officer at the United Nations, I set off confidently by taxi for work. My confidence was misplaced. I had no training in the Thai language, and Bangkok taxi drivers had no training in Australian drawl. My journey to work was to become an Australian crawl, as mystified taxi drivers waved me away following my futile attempts to describe my desired destination. Finally, I arrived, drenched with perspiration, wringing with anxiety, in my green, flared pants. My boss, Benny Widyono, politely pretended not to notice I was more than three hours late, and introduced me to my colleagues, a Sri Lankan and an Indian. To my delight, I was assigned a secretary and typist, a pleasant, enthusiastic 18-year-old Thai woman named Pornrudee who laughed freely even when she couldn't understand what I was saying.

Our small group established the Joint Unit on Transnational Corporations between the New York-based Centre on Transnational Corporations and the Bangkok-based Economic and Social Commission for Asia and the Pacific. We inquired into the impact of transnational corporations on rubber and bauxite production, pineapple canning, tin mining, and just about every other conceivable economic activity. This was substantial policy work, but the bane of my life was the monthly report I was required to prepare for the Program Coordination and Monitoring Office, an outfit comprising UN staff so hopeless they were literally kicked upstairs: we were on the eighth floor; the PCMO was on the 14th. For each of our research projects, we were required to draw a red line on a planning calendar depicting the agreed implementation schedule. Beneath each red line, we were to draw a blue line, tracking progress, including by consultants the office had engaged to assist with the research work. Below the blue line was a space into which I was expected to write a monthly comment.

Soon I was to learn, having been hauled up to the PCMO, that comments such as 'on track' and 'proceeding according to schedule' were unacceptable. I was instructed to think up creative descriptions of progress for each of the dozen-or-more projects we had running at any given time. Comments such as 'pleasing progress', 'first draft submitted', 'ongoing consultations', and 'preparatory work underway' could take my reports only so far.

When my imagination was exhausted and several projects passed the deadline, I asked for advice from the PCMO on how to report that projects were overdue without embarrassing our office. The answer was remarkably simple: get out a red felt pen and a ruler, and extend the deadline. From that day forward, according to PCMO reports, not once did our Joint Unit on Transnational Corporations fail to meet a project deadline. Everybody was happy.

Meeting the expectations of the PCMO in my early months at the UN had been challenging, but satisfying the Thai Customs Service, whose task was to clear our furniture that had arrived from Australia, was impossible. Locally engaged UN staff, led by a Thai man named Jimmy, were responsible for navigating the Thai bureaucracy for such matters on behalf of expatriates employed at the UN. Week after week, I enquired of Jimmy when my consignment would be cleared at the port of Klong Toey. 'Tea money', Jimmy demanded—if I paid 'tea money' of US$60, my furniture would be released within days. Bribing customs officials didn't seem to be an auspicious start for a young UN official on a mission to save the world. I refused. Months later, Customs finally released the furniture, probably because it was cluttering up the port, and no tea money was in sight.

A legal privilege was available to all expatriate UN officials: customs duties on new imported luxury cars were set at 200 per cent, but the vehicles could be imported duty-free for foreign UN staff. As a fresh recruit, I was encouraged by Jimmy and others at the UN to buy a new Mercedes Benz, drive it for the mandatory two years, and then sell it to a Thai national at a handsome profit. Jimmy could organise the finance. Having said no to importing a bottle of Johnny Walker Black Label into Burma, I recoiled at the image of a 23-year-old UN official cruising the streets of Bangkok in a Mercedes Benz. My unwillingness to cooperate incurred the wrath of Jimmy and his colleagues, who missed out on their commission.

Sharing the Bangkok apartment block with us were three German men around our age; an Englishman named Mike; an American representative of the John Deere farming equipment company named Karl Frank; his wife, Bev, and daughter, Cricket; a Russian who worked at the UN; and the owner of our apartment compound, who was a rich, attractive Thai woman dedicated to fashion. Around the UN, it was well known that the Russian was a spy—an affable spy, but a spy all the same.

American Thanksgiving Day had arrived, and the Franks prepared an amazing spread of turkey and all manner of food to be shared in the apartment's common area. In a gesture towards ending the Cold War, the Russian brought a bottle of duty-free vodka. The American businessman and the Australian academic hoping to save the world joined the Russian spy in demolishing the bottle, causing him to produce another.

Our glamorous landlady entered in a resplendent designer frock, her hair beautifully permed, and her fingers and neck dripping with gold, emeralds, and pearls. We gathered around the pool, and she introduced us to her boyfriend, a uniformed Thai policeman. Having consumed a bellyful of vodka, I saw an opportunity to entertain our fellow thanksgivers by throwing our divine host into the pool. She was very good natured about it, returning to her private apartment and emerging 20 minutes later in another designer frock, her hair beautifully permed, and her fingers and neck dripping with gold, emeralds, and pearls. By now, the vodka had taken full effect and, in a flash of brilliance, I threw her in again. Her policeman boyfriend failed to see the funny side of this second dunking, and confronted me, so I jovially wrestled with him and threw him into the pool, too, holstered gun and all. He was not amused, but, in good news for me, he restrained himself as the revellers laughed at his misfortune.

Arriving at work the next day, I could not lift my head off the desk for the first three hours, so I caught a taxi home, went to bed, and concluded I had done nothing to advance the cause of détente or of Australian–Thai diplomatic relations.

SEVERAL MONTHS INTO MY MISSION in Bangkok, in July 1978, Dad had his second heart attack. He'd suffered his first one in the early 1970s, following our move to Sydney. Dad never adjusted to life in the big smoke, and was eventually sacked from John Lysaght's. He then gained employment as a printer for a large wholesaling business, but after a few years it went broke. Finally, Dad returned to selling hardware, working at a store in Ashfield, one suburb away from our house in Croydon Park.

For many years, Dad had been applying for the so-called TPI pension, a payment for war veterans who had been medically assessed as being totally and permanently incapacitated. The Department of Veterans' Affairs rejected his application, despite his heart attack, and Dad found it difficult to cope with tetchy customers at the Ashfield hardware store. Once too often, Dad told a customer to bugger off.

As soon as I read of Dad's dismissal in a letter from home, I rang to urge Mum not to give him a hard time. It was too late. Dad answered the phone, and told me Mum had locked herself in her bedroom; they were having a row. Dad said he'd try to get her to come to the phone. She did, and I pleaded with her to go easy on Dad; but, in her opinion, Dad had failed. They were very insecure financially, now relying on Mum's income as a clerk at the Medical Benefits Fund. People who lived through the Great Depression were extremely anxious about being financially insecure. Dad's sacking was a devastating blow to him. I knew it would affect his health badly.

Dad's second heart attack was as inevitable as it was tragic. It happened within a couple of weeks of him losing his hardware-store job. He survived, but was placed on blood-thinning medication and told to wear special stockings. He was instructed that the medication was dangerous if mixed with alcohol, so he was restricted to no more than two beers a day. Slowly, Dad's health began to improve, but he suffered from breathlessness, and his legs ached.

A month or so later, the phone in our Bangkok apartment rang. It was Mum. She was crying. She said: 'I'll put Lance on.'

Lance told me: 'Dad died today, Pud.'

I could only say, over and over: 'Poor Dad. Poor Dad.'

That was my reaction as a son feeling sorry for his father. But Dad's death also obliged me to confront the utter finality of the death of a parent. I remember thinking that Dad had done many things in my lifetime. He had laughed, he had carried me on his shoulders from the Baradine picture show, he had told me of the war, he had encouraged me through school, he had argued with Mum, but he had never died before.

I learned that Dad had walked the short distance from our house to the Croydon Park shops, where he ordered mince for tea from the butchers, and went on to the nearby Croydon Park Ex-Servicemen's Club. Bored from being at home alone, unemployed and incapacitated, he probably had more than two beers. He returned to the butchers, picked up the mince, and reached the street corner near our house. There he collapsed and died, on the footpath, alone.

I flew back to Australia, where Lance, Mum, and I arranged the funeral. A veteran from the Croydon Park Ex-Servicemen's Club played a tape recording of the Last Post. As Dad's coffin was about to be lowered into the grave at Lidcombe's Rookwood Cemetery, Mum put her arms around the casket and said: 'Goodbye, mate.' For all the arguments, all the acrimony, and all the name-calling, she loved the man who had introduced himself to her via beautifully written aerogramme letters from a prisoner-of-war camp in northern Germany.

When I returned to Bangkok after Dad's funeral, a letter was waiting for me at the post office near the UN building that expatriates used as their postal address. Dad had written it on the morning of his death. He had that same morning received a letter from me, and was replying to it. He informed me the country had been hit by a strike by telecommunications workers. 'John Laws had Malcolm Fraser on the phone this morning', he wrote, 'and was interrupted by the operator to say the three minutes was up.' Dad complained about the recent budget having increased beer excise by six cents per middy, but concluded: 'It doesn't worry me now though because with this anti-coagulant dope I have to take I am only allowed two middies per day.'

I had tried in my letters to cheer Dad up from so far away. He was glad I found his recent letters more cheerful, explaining that, earlier, 'I was sore in the legs and swollen. I suffered shortness of breath day and night and was prepared to give the game away. However, I am now on the improve and I'm certain that as the weather warms I will make a very speedy recovery.' He signed off, 'Well mate, will write again soon. Your old Dad.' He didn't write again. He couldn't. He was gone, my old Dad. Oh, how I loved him, and how sad I am to be reliving my last time with him. I miss you, Dad.

10

Death at Sa Kaeo

IT WAS ONLY A FEW MONTHS until Christmas, which we shared with Mum and Lance in Australia. We then brought Mum back to Thailand for a holiday. It was her first time out of Australia since emigrating from Wales in 1945, and on the flight to Bangkok, Mum was so stressed that she disembarked the plane at Singapore. My young wife coaxed her back on board, but she behaved so badly when she arrived, being abusive and locking herself in the spare bedroom of our apartment, that I threatened to call the Thai police. We managed a few outings together, but they invariably ended in conflict. After spending a difficult fortnight with us, Mum returned to Australia.

Mum struggled without Dad. We had been in Thailand for only eight months in what was a planned five-year commitment to helping the poor. Now, in my mind, I had reduced the time to two years, since Mum could not cope without me and I was so homesick. Bangkok in the late 1970s was a world away: there was no Internet, the only English-language television station routinely broke down, telephone calls were horrendously expensive, and regular mail was the main link back to Australia.

Around this time, having been flattened by a lengthy bout of glandular fever, I fell asleep in the early evenings, waking around 10.00pm for a couple of hours and back to sleep till morning. Music offered a connection to Australia. On a holiday in New Zealand in 1975, I had bought a Marinucci handmade guitar. In Thailand, that guitar became my friend. Having never been taught music, I learned as many chords as I could.

Not only were music cassettes pirated in Thailand, so was the sheet music with chords and lyrics. At a street stall, I had procured a Bee Gees cassette titled 'Gotta Get a Massage to You', an appropriately Thai translation of 'Gotta Get a Message to You'. Then I got really lucky, coming across a 488-page book of every conceivable song under the sun, with accompanying chords. In those homesick nights between 10.00pm and midnight, I learned the lyrics and chords of more than 150 rock-and-roll songs. Poorly sung music would be a great source of personal joy for the rest of my life, though not so for my long-suffering family, friends, and conscripted audiences.

As we moved further into 1979, life was to go on in Bangkok. Some would say 'On, on!' Mike, the Englishman from our apartment compound, had joined the Bangkok chapter of the Hash House Harriers, a social jogging club that comprised expatriates who ran, lumbered, walked, and staggered around the city's outskirts, pretending to be hounds in pursuit of a fox. Thereafter, the pretend hounds consumed copious quantities of Thai Amarit beer, diluted with Sprite, from plastic beer steins.

Mike invited me to join the Bangkok Hash. Each weekend, two hounds took on the responsibility of laying the trail for the hounds, using tapioca flour and shredded paper for trail markings. A good trail contained loops and dead ends to confuse the hounds, which were led by a bugler. When the hounds temporarily lost the trail, they spread across the paddy field, or through the village or local temple until one of the pack picked it up again. 'On, on! On, on!' the clever hound howled, the bugle sounded, and the chase of the imaginary fox resumed.

Soon it was our turn to lay the trail. We had carefully surveyed our planned route during the week before returning early Saturday afternoon to lay our tapioca flour on the dry paddy field and through a village for the late afternoon's Hash. With no sign of rain, we had not a worry in the world. Ours would be a long, intriguing trail, ending happily for the sweaty expatriates eagerly anticipating the quenching of their enormous thirsts.

Bangkok's topography, it transpired, was a special place where rain not only fell from the sky but could also rise from beneath the ground. In the lower basin of the Chao Phraya River bisecting Bangkok, much of the land lies below the level of the Gulf of Siam. As we were to learn, the conjunction of a river swollen with rain from Thailand's north, and king tides in the Gulf of Siam, can cause water to rush upwards through the cracks in paddy fields, inundating them within hours. By the time the eager pack of Hash House Harriers had arrived, our trail of tapioca flour was submerged and largely dissolved beneath calf-deep water. Lacking even a feeble excuse to drink beer, our fellow hounds grumbled off to their cars, muttering about two incompetents, and leaving us to lament our ill fortune in failing to plan for rain falling upwards through the ground.

We resolved to drown our sorrows at the nearest available restaurant. During our meal, a small group of Thai men from a nearby table began staring at us. A grumpy, dispirited hound, I stared back. One of them shouted: 'What you looking at?' to which I responded by blowing him a kiss. Big mistake. Mike and I completed our dinner, paid the bill, and headed out towards Mike's car, where our three interlocutors confronted us. Not to worry. We were much bigger; Mike the Englishman was a martial-arts exponent, and I'd learned origami at school.

Although the area was only dimly lit by a distant neon streetlight, nothing adequately explains why I did not see my Thai aggressor's arms move, yet felt a punch to each side of my head. It was my first experience of Thai boxing, and more kicks to the head would surely follow. Fortunately for me, the kick boxer gave a higher priority to immobilising Mike, who was warming to his martial-arts pose. He received a couple of blows to the head, knocking his spectacles to the dark ground below and into an open drain. Without his spectacles, Mike's martial-arts skills were neutered. My most dignified response was to crawl around on my hands and knees, reaching into the drain in search of his glasses. I found them, and handed them to him. He put them back on. 'Let me at them! Let me at them! I do martial arts!' Mercifully for two hopelessly defenceless hound dogs, our assailants had melted into the night.

If you stay in the Hash House Harriers long enough, memories fade, and the hounds extend forgiveness to those who have stuffed up laying a trail. My second chance came when a Scotsman named Andy invited me to join him in mapping out a trail for the following week's Hash. We chose the higher ground of a village and adjacent paddy fields, surveying a route along the top of bund walls that formed the banks of the fields and served as a convenient walkway for the villagers. Where they lay beneath banana and coconut trees, the intersecting bunds were also a handy place to tether a village dog. Rabies was prevalent in rural Thailand, and village dogs were universally mangy, riddled with scabs and sores, and offering a safe abode for lice and fleas. Anxious about the consequences of being bitten by one of these four-legged disease carriers, I picked up a length of bamboo and led the surveying work for our trail. As I reached the intersection of two bunds, a terrifying dog lunged at me from the cover of a banana tree. Its snarling, bared teeth, along with its aggression and appalling appearance, so startled me that I struck it with my bamboo stick.

Unfortunately, Andy the Scotsman had been some way behind me around a corner, and hadn't witnessed this violent confrontation. I had quickly moved on to avoid any further contact with the enraged dog; but before I could warn Andy, he had drawn level with it. Frothing and growling, it lunged at my friend, biting him on the leg and drawing blood. We drove back into Bangkok and presented the wound to the doctor in the emergency department of a major hospital. The doctor disinfected the cut, but our worry was rabies. The doctor explained that the gestation period for rabies in humans was longer than for dogs. He advised us to return to the village twice weekly to check whether the dog was still alive. If it died, we were to return to the hospital, where Andy would be given a series of painful injections in his stomach. If that dog had not bitten my friend, I would have been happy to see it die; but since it did bite him, I was relieved to learn that it went on living its miserable existence.

IN LATE 1978, Vietnam had invaded Kampuchea—the name the murderous Khmer Rouge had given Cambodia. As the Vietnamese army pushed west, the Khmer Rouge sought sanctuary in the mountainous areas adjacent to the Thai border. Khmer civilians fled the fighting, crossing into Thailand. By October 1979, the refugee camps around the border town of Aranyaprathet were being shelled almost daily, causing the Thai army to hastily relocate tens of thousands of refugees further into Thailand.

A group of UN staff members volunteered to help establish a new refugee camp. As we stepped out of the bus hired by the United Nations High Commissioner for Refugees, and walked the short distance to the barbed-wire entrance to Sa Kaeo refugee camp, it wasn't the sight that overcame our senses, but the sound and smell. Guarded by Thai soldiers carrying automatic rifles, the entrance to the camp housing 30,000 refugees was an open gate.

Seagrass matting covered the makeshift hospital of eight tents. Roads had been carved into the mud of the disused paddy field. Plastic sheeting, bamboo, and seagrass matting had been thrown together to shelter the sick, emaciated refugees from both the burning sun and the afternoon monsoonal rains. From the mouths of these refugees, other than the infants, came only one sound: coughing from the pneumonia they had contracted on their arduous journey. No one spoke. The able-bodied refugees silently queued for water and food.

Backhoes had been used to dig trenches for use as open latrines. Lime was spread into the ditches and along their edges in the hope of disinfecting the human waste being dumped there by enfeebled refugees.

As we stepped under the seagrass matting of hospital roofs and past the stagnant water pooled on the ground, we encountered scores of women and children lying on mats, too weak even to move their limbs. The hospitals accommodated 1,400 refugees in urgent need of attention, but the Red Cross and World Vision medical staff told us that another 4,000 would have been hospitalised had there been sufficient doctors, nurses, and volunteers to treat them.

These poor, gaunt people were barely alive. Their bodies had no strength or resistance to fight the illnesses afflicting them—pneumonia, malaria, dysentery, and malnutrition. In the thick, steamy air trapped under the matting roof, the smell of death was unmistakable, like no other smell—a sickly, pungent odour that frightened us.

We needed no training for our first task. It was to lift listless women and children out of the puddles of water that had formed under them from the torrential monsoonal rainstorms. But if we lifted them up and tried to move them to another space, it would have killed them, so we packed donated blankets into the muddy pools.

When we volunteers began washing the patients, others beckoned limply in the hope they might be next. As we lifted the legs and buttocks of an elderly woman, who was too weak to move, out of the water she had been lying in, we could see that her skin had begun disintegrating. We wondered how she could survive. She probably didn't.

My wife and I had been given a baby's bottle with a teat, filled with infant formula, to try to get some nourishment into a tiny newborn girl. The teat was much bigger than the baby's mouth. We squeezed drops of the formula onto her lips, spreading it with our fingers. We tried to open the baby's mouth. Nothing worked. She just stared blankly into space. She was dying. Out of frustration, I rammed the teat between the baby's lips. Amazingly, the teat forced the baby's little mouth open, and her sucking reflex activated. She didn't stop sucking on that bottle until it was almost empty. We were so thrilled. This little one probably—hopefully—survived.

Among our group of volunteers was a trained nurse from Belgium. Her job was to inject antibiotics into the buttocks of refugees lying on hospital mats. She was an emotional mess. The Khmer people were so emaciated that there was no fatty tissue and precious little flesh into which to inject the medicine. As the Belgian nurse approached them with a syringe, they cowered and cringed in fear of the pain they had witnessed others enduring from the needle. She sobbed as she later relayed to us the trauma of injecting directly onto bone.

AS WE CONTINUED TO HELP in the hospital, a commotion erupted outside. We rushed out to find Thai soldiers shouting at young Khmer men. Brandishing their automatic weapons, the Thai soldiers angrily motioned the Khmers to the centre of an open area in the field. 'They're going to shoot them!' I yelled. I asked a Thai volunteer what was happening. He explained that the refugee camp was full of Khmer Rouge soldiers in civilian clothes. These young men were in far better physical shape than the elderly, the women, and the children. They, like the genuine refugees, had escaped the advancing Vietnamese army. The Khmer Rouge ran the camp internally, which helped explain the silence of the refugees. This group of men, with automatic weapons trained on them, had jumped the queues lining up for food. The Thai soldiers tied them up and forced them to stand, bare chested, in the sun, the heat, and the humidity until dusk.

From time to time during the day, we heard the panicked voices of refugees running from deep within the camp. Fearful of the Khmer Rouge and the Thai army, they had tried to care for sick family members under their allocated sheets of plastic roofing. But as the dying refugees' health deteriorated past all hope, their family members came screaming to the authorities. Volunteers lifted them onto plastic sheets and rushed them to the hospital tent, all too late.

In the haste of setting up the refugee camp, supplies of charcoal, rice, fish oil, blankets, and matting had been dumped onto an adjacent field. I organised local Thais who had been paid small sums to help set up the camp and, together, we spent much of the day separating the various supplies so the volunteers would know what was available and what was needed. Beneath a pile of matting and blankets, I discovered a mobile operating theatre and other medical supplies that were desperately needed but whose existence was unknown to the hospital staff.

As the sun began setting, I checked on the tethered Khmer Rouge men. They were still there, hands bound, tied to a post. A large truck pulled alongside the hospital. Men began emerging from beneath the hospital roof, one at each end of a length of seagrass matting wrapped around a blanket. They heaved their loads onto the truck, where they were stacked side by side. I waited and watched as 20 bodies of refugees who had died that day were loaded onto the truck for burial. No husband was there to lament the loss of his wife; no mother there to farewell her baby. They were all sick, exhausted, missing, or dead.

11

Climbing ivory towers and monuments

While living in Thailand, I maintained contact with Professor Ross Garnaut at the Australian National University, who had helped me with my masters thesis on mining taxation. Ross suggested I do a PhD under his supervision. After almost two years of running like hounds around the villages adjoining Bangkok, taking perilous bus trips to the Thai resort town of Pattaya, visiting the hill tribes of the north, undertaking official missions to most countries of the region, preparing many reports for the United Nations Unit on Transnational Corporations and countless progress reports for the PCMO, enduring six months of exhaustion from glandular fever, learning of the death of my father, and experiencing persistent bouts of homesickness, now, at the age of 25, I was keen to head home.

I had been overwhelmingly disillusioned by my time at the UN in Bangkok. The Economic and Social Commission for Asia and the Pacific was largely a sinecure for politically influential members and associates of the ruling elites from developing countries. Its work produced no obvious benefit for the poor in its member countries. Mercedes Benz cars were procured, conferences were held around the region, meetings organised, papers prepared, resolutions passed, minutes recorded, and generous per diems paid, but nothing really changed.

As a final mission in Bangkok, I was asked to represent the UN at a January 1980 meeting of the Organisation for Economic Cooperation and Development in Paris. Flying by Air France to Paris, I hadn't realised that the plane would be refuelling in Tehran, where 66 Americans were being held captive in the Iran hostage crisis. As we descended through the darkness, I was amazed to see more than a metre of snow piled up along the runway's edges. During refuelling, bearded Iranian military personnel carrying weapons boarded the plane, walking up and down the aisles. It was a mighty relief when they left and allowed the flight to proceed, taking only the airline food to which I considered they were welcome.

Arriving at Paris around 8.00am, the city still cloaked in darkness, it occurred to me that I knew barely a word of French. Neither did a Malaysian or a Korean who accompanied me, having been appointed to represent their countries at the meeting. Following each day's meeting, we familiarised ourselves with the Louvre, the Trocadero, the Eiffel Tower, the Arc de Triomphe, and the Crazy Horse Nightclub. It was my first visit to Europe and to this wonderful city.

BEFORE ENROLLING FOR MY PHD, an opportunity arose that would take me back out of Australia for three months. During the mid-1970s, Ross Garnaut had been an adviser in Papua New Guinea's Department of Finance. Ahead of PNG attaining independence in 1975, Ross was involved in renegotiating the generous tax arrangements that had been granted by the Australian colonial administration for the new Bougainville copper mine. This experience had helped inspire Ross to develop his profits-based Resource Rent Tax (RRT) proposal with his colleague, Anthony Clunies Ross.

A big new gold, silver, and copper mine would be opening soon in PNG's remote Western Province, bordering Indonesia's Irian Jaya. The PNG government wanted to ensure that the Ok Tedi mine offered benefits to the people of Western Province on top of the national taxation revenue it would generate.

Ross's PNG colleagues asked him if he knew of an Australian economist who could join a small team to assess the social and economic impacts of the Ok Tedi project. Ross suggested to me that this could form a useful case study for my PhD thesis, and I agreed. We rented a house owned by the ANU in Port Moresby that was surrounded by a high barbed-wire fence. Working with an expatriate professor at the University of Papua New Guinea and an American anthropologist, I spent a good deal of time chartering light planes to the Star Mountains in Western Province, where most afternoons the weather closed in to produce torrential downpours averaging eight metres per annum, making it one of the wettest places on earth.

Kiunga, a town on the Fly River in the Western Province lowlands, was a place that potentially could benefit from the Ok Tedi mine. The American anthropologist and I chartered a plane to Kiunga with an Australian expatriate who was an employee of the department of Minerals and Energy. We arranged for the charter flight to return to Port Moresby so that we could meet people around the town and catch a scheduled flight back to the capital the next morning. Over dinner at the house of a friend of the expat, we asked what time we needed to be awake to catch the next morning's plane. Our host told us that, since the flight was usually late, we should wait until we could hear the plane's engines before we got up, and he would then drive us to the airstrip.

Sure enough, the next morning we heard the buzz of the plane approaching Kiunga's airstrip. But our host had not accounted for two exigencies. One was that it had rained heavily overnight, making the road to the airstrip a slippery bog. The other was a local farmer who decided to drag a plough behind his tractor along the sodden track to the airstrip. Passing this laid-back farmer on the bog track was impossible. He was travelling at barely 20 kilometres per hour while the plane was readying for take-off.

By the time we passed him, the plane was revving its way along the runway. It was several days before the next scheduled flight, so when we spotted a gap in the fence dividing the road and the runway, the expat told his host to drive through the break in the fence. By now, the plane was at full throttle. So were we. As we reached top speed, we drew slightly ahead of the plane and waved down the pilot. He aborted the take-off, returned to base, and welcomed us aboard.

While in PNG, I also travelled to Bougainville to assess the mine's contribution to both the national economy and the local community. It, too, would be a case study for my PhD thesis. A few weeks after our return to Australia from PNG, we received news that the American anthropologist who had accompanied me had disturbed robbers in his apartment and had been stabbed in the stomach. He barely survived.

NOW AT THE ANU, I lined up for a cup of tea with fellow graduate students, academics, and Gough Whitlam, who had been appointed to an honorary position in our honeycomb-shaped building named after a great post-war economic adviser, HC (Nugget) Coombs. Wonderful economists such as Professors Max Corden, Fred Gruen, Bob Gregory, Peter Lloyd, and Peter Warr supported Ross in guiding me through my PhD thesis.

As PhD student colleagues in other disciplines, such as demography, within the Coombs Building struggled to match the data they had collected from extensive fieldwork with academic theories, I took the advice of Max Corden. 'Sit in your room and think', he counselled. He also suggested that most economic theories and thinking could be represented on a simple diagram comprising two axes and a couple of lines. Max and I walked together to a seminar in another building being conducted by a mathematical economist. Around 20 minutes into the presentation, Max interjected after the nth equation, where n is a large number, confessing: 'I don't understand.' If one of the world's leading economists could say he didn't understand, so could I. In fact, I have been saying it ever since.

To bolster my income from a PhD scholarship, I took up tutoring in first-year economics at the ANU. My students included Anna Cronin, who became economic adviser to opposition leaders Andrew Peacock and John Hewson, and chief of staff to Victorian premiers Jeff Kennett and Denis Napthine; Ruth Webber, who was elected as a Labor senator from Western Australia; Stephen Booth, later a senior office-bearer of the Australian Workers' Union; Michael Kerrisk, assistant national secretary of the Australian Labor Party; and Stephen Conroy, a senior cabinet minister in the Rudd and Gillard governments. It was at this time that I enjoyed my first experience as a newspaper columnist, writing a two-part exposé for *The National Times* on the flourishing tax-avoidance industry.

I also started playing volleyball. With meagre playing skills but better management capabilities, I helped organise a social team I named the Coombs Cavaliers, which included my roommate and fellow PhD student, Mike Nahan, who later became treasurer of Western Australia. We entered Canberra's volleyball competition and, before long, I organised additional teams to join the university's volleyball club. In a short time, we had grown from three to 13 teams, including two in the ACT state league competition. Among the players we attracted to the club were several Australian representatives, the retired captain of Poland's national team, and my former economics student, Stephen Conroy.

An American, David 'Crockett' Huntington Roberts, was studying for a PhD in science at the ANU. Crockett and I not only organised the 13 teams, but we also wrote the ANU Volleyball Club weekly newsletter, which we called *Ten Bricks Up*.

Not content with our achievements in winning the ACT state league competition and the intervarsity competition while offering enjoyment to the mixed social teams, Crockett and I decided to form another, much more exclusive, club. The ANU Monument Climbing Club had just two members—Crockett and me. I nominated for president and, there being no further nominations, was elected unanimously. Crockett won the position of honorary secretary. As novice monument climbers, we wanted to start modestly, choosing the Academy of Science. This dome-shaped building would surely be a pushover. To our disappointment, we found ourselves slipping down its gentle slope. Crockett, the industrious scientist, returned to his laboratory and created a sticky substance that we applied to our hands and feet. The Academy of Science then became our first conquest.

Next on the list was the ANU Refectory, where we came face to face with a surprised possum; then the Australian War Memorial, where we came face to face with a surprised security guard. When we explained we were representing the ANU Monument Climbing Club, the bemused guard let us go, but warned us against returning.

Our greatest conquest, however, was to be outside the nation's capital. Several years prior, my second-row partner from rugby days at St Pat's, Paul 'Bluey' Godsell, had observed while driving across the Sydney Harbour Bridge that large metal spikes radiated from the ladder leading towards the bridge's arch. Presumably, these spikes had been welded in place to deter would-be bridge climbers. Following another reconnaissance mission, I assessed that we could use our arm strength to lift our bodies out and beyond the spikes to the other side of the ladder.

Bluey and I chose a cold, wet, windy night that was otherwise perfect for bridge climbing. Levering ourselves beyond and above the spikes was the easy part. The greater challenge was the height and the wind. But we made it to the red light at the top of the bridge. Since this was long before organised, safe Sydney Harbour Bridge climbs, and therefore highly illegal, our worst fear was of being greeted by police as we climbed down onto the roadway on the northern end. From above, we could see every vehicle in perfect detail, and it seemed implausible that no one below had noticed us. They didn't, and we had conquered the bridge. Crockett and I went on to repeat the effort once more in our capacity as members of the ANU Monument Climbing Club, this time on a still, starlit night.

12

A doctor in the house

Having finished my PhD, I took up a position of post-doctoral fellow at the Australian National University, which Ross Garnaut had offered me. Ross had been seconded into the office of the recently elected prime minister of Australia, Bob Hawke. Since my PhD had been on mining taxation, and Hawke was committed to introducing Ross's RRT, Ross persuaded the resources and energy minister, senator Peter Walsh, to meet with me to assess my suitability as an economic adviser on his personal staff.

The RRT was based on the legal principle that a country's citizens owned the mineral and petroleum resources beneath the ground and were therefore entitled to a fair share of the profits made by corporations that extracted those resources. By basing the tax on profits, the RRT permitted corporations to recover the costs of exploration, project development, and operations. This gave them strong incentives to invest. But a large share of any profits greater than those needed to undertake the exploration and development — otherwise known as the resource rent — would accrue as taxation revenue to the government on behalf of the people. My PhD had demonstrated that this tax was superior to alternative taxes, since it was capable of maximising government revenue over time by encouraging exploration and development while collecting a large share of any excess profits.

In November 1983, Peter invited me over for an interview. We met in his office on the second floor at the back corner of the Senate side of the Old Parliament House. The whole area had a slightly musty smell;

old carpets and upholstery had absorbed decades of cigarette smoke. Even the polished wood smelled old. All the carpeting on that side was red, just as the carpet on the House of Representatives side, across King's Hall, was green.

Peter introduced me to other staff members. The advisers' offices around his suite were more like over-sized pigeonholes. Pointing to a seat at a bench in the open area just beyond his ministerial office, Peter said: 'That's your office.' Access to the minister wouldn't be a problem, I reasoned. He wouldn't be able to avoid me, even if he tried.

As I surveyed the tiny work area, I noticed a three-drawer filing cabinet adjacent to the workbench. On the front of the bottom drawer, where presumably a typed label was to be inserted, was instead a piece of paper with the handwritten word 'DIRT'. I was to learn that this drawer contained Peter Walsh's renowned dirt file on his political opponents, most of whom, but not all, were members of other political parties.

At this point, the interview seemed to be going well. Peter had not asked me a question about my background or expertise; he had been content to accept Ross's assurances about those. Indeed, Peter held economists in high regard—so much so that, as a farmer from the Western Australian wheat belt, he had decided to teach himself economics in order to become better equipped for a career in politics. I sensed my biggest hurdle lay ahead of me when Peter said: 'Let's adjourn to the Non-Members' Dining Room.' This was to be my initiation.

Peter ordered a bottle of Houghton's White Burgundy. Before we were halfway through the entrée, we had demolished the bottle. He said: 'I don't doubt your economic expertise, but what do you think we ought to do about the tax dodgers?' He despised wealthy people who refused to pay their fair share of tax.

It turned out he was a close friend of Brian Toohey, editor of *The National Times*, to whom I had submitted my research pieces while at university. Peter had read my feature on the tax-avoidance industry, and was very impressed. Movers and shakers in the West Australian Liberal Party had been heavily involved in the notorious 'Bottom of the Harbour' tax-avoidance schemes in which they set up or bought companies, made profits, and, before company tax was payable, closed the companies down and destroyed their financial records, figuratively putting them in filing cabinets that they dropped to the bottom of the harbour.

Sir John Crawford, ANU's chancellor and, with Nugget Coombs and others, a key architect of Australia's post-war development, had learned of the possibility of me working at Parliament House. He warned me that these people drank a lot and that I needed to be very careful not to participate in that sort of activity. It was too late.

After finishing off the second bottle, with Peter railing against the 'crooks' of the New South Wales right wing of the Labor Party, the 'spivs' of the business community who demanded of governments and obtained income-tax rorts, the 'hairy-legged Stalinists' of the women's movement whose elitism betrayed the interests of low-income working women, and the 'economic treachery' of the maritime unions for blocking Australian export cargoes on the wharves, he considered I had the necessary qualities to be his economic adviser. I was 29 years old, and my starting salary would be $29,000 a year — far in excess of anything I could have expected as an academic at that early stage of my career.

BY JANUARY 1984, I was working in Peter's office, designing the RRT in collaboration with Ross in the prime minister's office. Taking on the role of economic adviser to a federal cabinet minister was a turn in my early career I had not envisioned during my school and early university years. But, having seen the possibilities in my masters thesis of applying the RRT in mineral-rich developing countries to help the poor, my move into Peter's office had a certain logic to it.

In my mind, a Labor government was more likely to use taxation revenue for the alleviation of poverty, as was already evident in the Prices and Incomes Accord that had been reached with the trade union movement. The accord was designed to achieve economic recovery and job creation through wage moderation, while boosting the social wage through Medicare and the provision of income support for families in need. Now I had the opportunity to pursue my missionary service through my training in economics.

Within days of me taking up my new job, Peter and I, along with his personal assistant, visited state resources and energy ministers to seek their cooperation with our proposal that the federal government apply the RRT and the states remove their own taxes, the two levels of government then sharing the proceeds of the federal tax. With remarkable consistency, the states told us to get stuffed.

Having already been rebuffed by several states, we landed in Adelaide on 27 January for discussions with the South Australian resources minister, Ron Payne, and his economic adviser, David Cox. David later became a federal Labor shadow minister and a good friend. Ron Payne, like his colleagues from the other states, but with all the good grace he could muster, also told us to get stuffed.

Left in no doubt about where the states stood, Peter made the strategic decision that we should seek to apply the RRT only in territory controlled by the federal government. Essentially, this was in waters three miles from the Australian coast. It became the Petroleum Resource Rent Tax (PRRT).

The departments responsible for the taxation of resources, Treasury and the Department of Resources and Energy, opposed the RRT. They liked the existing Crude Oil Levy. However, there was a major problem with the levy: it was payable regardless of whether the oil companies made a profit from extracting the oil, causing them to leave oil in the ground that otherwise would be profitable to extract for the benefit of the Australian people.

Before I had joined Peter's staff, his department had already tried to talk Peter out of the tax, but he remained committed to it. Despite the circulation of a discussion paper written by the government and a series of face-to-face meetings to discuss design features of the tax, industry mounted a heavy media campaign, including full-page newspaper advertisements, against any new resources tax.

In late February, Peter and I met with millionaire entrepreneur Sir Robert Holmes à Court in Perth. Robert, a thoughtful, tall, gentle man, told us that one day he would control BHP. He said the RRT was a sound concept and that he was not opposed to it as long as the tax rate was not too onerous. One businessman, zero states, and zero government departments supported the RRT.

Implementing my PhD thesis almost straight out of university was a unique opportunity for me, pushing me to acquire the skills to convert economic theory into practice. In order to give it more time to escalate its campaign of opposition, industry applied intense pressure on the government to defer consideration of the RRT beyond Peter's favoured announcement date of 1 July 1984. Ross arranged a meeting in the prime minister's office on 27 February to discuss the tax.

Although I had been around to the prime minister's office, I had never been in Bob Hawke's personal suite. As we arrived with departmental officials, we were told to go straight in. Bob Hawke sat facing us from behind a large wooden desk in a high-backed swivel chair, with Ross sitting on an ordinary chair on the same side of the desk as Bob. All invitees to the office, including treasurer Paul Keating, sat in an arc facing the prime minister. Attendance at this meeting was so large that ministers, advisers, and officials formed two arcs.

Wow, this is big, I thought. *That's Bob Hawke, the prime minister of Australia, in person. And that's Paul Keating.*

In their company, Peter was quite reserved, presenting his arguments as an academic would, very accommodating of alternative views, even rehearsing them as if to give them legitimacy.

Peter's gonna get eaten alive, I worried, *and I'm too scared to speak up.*

Paul Keating had been one of the first Labor politicians to advocate the RRT, when he was shadow minister for resources and energy in 1976. The Labor Party adopted it as policy at its 1977 national conference. But now, as treasurer, Paul was worried about the industry's reaction to the tax—proposing instead a continuation of the Crude Oil Levy. Hawke and Garnaut spoke in favour of the RRT. Hawke called for more work to be done to try to bring the departments together. He had saved the day, but I knew from that near-defeat that the going would be tough in getting the RRT adopted as government policy.

An inter-departmental committee was formed, and I was to represent Peter at its meetings. Bernie Fraser asked me whether I would support the RRT only on offshore 'greenfields' projects—ones that did not yet exist—exempting Bass Strait and the North West Shelf. I reserved my position, so as to have some leverage over the final design of the tax.

Back in my office, I developed two alternative designs for the RRT, based on the thinking I had done for my PhD thesis. One had the government contributing towards exploration costs, but collecting a large share of profits from successful discoveries. The other option involved no government contribution towards exploration costs, but a smaller share of profits.

One month later, we met again in the prime minister's office. Meanwhile, Paul had met with senior executives of Esso and BHP, who remained implacably opposed to the RRT. Bob asked: 'Where are we up to?' Paul declared that we supporters of the RRT could 'kiss Bass Strait goodbye'. The Crude Oil Levy would continue to apply.

Paul, fully aware of the views of officials from Treasury and the Department of Resources and Energy, suggested to Bob, 'Let's hear what the officials have to say.' We were effectively now discussing only whether to introduce an RRT for offshore, 'greenfields' developments. Bernie Fraser spoke against our proposed announcement date of 1 July 1984 for the greenfields RRT, arguing that it was all too rushed. Another deputy secretary from Peter's own department, who had been under Peter's explicit instructions to work with me to develop the RRT proposal, argued against it at this crucial meeting, effectively pulling the rug from under his own minister. Peter was losing the debate badly.

Peter didn't want to walk out of the room with nothing, so he pressed the case for a 1 July announcement date. Bob agreed. The government would release an options paper for industry comment, with two alternative designs for the tax that I had developed. As everyone else filed out of the meeting through the narrow entrance to the prime minister's suite, I lingered so that I might have the opportunity of a word. At that stage, even Ross had left the room. It was just Bob Hawke and me, a frightened young staffer who had marvelled how the prime minister had salvaged the policy on which I had been working for more than three years.

Bob looked up at me from behind his desk and said: 'We can tolerate some blood now, but not later in the year when I want to call an election.' The prime minister had confided in me the 1984 election date, eight months ahead of calling it. I reassured Bob that Peter and I would have the RRT in shape for an announcement on 1 July.

The next day, I returned with Peter and Paul Keating to Bob's office for meetings with BHP, followed by Esso. Peter explained to BHP's Brian Loton and Russell Fynmore that the RRT would apply to offshore greenfields areas while the existing Crude Oil Levy would apply to Bass Strait. A special rate of the Crude Oil Levy set at 50 per cent would apply to the recently discovered Fortescue oilfield within

Bass Strait. The 50 per cent rate was an ambit claim; the government's true position was 40 per cent. To our astonishment, Loton expressed annoyance that the Bass Strait oilfields were to be treated differently from the other offshore areas. Bob leapt at the opportunity, offering to apply the RRT to Bass Strait if BHP wanted consistency.

Paul was surprised by Loton's position, reminding him that the proposed isolation of Bass Strait from the RRT was at Loton's personal request. Loton back-tracked, confirming BHP's position that the Crude Oil Levy should continue to apply to Bass Strait. The discussion then turned to the rate of the levy on the newly discovered Fortescue field within Bass Strait. Russell Fynmore said he would still have a slight smile on his face if the levy rate for Fortescue were 35 per cent.

At the next meeting, Esso's Jim Kirk conceded that the RRT was a reasonable tax for new greenfields developments, but argued it shouldn't be applied now; it should be applied, he suggested, when some oil had been discovered. A senior Esso executive was proposing that the government deceive oil explorers into believing no extra tax would apply to their discoveries. Kirk insisted that the maximum tolerable Crude Oil Levy rate for the Fortescue field was 20 per cent. Bob revealed that BHP had just moments ago offered 35 per cent. Kirk said he was confident he could talk BHP down from 35 per cent to 20 per cent. We laughed, confident that he could. Paul slipped me a note, asking how much revenue a 35 per cent rate would raise. I wrote '$350 million a year.' We settled on 35 per cent.

Following further consultation with industry, we implemented the RRT for offshore petroleum against industry's concerted opposition and that of the Peacock-led federal opposition. In 1989, BHP and Esso approached the Hawke government to request that the Petroleum Resource Rent Tax be extended to the Bass Strait oilfields in place of the Crude Oil Levy. We reminded them of our proposal to do just that five years earlier, against the companies' trenchant opposition. BHP told us it had been privately supportive of the RRT but, having been unable to persuade Esso, had locked in with its Bass Strait partner against the tax that the two companies now supported.

The Petroleum Resource Rent Tax has collected tens of billions of dollars for Australian governments on behalf of the people of Australia. Few academics are given the opportunity to convert their recently completed PhD theses into government policy. I was one of the fortunate ones.

TWENTY YEARS LATER, I was appointed a minister in the newly elected Labor government led by prime minister Kevin Rudd. Although I was in the outer ministry, not in the cabinet, I was aware that the government was contemplating the introduction of an extra tax on the mining profits associated with China's voracious demand for iron ore and coal. Several times, I offered to provide advice on my experience with the Hawke government's RRT.

To my dismay, when the taxation review committee's report was released a few days before the May 2010 budget, it recommended not the RRT but a different tax, which it called the Resource Super Profits Tax (RSPT).

In my PhD thesis I had carefully considered this alternative tax. But I had concluded that, while it was theoretically elegant, it was also impractical, since it would require the government of the day to make large cash payments to mining companies if projects turned out to be unprofitable. Companies would not be confident about a government following through on the promises of political predecessors to write out big cheques to them if mineral prices collapsed in a global economic slowdown. In such circumstances, governments would have higher priorities, such as assisting the unemployed and stimulating the economy.

Predictably, the mining industry's reaction was of great hostility to this flawed tax, launching a multi-million-dollar advertising campaign against the Rudd government. As the industry's advertising campaign continued to escalate, I tried helping behind the scenes, proposing a Minerals Resource Rent Tax based on the Petroleum Resource Rent Tax.

Long-simmering tensions between Julia Gillard and Kevin Rudd over a lack of policy direction burst into the open when Julia successfully challenged Rudd for the prime ministership. The new Gillard government began negotiating with the mining industry to replace the RSPT with a Minerals Resource Rent Tax; but in order to prevent the resumption of the advertising campaign, the design of the replacement tax was so favourable to the industry that the tax was incapable of collecting any significant revenue from the China boom that by then was well underway. As Australia's new minister for trade, I was not involved in the design of the new tax. The whole debacle ended with the incoming Abbott government scrapping the Minerals Resource Rent Tax before it could do its job and begin collecting revenue.

13

We want you as a new recruit

From time to time, Stephen Conroy, my friend from volleyball and ANU economics, visited me in my small office at the Senate side of the Old Parliament House. Stephen had taken a position as electorate officer for the member for Canberra, Ros Kelly. Ros was in the right of the Labor Party, and Stephen considered that either she or the education minister, Senator Susan Ryan, of the centre-left faction, might come under threat from the left to retain her endorsement as a member of parliament. The left faction was signing up members to the Mount Ainslie branch. Stephen informed me he could not find my name on any branch listing in the ACT, and I confirmed I was not a member of the Labor Party. Peter had never asked me if I was a party member and, when I casually told him I was not, he hadn't suggested I should join. But, of course, I was a Labor supporter and, at Stephen's request, I was happy to join the party to help counter-stack the Mount Ainslie branch against the left.

My first meeting as a branch member was dominated by an argument over which branch member we would nominate for membership of the Electoral Boundaries Disputes Committee. This sounded to me like the Project Coordination and Monitoring office at the United Nations in Bangkok. Why bother with substance when you could immerse yourself in process? When the discussion moved on to the more substantive issue of a wine-bottling fundraising evening, I naively suggested the proceeds could go to the St Vincent de Paul Society. I was left in no doubt that funds raised were to assist ALP candidates in local elections.

My introduction to ALP branch meetings confirmed my naivety. It was neither endearing nor uplifting.

About a year later, Susan Ryan did indeed come under pressure for her nomination as the Labor Senate candidate for Canberra at the coming election. Stephen again visited me to seek my support. I assured him I would vote for Susan. But to be eligible for a preselection vote, I needed to have attended a minimum of three branch meetings in the preceding twelve months. I had attended only one, having to advise a dismayed Stephen Conroy that I was ineligible to vote. Susan survived without me, and I lifted my branch-meeting attendance thereafter. Stephen and I became lifelong friends and cabinet colleagues. I am grateful for his forceful encouragement of me to join the Labor Party.

FOLLOWING THE DECEMBER 1984 ELECTION, Bob Hawke promoted Peter Walsh to finance minister, whereupon Peter doggedly pursued budget savings in endless meetings of the Expenditure Review Committee. Nearby our office was Susan Ryan's. Susan often came around to our office with her staff and, much to Peter's bemusement, we sang all the old Catholic hymns, especially *Hail, Queen of Heaven* and *Soul of My Saviour*. Susan was also the minister assisting the prime minister on the status of women. Although Peter irritated her with his persistent references to feminists as 'hairy-legged Stalinists' and 'the hairy-armpit brigade', the two were quite fond of each other.

On Wednesday nights, the Senate rose early, allowing politicians and their staff members to go out to dinner. Every Wednesday afternoon, the following conversation occurred.

'Where will we go for dinner? Craig, can you look up a few restaurants?'

During Question Time in the Senate, I would routinely check the Yellow Pages to identify some possibilities.

According to this routine, by early evening, Peter would ask: 'So, where are we going tonight?'

I ran through the names of restaurants, which, one by one, Peter dismissed. Then came the serial question: 'What about the Palace Garden?' adding, 'It's lurching distance from the sty.' The sty was Peter's apartment in the Canberra suburb of Kingston.

'Good idea', I replied on each occasion, and we headed for the Palace Garden to order the obligatory set-piece Chinese banquet and several bottles of Houghton's White Burgundy.

At the end of each parliamentary session, various parties were thrown to celebrate the release of politicians and staffers to their families back home. Across the political spectrum, it was generally agreed that John Howard hosted the best parties. In the Old Parliament House, ministers' offices were intermingled with those of backbenchers and members of the opposition. A few doors along the corridor from Peter's office was that of a Liberal senator, Tony Messner. We all got on well, and Tony ushered me around to Howard's parties, where I never attracted a sideways glance.

Regular mingling occurred in the Non-Members' Bar, too. Here, politicians of all parties, staff members, and journalists gathered to drink and gossip. A living institution in Parliament House was Mungo MacCallum, a man committed to holding up the bar to avoid any risk of it collapsing onto patrons. The ever-affable Mungo elicited more stories than most other journalists from lubricated-lipped politicians and staffers.

BACK AT WORK, Peter Walsh, Ross Garnaut, and I were in regular discussion about a white paper on tax reform that Paul Keating and Treasury were preparing. Paul was a strong advocate of a broad-based consumption tax, which came to be known simply as a BBCT. Ross was worried that the trade union movement would successfully demand large wage rises to compensate for the tax's impact on the cost of living, preventing a necessary improvement in Australia's international competitiveness.

My view was that the economic benefits of the BBCT were exaggerated, and that these benefits were not large enough to compensate for its inherent unfairness. In its draft white paper, Treasury described the compensation going to the poor as 'rough justice': some being over-compensated, with others being left to pay more. I described Treasury's compensation proposal for the poor as 'scattering around money like confetti', hoping it would fall in the right places but not caring too much. Stephen Conroy repeated the metaphor around the corridors of Parliament House.

The unfairness of the compensation proposals seemed bad enough, but I was incensed when I read, in the Treasury documents, that the BBCT was needed to fund reductions in the higher marginal rates of income tax on the basis that high-income earners were the most productive members of society. Had Treasury never heard of inherited wealth? Why did highly paid business people and Treasury officials need more incentives to be productive when the real task was to lift people out of poverty—people such as those living in tin sheds on the outskirts of Baradine?

Peter and the Department of Finance were sceptical. Peter shared my view about the unfairness of using the BBCT to provide tax cuts for high-income earners.

As the debate see-sawed within the government, I spent an increasing amount of time strolling across King's Hall to the prime minister's office to confer with Ross and his fellow advisers. Not one of them supported the consumption tax. As finance minister, Peter was a high-ranking and respected member of cabinet. The prime minister's office was not unhappy that I was advising Peter against the tax. From time to time, one or another of them would ask: 'How goes the battle?'

Peter was in the Centre Left faction. By now a committed ALP member, I had joined the faction and regularly attended its meetings, where I got to know the likes of Bill Hayden, John Button, John Dawkins, Mick Young, Neal Blewett, Barry Jones, and its convenor, Senator Peter 'Cookie' Cook. Cookie was a backbencher whose office was close to ours. We became good friends. We convened a daylong seminar, where I used butcher's paper and a felt pen to bring the ideas of the various members of the faction into a set of proposals for tax reform that did not include a consumption tax.

A dinner of Centre Left ministers and backbenchers was organised at the Santa Lucia restaurant in Kingston. Bill Hayden arrived late from a prior commitment, and by the time he got there, the group had resolved to oppose the BBCT, subject to Hayden's view. Hayden concurred. As factional convenor, Cookie agreed to deliver a speech against the BBCT if I wrote it for him. I did, and he did.

By now, I was pretty nervous about being on a collision course with Paul Keating. He phoned me after talking to Cookie about his speech. It would be fair to surmise, based on Cookie's account of the conversation with Paul, that the treasurer was unimpressed with the content of the speech and, indeed, with its very existence. It seems Cookie let slip that I had a role in the speech's preparation. I was a junior staffer. Paul could have monstered me in that phone call but, instead, was remarkably civil, criticising Ross for talking Bob into announcing a tax summit during the 1984 election campaign, which, Paul complained, left him holding the can to come up with a tax-reform package. Paul did not criticise Bob, but he did tell me I should not remain involved in the debate within the government.

Although receiving such a phone call from Paul Keating was disconcerting, I felt in all conscience that I could not withdraw from the process. Working with the Department of Finance, Peter and I, in consultation with Ross, developed an alternative proposal: a sales tax set at the modest rate of 5 per cent compared with the BBCT's 12.5 per cent rate. It became the white paper's Option B. Option A involved the introduction of a capital-gains tax and a fringe-benefits tax. Option B included those taxes and the 5 per cent sales tax. Option C also included the capital-gains tax and fringe-benefits tax, but with the full 12.5 per cent BBCT.

Following the white paper's release, Paul passionately championed his Option C. Every time Paul thought he had persuaded Bob to support his option, Bob's advisers cautioned him against it. Ross and I stayed in close contact. Bob was attracted to our Option B, but Paul bitterly opposed it, resenting the involvement of Peter, Ross, and probably me. When, 13 years later, prime minister John Howard advocated a consumption tax in the form of a 10 per cent GST, I had all the arguments against it at my disposal, using them as one of the newly elected backbenchers to support shadow ministers Peter Cook and Stephen Conroy in a Senate inquiry into the effects of the tax.

At a July 1985 tax summit to consider the white paper proposals, every group, including the business organisations, trade unions, and charitable organisations, spoke against the BBCT. Over the following weeks, the government considered its position, and adopted Option A. Australia was to have a capital-gains tax and a fringe-benefits tax, but no consumption tax.

ON THE NIGHT of the government's announcement, I was celebrating with MPs and representatives of the Australian Council of Social Services. At 10.00pm, Lance rang to advise me that Mum, who had been in hospital for three days and had been improving, was now deteriorating.

'You'd better come tomorrow, Pud. I've never seen Mum like this', he said.

'No, I'll come now.'

I drove to Sydney and went to the hospital with Lance. To avoid alarming Mum, Lance and I agreed I should go to her bedside alone and that he would join me afterwards. Mum was asleep, her breathing assisted through an oxygen mask as she struggled with acute emphysema.

I gently woke her, nudging her arm.

'Mum, Mum, it's Pud', I said.

Mum turned her head towards me, looked at me, and died. I think she would have waited for me the next day, but she only wanted to see me at her bedside, and was content to go.

I walked out to Lance to tell him Mum had died. He came into the room, we cuddled each other, and Lance cried: 'It's just the two of us now, Pud.'

14

Life in the prime minister's office

Late in 1985, Bob Hawke appointed Ross Garnaut to the position of ambassador to China. I was astonished. Here was Ross, designing and carrying in his mind the intellectual framework for the economic reforms that the Hawke government was pursuing, at the height of his influence, and he had asked to be sent to China. We arranged to meet at Ross's house in south Canberra, where we had met so many times before. Disappointed, I quizzed Ross about why he was throwing it all away. He explained that China would resume the position it had occupied in the centuries before the Industrial Revolution as one of the world's two largest economies, previously alongside India and shortly to be alongside the United States. Ross had accompanied Bob on an official visit to China in 1984 and, with Bob, foresaw China's rise.

Amazed at Ross's exposition, I understood that something big was to happen to Australia, and that Ross wanted to be in China to help forge it. Twenty-five years later, as Australia's minister for trade, I said in a speech: 'Australia is in the right place at the right time, in the Asian region in the Asian Century.' It became the basis of the white paper on Australia in the Asian Century that prime minister Julia Gillard and I launched.

With Ross's departure for Beijing imminent, Bob and his office were looking for a replacement economic adviser. Bob appointed the highly capable and professional Steve Sedgwick from the public service as his senior economic adviser, but was interested in bringing me on board as an adviser on microeconomic reform, which was my particular strength.

Bob's chief of staff, Graham Evans, approached me with a proposition for a very unusual dual role: assistant secretary in the Department of Prime Minister and Cabinet, and personal consultant to the prime minister. Bob signed the consultancy agreement, and I began the role in early 1986, located in the prime minister's department.

Several years later, Bob said at my farewell gathering in his office: 'I have a very clear memory of when Craig first came to the office. This was before he was working for us. I can remember this bouncing, enthusiastic bloke jumping around the place. He was in and out of my office, and I thought: *I like the cut of that young bloke.*'

A couple of months after taking up my appointment in the prime minister's department, reporting to first assistant secretary Rod Sims and secretary Mike Codd, I was asked to be the official note-taker at a meeting with business representatives and Paul in the prime minister's office. As I was leaving, Bob grabbed my arm and congratulated me on my critique, written as his personal consultant, of a paper prepared by a left-winger in the Labor caucus that had advocated a return to high tariffs to achieve the 'reindustrialisation of Australia'.

Bob asked Paul to join us, outlined my rebuttal paper to him, and told us he intended to give it to a newspaper. My paper argued that a country like Australia could not successfully rebuild its manufacturing sector behind high tariff walls, since the protected manufacturers would have no incentive to be efficient and would call for ever-higher tariffs, as they had done in the past. Yet, at the same time, Australian consumers on low incomes would be required to pay more for basic items, such as their children's underwear and shoes, in exactly the same way as a consumption tax—which the left vehemently opposed—would oblige them to do.

Bob's fondness of my paper confirmed that our economic philosophies were aligned. *Wouldn't it be fantastic if I could move over here to his office?* I thought. As I left the office, Bob asked me to write what he called a 'ripper speech' for him to deliver following his return from China in late May, setting out his government's response to the ever-widening current-account deficit with the rest of the world. Australia's agricultural prices were collapsing, and, with its high cost structure created by decades of protectionism, the country was unable to compete on non-agricultural international markets.

Bob and his key staff members travelled to China in mid-May, where Bob met its leader, Deng Xiaoping. They discussed China's plans to open its economy to the world. At the end of that visit, Bob's trade adviser announced he was leaving, after a couple of years in the job. Upon his return from China, Bob phoned me in the prime minister's department and asked me to be his microeconomic and trade adviser. Yippee! I was to return to life in the fast lane at Parliament House, this time as one of the prime minister's personal staff members.

On 2 June 1986, I moved into the prime minister's office. It was a scary day for a 31-year-old academic. I was shown my seat and a small bench in a tiny area that I would be sharing with another adviser. Most of the steno-secretaries and executive assistants in the open area at the front of the office smoked, thickening the air along the narrow corridor separating advisers' offices that led into the prime minister's suite. Despite my childhood aversion to cigarette smoke, I found the front-office staff to be a happy, pleasant, and welcoming group.

The most senior advisers—such as Bob's chief of staff, Graham Evans, his political advisers, Peter Barron and Bob Hogg, and his foreign-policy adviser, John Bowan—were on the side of the corridor with windows facing the front of Parliament House. My nook was on the darker side, but with a view through to their well-lit but small offices.

Barron, Bowan, and Hogg were considerably older than me and much more battle hardened. Although they were kind and friendly, they frightened me with their self-assuredness, using terms such as 'fucking bullshit' and 'crap' to describe any views that were contrary to their own. I knew I would need to have my arguments well honed when putting a viewpoint to them; but, to their great credit, they never sought to bully or intimidate me into agreeing with them.

Equally terrifying was Bob Hawke's chief media adviser, Geoff Walsh, who was to become a lifelong friend. Having been a journalist himself, Walsh was as hard-bitten and cynical as any member of the national press gallery, but retained his ideals—like Evans, Barron, Bowan, and Hogg did—and was determined to keep Labor's prime minister and government in office. It came as a pleasant surprise to me that these advisers routinely greeted each other and me as 'comrade, fellow worker', and it was a delightful shock that Bob Hawke used the same term in talking to his staff. Their camaraderie in the cause of economic progress for workers, and their support for the underprivileged, was an inspiration to a young bloke starting out in the prime minister's office.

As frightened as I was of working with such experienced advisers and a famous leader, I felt I had been given an opportunity that I could not have imagined back in Baradine running along the sideline for the Baradine Juniors rugby league team, bereft of confidence, dropping the ball and letting the team down.

Within days of me starting work in the office, Peter Barron and Bob Hogg made it clear that I would have an additional role that did not appear in my consultancy contract. The workload Bob took on as prime minister was hard and unrelenting, and he had few opportunities to escape for a bit of amusement. I was to be his accomplice in fun, a mate he could turn to for a few laughs and diversions. Over the following months and years, this informal, enjoyable role drew Bob and me close together, to a point where others described me as Bob's surrogate son. This was no reflection on the relationship with his true son, Stephen; it's just that Stephen was living with and supporting remote Aboriginal communities far away in Western Australia at the time and didn't get to Canberra very often.

WHILE BOB WAS IN CHINA, Paul had done a radio interview with John Laws on a telephone attached to the kitchen wall of a restaurant, from where he warned of the dangers of Australia becoming a banana republic if it failed to address the blowout in its current-account deficit. Whether or not Paul intended it, his 'banana republic' statement jolted the nation; but, as an academic economist, I thought it was just what was needed to create national support for economic reform. Bob and his travelling party had a different view, considering it ill disciplined and irresponsible, creating unnecessary panic and the sense of a government that had lost control of the economy. Both views are legitimate and need no adjudication but, from a strictly personal perspective, Paul's banana republic statement certainly raised the stakes.

My 'ripper speech' was now to be replaced with an address to the nation. All the resources of government were mobilised, with the prime minister's department in the driver's seat. Nevertheless, Bob was very open to any policy ideas I might have.

One of those ideas was formed when shopping for new clothes for my job in the prime minister's office. By this time I had a new partner, Cathy Hudson, having met her at a party hosted by Paul Keating's chief of staff, Don Russell. Cathy worked for the special minister of state, Mick Young, half time in his electorate and the other half in Canberra at his Parliament House office, which was downstairs and along the corridor from the prime minister's office. We went shopping at a menswear store in Canberra's Civic Centre, where we bought a bunch of clothes: a new suit, a pullover, a couple of neck ties, and some shirts. It was only when we got back home that we checked the labels on each item, learning that I had personally worsened Australia's current-account deficit: all but one item of my new clobber had been made overseas.

It occurred to me that if I had been able to find in that store some items bearing a green-and-gold logo to signify they were made in Australia, I might have chosen the Aussie items over the imported ones. So I put the idea of an Australian Made campaign directly to Bob. He liked it, and pushed it through cabinet against Peter Walsh's scepticism about its value for money and effectiveness, announcing it as one of the new policies in his address to the nation on 11 June 1986. John Singleton became the successful tenderer for the Australian Made campaign, and Bob and Singo went on to form a strong and enduring friendship.

The address to the nation did not halt the slide in the value of the Australian dollar as the current-account deficit continued to widen. Every day, Bob entered the Old Parliament House via the front steps instead of through a private entrance directly into his office. He strolled from the front of the prime minister's office along the corridor towards his suite, saying hello to steno-secretaries and a couple of the advisers on the way down. Then he would stick his head into my cubbyhole and say: 'Where's the dollar today, young fella?'

My answer was always the same: 'I don't know; I haven't checked.'

My attitude was that if you floated the dollar—which the government had done in December 1983—it would float, up and down. After a week experiencing my indifference about the exchange rate, Bob stopped sticking his head into my cubbyhole. I was disappointed that he walked right past me without saying hello, so one morning I told him the exchange rate, and he started talking to me again.

Soon after that, Bob no longer needed me to advise him of the rate. Paul had been handed a new device that he carried around with him all the time. It was called a Reuters screen, and he was able to give Bob and his other colleagues a running commentary on the value of the dollar against a multiplicity of currencies. That lifted a burden from my shoulders.

To provide a bit of merriment, I brought my guitar into the office. When Bob wanted a break from work in the evenings, he came to my cubbyhole, where I played and he sang. But still the dollar kept falling. The economic ministers met at least every day during this crisis. They eased foreign-investment rules, reduced taxes on foreign-investment income, and worked with the trade union movement to restrict wages growth — with Peter Walsh muttering all the while about the International Monetary Fund having to bail Australia out if the current account continued to deteriorate.

We needed to explain better to the public what was happening. In his address to the nation, Bob had said that Australia had suffered a 3 per cent decline in our terms of trade. I suggested to Bob that to everyday Australians, 3 per cent wasn't a big number, and they didn't know what the terms of trade were anyway. I calculated that this 3 per cent amounted to more than $6 billion. Then I reasoned that most Australians didn't really know what a billion dollars was, other than it being a large number. So I changed it to $6,000 million.

From our conversation, Bob adjusted the story in future iterations to say that a collapse in the prices the world was paying Australia for our agricultural exports had slashed $6,000 million from our national income, and that because of this we needed to tighten our belts. Bob and Paul were a formidable team in explaining Australia's economic predicament to the public in simple terms.

PETER BARRON had been with Bob from the start, and was the epitome of a fearless and frank adviser. He argued with Bob most days about Bob's delivery during Question Time in the parliament. On many occasions, they brushed past me and the other advisers when returning from the chamber, entered Bob's suite, and 'Boom!', the door slammed shut as the argument continued. After three years, Bob and Peter grew a little weary of each other. Having not spoken a word to Bob on a particular day, Peter leaned back on his chair one early afternoon to catch my eye across the corridor separating our offices.

'Righto, I'm off home', he said. 'I've advised me little head off today.'

This was the same Peter Barron who, on an earlier trip to China, had sat at the front of a bus that the Chinese hosts had commandeered to take Bob's staff to visit the Great Wall of China. Geoff Walsh was at the back of the bus. The guide boasted to the travelling party that the Great Wall of China was the only man-made object visible from the moon. Barron shouted down the bus to Geoff: 'Hey, Walshie, does Hawkie's ego count as a man-made object?'

It was this irreverence and basic instinct about how 'the mob' thought that made Peter Barron such a valuable adviser. Barron's irreverence, however, wasn't limited to the prime minister. Senior departmental officials always accompany the prime minister and his personal staff on overseas trips. As Barron and the secretary of the prime minister's department, Sir Geoffrey Yeend, were feeling each other out in the early period of the Hawke government, Barron decided to leave a lasting impression on Sir Geoffrey during a visit to the Cook Islands for the South Pacific Forum.

Security for a visiting prime minister is always tight. Barron approached the security contingent and told them the travelling party had been tipped off that a man masquerading as the secretary of the prime minister's department would try to enter the restricted area. Barron described this poser, and advised the security contingent that the man would give his name as Sir Geoffrey Yeend. As Barron had foretold, a man calling himself Sir Geoffrey Yeend approached the restricted area, where security officers detained him. Satisfied with his work as Sir Geoffrey protested his detention, Barron told the security officers that this man was the real Sir Geoffrey Yeend and that it was safe to allow him to pass.

Barron decided to leave the prime minister's office in July 1986, a little over a month after I started working there. The day Peter's successor, Bob Sorby, arrived, the dollar fell below 60 US cents for the first time in history. Sorby remarked about the calmness of the prime minister and his ministers, who were meeting to discuss the government's response to a full-blown economic crisis.

Yet it didn't seem like a crisis, sitting in the most powerful office in the country. You can only do what you can do, pulling some policy levers here, pressing some buttons there, and hoping the country's economic engine will respond favourably. In truth, the most that could be done was to send some positive messages to nervous markets and international investors about the government's commitment to reform. That's what the address to the nation had been designed to do, and it was what Bob and Paul sought to do every day through their media appearances.

Here the trade union movement was pivotal. At that time, almost half of working Australians were union members. If Australia were to achieve international competitiveness in industries beyond farming and mining, it would need to reduce its wage costs. Under the Fraser government and the centralised wage-fixing system, wages and prices followed each other in an upward spiral, even when unemployment climbed during the 1981–82 recession. In what Bob called Fraser's quinella, the Liberal prime minister had presided over double-digit inflation and double-digit unemployment. If that spiral were to be broken, the union movement would need to agree to restrain its wage claims when the cost of living rose.

The secretary of the Australian Council of Trade Unions, Bill Kelty, understood this well and, with ACTU president Simon Crean, had the unenviable task of persuading the affiliated unions of its merits. Many union leaders, more comfortable in class struggles with the evil capitalists, were severe critics of Bob, Paul, and their pro-market philosophy, but Kelty used his skills of persuasion to keep them at the negotiating table.

Although I was Bob's microeconomic, not macroeconomic, adviser, he invited me to sit in on discussions with Kelty, Crean, and Paul. Much pre-agreed chest beating by Kelty and his comrades heralded meetings with Bob and Paul, enabling Kelty to demonstrate to the membership that he was putting up a good fight against the economic rationalists running the country. Briefing notes arrived from the prime minister's department for key meetings with Kelty and Crean, filled with expressions of alarm and threatening newspaper clippings, warning of a wages breakout that would destroy the economy.

From time to time, we met with the leaders of affiliated unions in the cabinet room, where they could vent their anger at wage restraint, and raise issues that mattered to their members beyond wage rates — such as health care, education, and family-income supplements for the lowest-paid workers. It was through these meetings with union leaders and the private meetings with Kelty and Crean that I developed a great fondness for the trade union movement. Despite all the shouting, table thumping, and abuse, the unions accepted and many even relished their responsibility to steer the economy in the right direction after a decade of high inflation and continuing decline in Australian manufacturing.

Yet, throughout the crisis, Bob sought to reassure money markets of his government's commitment to economic reform by stating the amount by which wage costs had fallen under the accord with the trade union movement, enraging rank-and-file union members. As images of Bob dining at black-tie events with the likes of Kerry Packer and Alan Bond appeared in newspapers, members of unions that had the ability to achieve large wage rises through direct industrial action applied enormous pressure to their leaders to break out of the accord. Many public threats to do so were made, but the accord held firm.

Through this experience, I learned from observing Bob how much could be achieved by keeping doors open, listening, copping ill-tempered abuse, and never seeking to belittle critics. Fits of temper and bursts of abuse from people with power and authority were a sign of weakness, not strength. After the most robust, profanity-riddled exchanges, Bob kept the lines of communication open with his union critics. At this early stage of my career, I concluded that it was important not to go out of my way to make enemies; many would come my way without my behaviour adding to their number. And they inevitably did, starting from my earliest days in the prime minister's office.

15

Skirmish over Jackeys Marsh

'Who's going into the meeting with Richo and Bob Brown?' Bob Hogg shouted from his office, looking for a volunteer.

'I will', I said. With that exchange on 12 June 1986, less than a fortnight after starting as Bob's economic and trade adviser, I became his environmental adviser as well.

Having spent my youth shooting birds, chopping down cypress-pine trees to make our Baradine tree house, catching yabbies, and killing ants, I had no obvious environmental credentials. My reason for volunteering to attend the meeting with Labor backbencher and powerbroker Graham 'Richo' Richardson and the Tasmanian Greens' leader, Bob Brown, was that I thought Brown was a beautiful speaker, and I wanted to meet him.

At that meeting, the Hawke government's environmental revival began. The government had developed an unwanted reputation as having lost its way on protecting the environment after a courageous decision in 1983 to block the damming of Tasmania's Franklin River for the diversion of its water into a hydroelectric power station. Australia was a signatory to the World Heritage Convention, and the High Court upheld the Hawke government's argument that it had an obligation to protect identified World Heritage values. But, after that early decision, a public perception took hold that Labor was quickly abandoning its commitment to the environment.

One reason for the public's unfavourable perception was Bob's support for the American alliance during the nuclear arms race between the United States and the Soviet Union. Bob's pro-American posture had alienated young voters, not because they were necessarily anti-American—although some were—but because they were anti-nuclear. Then the Labor Party's 1984 national conference opened the way to uranium mining at Roxby Downs in South Australia. For many young people, uranium mining had become synonymous with nuclear weapons.

At the 1984 federal election, a new party entered the political stage from the left. Midnight Oil's lead singer, Peter Garrett, led the formation of the Nuclear Disarmament Party, and Peter stood for election to the Senate. Peter's party received a lot of votes, including mine. But it didn't get enough for Peter to be elected, thanks to a deal between the New South Wales Liberal and Labor parties to give Senate preferences to each other, in order to keep out of the Senate this radical new party that wanted to prevent nuclear war.

Hawke was, in truth, a strong opponent of nuclear weapons. He argued that the only redeeming feature of the policy of mutually assured destruction, which had become known as MAD, was that it worked. The superpowers had such massive nuclear arsenals that neither side would risk nuclear war. But faced with a choice between a rock star campaigning for world peace and a prime minister who had developed a close relationship with US president Ronald Reagan, young voters were keener on the 'Power and the Passion' of Midnight Oil.

Accelerating the decline in the Hawke government's environmental credentials, Queensland's premier, Sir Joh Bjelke-Petersen, who loved nothing more than a stoush with Canberra, had authorised bulldozing a road through the Daintree Rainforest in tropical North Queensland. Bob was worried that if his government took on Sir Joh over this issue, the local Labor member for Leichhardt would lose his seat. Bob was even more worried that the issue itself could become a statewide rallying call for the conservatives in such a parochial state as Queensland, costing seats up and down the coast, including as far south as Brisbane.

At the meeting of 12 June, the numbers man from the New South Wales right, wearing a silk shirt covering a pudgy belly, spoke glowingly of the tall trees, some of the earth's largest organisms, that were in the path of the chainsaws. Bob Brown implored the prime minister to save the centuries-old trees, their hollowed branches providing homes for rare and threatened birds and animals, including pigmy possums and soaring eagles. Bob Hawke was very receptive, but cautious about what such an intervention might mean for the jobs of forest workers. While I was excited about the proposed great environmental adventure, I reflected on my father's loss of work in our hometown of Baradine that had been dependent on timber cutting in the Pilliga Scrub.

Of all the locations to stage the fightback for environmental credibility, Richo and Bob Brown picked a place called Jackeys Marsh. Far from being pristine, Jackeys Marsh had been logged repeatedly, and much of it was cleared. Nevertheless, the area had been nominated for inclusion on the Interim Register of the National Estate. Most Australians confused the National Estate with national parks, thinking that logging at Jackeys Marsh was logging a national park.

As Bob's new environmental adviser, I enquired of the environment minister's consultant, Jonathan West: 'How do you put a piece of land onto the Interim Register of the National Estate?' Jonathan, who was also director of the Tasmanian Wilderness Society, told me it was pretty straightforward: a conservation group would submit a written description, a few photos, and a map, and ask the Heritage Commission to put it on the interim list. Then an under-staffed but independent Heritage Commission would most likely place it on the Interim Register of the National Estate, pending further investigation. Any such investigation could take a very long time. In the meantime, the area would enjoy iconic status, and eventually would probably be inscribed on the Permanent Register.

Jackeys Marsh had gained that status. Bob Hawke gave Bob Brown a commitment to save Jackeys Marsh from logging while a full assessment could be done of its National Estate values. Bob Brown actually wanted an unqualified commitment to ban logging, not only at Jackeys Marsh but also in all Tasmanian National Estate forest areas. Bob Hawke and I didn't even know which forests in Tasmania were on the interim or permanent registers of the National Estate. We didn't know their environmental values, and we didn't know the number of workers who would be affected by a ban on logging. Bob Hawke wouldn't go any further than committing to protecting National Estate values, not areas.

After the meeting, Bob asked me to finalise the details of his agreement with Bob Brown by working with the offices of the primary industries minister, John Kerin, and the environment minister, Barry Cohen. Jonathan West helped me convince Bob Brown that protecting National Estate values was as far as the prime minister was willing to go. Through the afternoon, we worked on a press release. I wrote these words: 'In the event of a disagreement with Tasmania, where forestry operations would adversely affect National Estate values, all the Commonwealth's powers would be used to protect those values.'

Bob was heading back to the Lodge downstairs through the private entrance to his office for the night when I just managed to catch him with my draft media release. He looked back up the stairwell and said: 'It'll be right, mate. If you think it's right, just put it out.'

That media release started the mother of all fights with Tasmania's premier, Robin Gray, and his Liberal government. The same day, John Kerin and the Tasmanian forestry minister, Ray Groom, had signed a memorandum of understanding, which had been negotiated over many months. Kerin was incensed. He greatly resented Richo's intervention as a backbencher, which had effectively weakened the government's commitment to the memorandum of understanding.

My previous boss, Peter Walsh, acidly remarked that the 'Greenies and their co-conspirators in the Australian Heritage Commission' made a practice of giving romantic or mystical names to areas of previously logged forests to dupe the public into supporting a shutdown of the Tasmanian forestry industry. It's true that the Lemonthyme, the Valley of the Giants, and the Walls of Jerusalem are evocative placenames, but Jackeys Marsh sounded more like a swamp to me. Anyway, we were going to save it.

Robin Gray immediately returned fire. Angry letters flew between Hobart and Canberra. As soon as a missive arrived from Hobart, I would prepare a sharp response to be typed up in the office for Bob's signature. Each Robin Gray accusation that the Hawke government had violated the memorandum of understanding was met with an equally vociferous allegation of an atrocity against National Estate values in contravention of the commitments given in an appendix to the same document. A committee had drafted the memorandum of understanding, making it all things to all people.

But my return missives began missing the mark. Some of the prime minister's claims in the letters back to Gray were factually incorrect. These were errors on my part and, to put it plainly, my 31-year-old arse was on fire. The prime minister's department began taking notice of this barrage of correspondence between Hawke and Gray. To his great credit, the departmental secretary, Mike Codd, quickly established an environmental section in the department to advise on the Tasmanian forest issue.

Before that, none had existed. The entire departmental environmental contingent comprised a single officer who also worked on agricultural issues. Suddenly, briefing notes began arriving from the department, which was a blessed relief for me and possibly for Bob, too.

Still, the skirmish with Tasmania continued. We commissioned a researcher from the University of Tasmania to scour Jackeys Marsh for any National Estate values he might be able to find. The place was littered with a species of wildflower. Maybe those wildflowers were of National Estate value? But stopping further logging at Jackeys Marsh was a lot easier said than done. Under what power of the Constitution could the Commonwealth legally intervene? While the Hawke government had successfully relied on the external affairs power to stop the Franklin Dam, Australia hadn't signed any international treaty to protect National Estate values, since no such treaty existed. And not even the Tasmanian Wilderness Society claimed that Jackeys Marsh was of World Heritage standard.

We knew that the Constitution gave the Commonwealth the corporations power, but it also bestowed land-use powers on the states. The corporations power could be used to regulate the activities of companies, but no one in the government had much stomach for invoking it; if it were used in one environmental dispute, the government would find it difficult to resist demands to intervene in other environmental disputes all over the country, no matter how great or small. In any event, since the corporations power could be used only to regulate the activities of companies, it could not be used to stop the government-owned, unincorporated Tasmanian Forestry Commission, which was planning to do the logging at Jackeys Marsh.

We were stuck, and Robin Gray knew it. The Tasmanian Forestry Commission continued to cut down trees at Jackeys Marsh. Lesson number one for me as environmental adviser to the prime minister was that if you want to start a battle, check your weapons first.

After our many conciliatory phone calls to Hobart, Robin Gray reluctantly agreed to suspend hostilities at Jackeys Marsh while the wildflower assessment was completed. But it was an uneasy truce. Bob had undertaken to protect all National Estate values in Tasmanian forests, not just the ones that might be present at Jackeys Marsh. Although the skirmish at Jackeys Marsh had ended, the battle over Tasmania's forests between the Hawke government and the Tasmanian government had only just begun.

16

Butch, the kid, and horses

Tasmania's forests were not to be the only location for the Hawke government's environmental revival. While we were slogging it out with the Tasmanian government over Jackeys Marsh, we turned our eyes to the north during the breaks in hostilities. To his great credit, prime minister Malcolm Fraser had, in 1981, nominated part of Kakadu National Park, known as Stage I, to the World Heritage List. Bob was keen to add an area comprising Stage II to the listing. We travelled to Kakadu, where I counted 17 crocodiles during the hour or so we spent on a boat trip on the Alligator River. It was never clear to me why it wasn't called the Crocodile River instead. It teemed with marine life and an astonishing array of birds.

Back on dry land, we organised a media conference for an important announcement. The travelling media party had suggested a beautiful shady spot with grass that looked like a well-tended lawn, almost a bowling green. Standing on this pristine area, Bob confirmed his government's intention to nominate Stage II of Kakadu National Park to the World Heritage List. A journalist asked Bob about further uranium mining in the area, since the original Stage I nomination had excluded an area in which the Ranger uranium mine was operating.

Bob said: 'How could anyone contemplate mining in this beautiful, fragile area? Under no circumstances will I allow it.'

Moments before Bob had started addressing the media, locals from the Ranger mine had alerted me that Bob was not standing in Kakadu National Park but on the Jabiluka uranium-mining lease, which had been excluded from the park. After the media conference, I told Bob he had just ruled out future uranium mining at Jabiluka. I was worried the media would report this if they realised he was standing on the lease.

'Don't worry, mate—we won't tell them', Bob reassured me. We never did. That evening's national television pictures of Bob Hawke at 'Kakadu National Park' were stunning.

That same night, Bob told me that his press secretary was leaving and that 'Butch' was to replace him. I had no idea who 'Butch' was, but I nodded approvingly. Only later did I learn that 'Butch' was Barrie Cassidy, the bloke I had been watching read ABC news bulletins for years. Within days of Barrie starting, Bob, inspired by the movie *Butch Cassidy and the Sundance Kid*, dubbed us 'Butch and the Kid'.

Bob dispatched Butch and the Kid to Cairns in August 1986 to report to him on the efforts of his trade minister, John Dawkins, in organising various agricultural-producing countries into what, by the end of that meeting, had been dubbed the Cairns Group of Fair Trading Nations.

The United States and the European Union were engaged in an agricultural trade war, subsidising their farmers to produce food, and subsidising them again to export it. These subsidies caused a global food glut, depressing prices and precipitating the blowout in Australia's current-account deficit. Now, thanks to John Dawkins, Australia and 13 other agricultural-producing nations—many of them developing countries—had joined forces and pushed for an end to the American and European subsidies war. Our job entailed sitting poolside at the Ramada Hotel during the day and telephoning the prime minister with the good news out of the meeting in the evenings. This job of working as the prime minister's economic and environmental adviser didn't seem too hard after all.

BEING AN ECONOMIST and the point man for the Australian Made campaign, I was asked by the senior advisers in the prime minister's office to travel with Bob as much as I could. We arranged Australian Made launches at local shopping centres all around Australia. Bob's many speeches contained the same message: *The rest of the world has slashed $6,000 million off our national income, and you can do your bit for* *your fellow workers by stopping and comparing the Australian-made product with the imported item.* Before long, the $6,000 million figure had blown out to $9,000 million as commodity prices continued to slide.

On these trips, I soon learned the secret of Bob's success: when we worked, we worked hard, but when we finished work, we played hard. Aboard the Royal Australian Air Force VIP flight, having read his briefing notes for the next day, Bob steered the discussion away from work to quiz me about mathematics. He asserted that, as an economist, I had to be familiar with probability theory. He further reasoned that anyone with a knowledge of probability theory had to have an interest in blackjack. Yes, prime minister.

Bob taught me the decision rules that maximised a player's chances of winning at blackjack—when to draw another card, when to sit, when to split two cards, and when to double the bet. If I strictly followed all these rules, I had better than a 49 per cent chance, but less than a 50 per cent chance, of winning. Oh joy!

We visited various casinos—in truth, most of them—while travelling around the country, but there was a problem: my preferred standard bet was $2, and Bob's was $200. The exclusive rooms we frequented didn't cater for $2 low rollers like me, but Bob wanted some company, so he made me an offer I couldn't refuse: I would be paid 2 per cent of any winnings, with no liability for any losses. At those odds, Bob had in me a loyal companion at the blackjack table.

Now that Bob had roped me into blackjack, it was only a matter of time before he got me interested in horse racing. This process began with Bob asking me to mark up 'the Bible'— *The Sportsman* magazine's form guide—identifying those horses whose trainers Bob knew personally. He studiously assessed the form of each runner while aboard a VIP flight, and rang his friendly trainers on race day for an assessment of their charges' chances. Bob's formula for taking a closer interest in a horse's prospects was that it needed to have run fast times and to be carrying a lighter weight than it had in its previous races.

Aided by my marking up the friendly trainers, Bob ploughed through *The Sportsman*'s form guide for Sydney, Melbourne, Adelaide, and sometimes Brisbane as well. He marked with an asterisk those horses he rated as having a good chance of winning or at least running a place, ready to ring the trainers early the next morning for their assessments.

It was this arduous process that almost led to the early termination of Butch's engagement as the prime minister's media adviser. We were on a Friday night VIP flight from Canberra to Perth. Bob had spent most of the time aboard assessing the form in *The Sportsman* while I marked up the trainers he knew, ready for phone calls very early on Saturday morning. As we were leaving the jet in Perth, Bob gave Butch a bundle of newspapers, including *The Sportsman*, and said: 'Here, take care of these.'

Butch noticed only the daily newspapers and, it being late Friday night, couldn't see any further use for them, so he threw the bundle into a corner of the aircraft cabin.

At around six o'clock the next morning, Bob woke to make his telephone calls back east, where it was already 8.00am. Bob needed to ring the trainers before they headed off for the races. He looked around his hotel suite, but couldn't find *The Sportsman*. He rang his accompanying Australian Federal Police security officers to ask them where *The Sportsman* was. They came around to my room. I told them I didn't have it. Then they went to Butch's room. Butch speculated: 'It's probably in the bunch of papers I left on the plane.' The cops returned to Bob's suite to inform him that Butch had left *The Sportsman* on the plane. They came back to my room to report they had just left the prime minister of Australia standing in the doorway in the nude, shouting: 'How could anyone be so fucking stupid?'

Despite its rocky start, Bob's relationship with Butch soon improved. Saturday morning's phoning of trainers had become a ritual when Bob and I were travelling. When we were not, I still gave him the form guide marked up with trainers, he rang them, passed on the tips to me, and I phoned them through to Butch. Almost every Saturday when Bob was at the Lodge, I joined him to listen to the day's races on the radio. If we were at Kirribilli House in Sydney, we usually went out to the Rosehill or Randwick racetracks for the day's racing.

As a young staffer, I didn't have a big stake to take to the races, so I usually bet a few dollars each way. Having checked the form on a maiden two-year-old race as best I could, since most of the field had not raced other than at barrier trials, I noticed that a filly, Pine Lodge Girl, had already contested a race and run fourth. The red-hot favourite was unraced, which I considered a risk, since it was inexperienced and lacked race fitness. When I approached our friendly bookie at the track, wanting to place $5 each way on Pine Lodge Girl, he laughed and gave me odds of 250–1.

To my delight, Pine Lodge Girl beat the favourite home by almost a length. As I walked towards the bookie to collect my winnings, a protest siren sounded. The stewards deliberated for what seemed like an eternity. They ruled that Pine Lodge Girl had caused interference to the well-beaten, red-hot favourite, reversing the result. It reminded me of the old racing story: How do you go home from the races with a small fortune? Go there with a big fortune.

At one race meeting, we backed a horse named Sound Horizon. As the field entered the straight, a member of our party said said: 'Bugger! Sound Horizon is blocked for a run behind a wall of horses.' Moments later, he observed: 'Great! A gap has opened up for Sound Horizon', which he immediately followed up with: 'but the gap's going faster than Sound Horizon'.

Months later, Sound Horizon was nominated for a major race. Cathy accompanied Bob and me to the races for the carnival race day. She noticed this handsome black horse parading in the mounting yard, and decided to bet on it. I pointed out that it was a 40–1 outsider and had no chance, talking her out of the bet. Of course, Sound Horizon won in a canter, and I have never been forgiven.

AT A MELBOURNE RACE MEETING, Bob took the opportunity to greet an up-and-coming trainer who, for reasons that will soon become obvious, shall remain nameless. The trainer had only a small contingent of racehorses, but one of them was lightning fast over short distances. To protecty the horse's identity, I will give it the name 'Lightning'.

Within ten days of the meeting between Bob and the trainer, Lightning was entered into a mid-week race in Melbourne. Bob phoned the trainer, who declared that Lightning 'will win'. Bob called Butch and me into his office to listen to the race call. Bob told us he had placed a modest bet on the horse. The gates opened, and Lightning raced immediately to the lead. Lightning maintained a big lead, but, into the home straight, the field began closing on him. Then, extraordinarily, horses in the chasing pack found trouble. One suffered a bump, falling back into the field. A new challenger emerged from the pack and actually fell over. Clear of interference, Lightning cantered to the finishing line, winning by six lengths. Bob collected, at long odds.

From that day onward, Bob was convinced that the interference had been, in some way, let's say, premeditated. Ahead of Lightning's next couple of outings, its trainer declared that the horse 'will win'—not that it 'has a good chance of winning' or that it 'will probably win', but that it 'will win'.

As the trainer predicted, Lightning won its next race, and the next, dashing to the lead and running the chasers off their legs.

Bob concluded that Lightning was a money-printing machine. The horse was nominated to contest a mid-week race in country Victoria. Bob phoned the trainer who, again, declared that Lightning 'will win'.

Now we were all going to cash in. Bob, Butch, other staff members with an interest in horse racing, as well as steno-secretaries with no interest at all, pooled our funds for a very big office bet on Lightning. Having won its previous three races, Lightning, while up in class, was at short odds. We would bet on it to win, not each way.

But if we put our large collective stake on the TAB, we ran the risk of shortening its odds further. We decided, instead, to dispatch one of our punting staff members, Grant 'Grunter the Punter' Nihill, to the Hawkesbury racetrack in the New South Wales Hunter Valley. Grunter's mission, if he chose to accept it, was to move quickly from one bookie to the next, wagering equal shares of our office stake with each, securing from them the odds they displayed at the time, before they could wind them in. This worked a treat; Grunter obtained the best possible odds from each bookie.

Bob and I were in the official prime ministerial car, travelling to Parliament House from the airport following our return from campaigning in marginal electorates. The car radio covered the race. The field jumped. Lightning raced to the lead. As they entered the home straight, Lightning maintained a lead of many lengths, the race caller declaring it home and hosed. At that point, the race-day compere announced that the station was interrupting the Victorian country race to cover an overdue Adelaide city race.

No matter, we concluded, Lightning had established an unassailable lead. We drove through the prime ministerial entrance of Parliament

House and strode triumphantly into the prime minister's office to be met by stony-faced staff members who had contributed hard-earned cash to the big bet. One of the steno-secretaries was close to tears, and the others looked dark and angry. Soon after entering the straight, they explained, Lightning had stopped running, slowing to a canter. He had been beaten by several lengths.

How could this be?

I checked the form guide. Lightning had won all his races over the short distances of 1,000 metres and 1,100 metres. Today's race had been run over 1,200 metres, which the horse had never attempted. None of us in the prime minister's office, including Bob, had taken this important detail into account. Over the extra 100 metres, Lightning had breathlessly walked home as his rivals sailed past him. As a matter of probity, Bob had insisted that Grunter take a day of annual leave. He returned that evening, tired, grumpy, and relieved of a large amount of pooled funds.

Despite this setback, the allure of the races attracted me, and I took up a suggestion from our favourite trainer, Brian Mayfield-Smith, to buy a share in a yearling he had acquired at the Easter sales. The 20-per-cent stake in Notorious Deed cost $30,000. Brian decided to enter the horse into a mid-week maiden race at Hawkesbury. At the time of the race, Bob and I, along with many racing identities, were attending the opening of Arrowfield Stud nearby. Having listened to the race on the prime ministerial car radio, I was able to walk up to my co-owner to inform him that our horse had won.

'Oh, that's marvellous', Sir Robert said. 'Where was it racing?'

Sir Robert's Sangster's share of the prize money for this mid-week maiden race would have made little impact on his accumulated fortune. Notorious Deed went on to win six races, but to lose many more. Win or lose, horses still eat hay and need veterinary care, shoes, training, and spells in paddocks. As Notorious Deed rolled in clover, I did not. My interest in owning horses ceased with a filly whose mother was a Lunchtime mare and whose father was named Valiant Prospect. Since a Valiant was a type of car, and lunchtime was a meal, I named the filly Meals on Wheels. She lost when she was expected to win, and won when she was expected to lose. Meals on Wheels soon made a good companion for a little girl on a farm.

Bob enjoyed having a bet on the mid-week races as an entertaining distraction from his heavy workload. One time before a cabinet meeting, he perused the form guide and identified a runner he considered might have a chance of at least running a place. Bob rang the trainer, who was astute at placing his horses to greatest advantage, preferring to win an easier race offering modest prize money to losing a big race offering top prize money. The trainer told Bob this mediocre horse had a good winning chance in a weak race.

Bob placed $100 each way on the horse before chairing a meeting of the federal cabinet. A minister was making heavy weather of trying to persuade his colleagues of the merits of his submission, which involved a substantial amount of new spending. Just when all seemed lost, an attendant delivered my note to Bob informing him the horse had won at 33–1. Bob looked over to the minister and said: 'That'll be right, mate. Your submission is approved.' While naming the fortunate minister would constitute a breach of cabinet confidentiality, let's just say that the science budget received a welcome boost.

17

War in the Lemonthyme

As 1986 drew to a close, Bob gathered his staff at The Lodge for drinks. After thanking us before heading off for a break, Bob turned to me and said: 'Mate, look after the Tassie forests while I'm gone, will ya?' He didn't want to be disturbed during his break. I assured him everything would be fine.

But Tasmania's premier, Robin Gray, still smarting from the skirmish at Jackeys Marsh, had no intention of wishing us a Merry Christmas and a Happy New Year. On Boxing Day, Tasmanian Forestry Commission bulldozers lumbered like Sherman Tanks into the Lemonthyme Forest. Cathy and I were holidaying at Jervis Bay. In those days, mobile phones did not exist. It seemed I spent more time with a pocketful of coins in a local telephone booth than on the beach.

Smoke had been reported rising from the Lemonthyme Forest. I was supposed to be looking after it for the prime minister, but now they were burning it down. Boy, those Tasmanian Liberals knew how to fight.

I arranged an urgent meeting in Sydney with acting prime minister Lionel Bowen. Lionel, a laid-back sort of guy, said we shouldn't do anything until Bob returned from leave. But half the Lemonthyme would be gone by then. Bob Brown and the Tasmanian Wilderness Society were hysterical about this incursion, and demanded federal intervention. I knew Bob would expect us to act.

A deputy secretary in the Attorney-General's Department, Dennis Rose, attended the meeting with Lionel. Dennis advised us that in order for a federal government to intervene legally, we needed evidence of the destruction of possible World Heritage values. I asked what evidence was required. Dennis said we needed photographic evidence.

My mind flashed back to the F111 flights over the Franklin River taken in 1983 to collect photographic evidence to enable the Hawke government to stop construction of the Franklin Dam. Apparently the F111 was meant to take its photographs from a height of several kilometres, but the pilot decided on a last pass to snap a few close-up pictures. He frightened the living daylights out of every human and animal in the area by flying at a couple of hundred metres above ground level. I think the sonic boom might have given him away. I didn't want a repetition of that episode, so we quickly ruled out aerial photography. That left only photos taken from the ground. Lionel was beside himself with indifference, but Jonathan West and I decided to obtain the necessary photographs ourselves.

I took a flight to Hobart to join Jonathan, who had organised to meet with a bloke named Geoff Law near the Lemonthyme Forest. Geoff was a senior member of the Wilderness Society, and he had wrapped a camera in a sealed plastic bag. We figured that if we approached the logging activity by the forestry road, the Tasmanian Forestry Commission and maybe even the police would be ready for us — we would either be turned back or arrested. The only way to enter the Lemonthyme Forest unnoticed, therefore, would be by swimming across the Lemonthyme River.

We left Hobart in Jonathan's dilapidated old bomb of a car, radio blaring, heading out on the highway, looking for adventure, born to be wild. Twelve kilometres outside Hobart, Jonathan's car spluttered, stopped, and died. It just died. Nothing would revive it. We tried for four hours, and for all I know, the wreck is still there on the roadside, a rusting testament to our attempt to save the Lemonthyme Forest. We had no photos, no evidence, and no way of stopping the logging.

But at least the conservation movement knew that the Hawke government was serious about trying to save the Lemonthyme. After all, the prime minister's environmental adviser had been prepared to swim a river and risk arrest to gather the evidence for Commonwealth intervention. Our pathetically failed attempt had, ironically, taken the immediate pressure off the government. With Bob still on leave, and

Lionel unwilling to do anything, I returned to our holiday at Jervis Bay.

By now, departmental secretary Mike Codd was turning his mind to solving the problem of how to stop the logging. Dennis Rose and Mike conceived the idea of a special act of parliament to empower the federal government to stop forestry operations in areas such as the Lemonthyme while they were being assessed for World Heritage values. Bob returned from leave, and obtained cabinet approval for a bill to be introduced into parliament when it resumed in early February.

By this time, Bob Brown and the conservation movement were demanding that the Hawke government prevent other scheduled logging activity in National Estate areas in the adjacent Southern Forests of Tasmania. Many cabinet ministers were opposed to this grand intervention into Tasmanian land-use issues. I had become very familiar with the detail of the proposed intervention, the areas affected, and what it could mean for forestry jobs. To the astonishment of Bob's cabinet colleagues, he arranged for me to accompany him into the cabinet room for the debate, seated beside and just behind him.

With a great sense of foreboding, the cabinet acquiesced in or did not actively oppose Bob's recommendation, ensuring that the bill before the parliament covered not only the Lemonthyme Forest but also the Southern Forests. This decision gave the government time to set up a full commission of inquiry into the region's environmental values in order to determine if they were of World Heritage standard, while at the same time empowering the federal government to stop logging within the designated area.

The Tasmanian government took the Hawke government to the High Court over the constitutional validity of the Lemonthyme and Southern Forests Commission of Inquiry Act. Based on the precedent set in the High Court's judgement in the Franklin Dam case, the Hawke government won.

A retired Supreme Court judge, Justice Michael Helsham, chaired the commission of inquiry. When it eventually reported, it recommended, by a majority of two commissioners to one, that only five small areas within the Lemonthyme and Southern Forests be nominated for World Heritage listing—just 10 per cent of the inquiry area.

The minority report by Dr Peter Hitchcock concluded that almost the entire area was of World Heritage standard. This created a conundrum for the Hawke government, which Bob solved over the course of three very long cabinet meetings stretching over many weeks. Ahead of the first cabinet meeting, Bob and I discussed my briefing note, and accepted that the government needed to protect the large area recommended by Peter Hitchcock. As Bob was leaving his office for the cabinet room, I said: 'It's really important that you get this through cabinet.'

Bob turned to me and said: 'I will, mate, but I want to bring my colleagues with me.'

Senator Peter 'Cookie' Cook had become the minister for forests. He worked assiduously with his department on a compromise proposal to save the most environmentally sensitive areas while allowing logging to continue on a limited scale. Cookie came to a meeting of Bob and me with his maps and papers. Bob was a great admirer of Australian artist Lloyd Rees, and had one of Lloyd's paintings hanging in the anteroom to his office. Lloyd's son, Alan, was living in Hobart. Bob thought if Lloyd could be persuaded to support Cookie's plan, it might gain some much-needed public credibility. Bob said to Cookie: 'If you can convince Alan Rees and he's willing to advocate your plan to Lloyd, I'll consider it.'

Cookie and I flew to Hobart, and met Alan at his home. After enjoying a cup of tea and cakes, we discussed Cookie's plan. At the outset, as Cookie began unfolding his maps, Alan asked: 'Why do you want to cut down the trees?'

Cookie explained his plan carefully and methodically, pointing to small logging coupes on his map, much larger preserved areas, the protections that would be assured for vegetation along the rivers and streams, and the periods that would be allowed for regrowth. This took more than an hour, Alan taking a keen interest in the contours on Cookie's map and his carefully considered plan.

Cookie rolled up his map and asked Alan what he thought of his forestry plan, to which Alan replied: 'Yes, but why do you want to cut down the trees?'

We returned to Canberra to brief Bob, Cookie bringing his maps and charts along with him. As Cookie unfolded them on Bob's desk,

Bob asked us: 'How did you go with Alan?'

Cookie replied: 'Pretty well, I think.'

After Cookie left the office, I told Bob that Alan's first and last question was: 'Why do you want to cut down the trees?' Alan, I advised Bob, was most unlikely to recommend Cookie's plan to his father. We would be going with the minority-report recommendation to protect almost the entire inquiry area.

In the ensuing cabinet meeting, an exasperated primary industries minister, John Kerin, sarcastically quipped: 'Why don't we use a set of crayons to decide which areas to log and which ones to lock up?' Metaphorically speaking, Bob did just that, colouring virtually the entire Lemonthyme and Southern Forest area green.

Following the cabinet decision in August 1988 to support Peter Hitchcock's minority report, Bob Brown began pressing me to urge Bob to add to the World Heritage nomination a number of areas that were not in the Helsham Inquiry area but were of no value for forestry operations. I considered this impossible, but Bob seemed to adopt the philosophy of 'In for a penny, in for a pound.' He added the Walls of Jerusalem National Park and the Central Plateau Conservation Area to the nomination, bringing the total World Heritage-nominated area to 262,000 hectares.

Bob Brown sent both Bob Hawke and me a bottle of champagne and a bunch of flowers. I drafted a letter to Bob Brown, which Bob signed. It read: 'Dear Bob. Thanks for the champagne and flowers. The World Heritage nomination is a magnificent achievement, one of which my government, all Australians and you in particular can feel justifiably proud.'

For my part in the decision to nominate the Lemonthyme and Southern Forests for the World Heritage list, the Tasmanian forestry union dubbed me 'Dr Death'. The rancour having subsided with the passage of time, the secretary of the national union, Michael O'Connor, now addresses me as 'Dr Death' or, in his more affectionate moments, 'Comrade Death' or, more informally, just 'Death'.

In an ironic twist, the federal Labor government and the Tasmanian Liberal government ended up jointly submitting the World Heritage nomination, signed by Bob Hawke and Robin Gray. Bob had offered premier Gray $50 million to develop plantation forests in the hope of avoiding such conflicts in the future. The nomination was sent to the World Heritage Bureau almost exactly two years after the Tasmanian Forestry Commission first rumbled into the Lemonthyme Forest. The war in the Lemonthyme had been won.

18

A crack in the wall

As the war in the Lemonthyme was escalating, Bob returned from annual leave, and we headed overseas for Jordan, Israel, Switzerland, and Egypt. Bob had a deep and abiding interest in peace in the Middle East. For various reasons, personal and professional, Bob was seen to be strongly supportive of Israel in the continuing conflict with the Arab states. Jordan was a moderating influence.

We arrived in the capital, Amman, aboard the Royal Australian Air Force Boeing 707, accompanied by a large Australian media contingent. Amman was a neat, attractive city in a rocky, hilly country. Only the hardiest of vegetation could eek out sufficient sustenance from the pockets of soil wedged between the rocks on the hills surrounding the city.

Australia's modest economic ties with Jordan didn't warrant my participation as trade adviser in most meetings, though we did hastily cobble together a simple commercial agreement between the two countries. We visited an amazing place—Petra—a deserted ancient city carved into deep ravines. After peace, all that seemed to matter to the Jordanian government was water. If the Jordanians could gain access to water they would be well off, but without it they would continue to struggle. Peace and water could flow together: if Jordan had an enduring peace with Israel, water could be piped through Israel into Jordan.

Our arrival in Jerusalem left with me one of the most striking impressions of my life. Here I was, a former altar boy at St John's Church, looking across the Holy City, bleached white with limestone buildings, with Australia's prime minister. The Garden of Gethsemane, the narrow alleys bearing the Stations of the Cross, and the Church of the Holy Sepulchre resting above the place of Jesus's crucifixion laid out a mystical world before my living eyes. The ancient book, so familiar to me through years of Catechism, Bible studies, and church attendance, was a travelogue, a street directory.

In my mind, I had assumed that these holy places would have been destroyed, or would have crumbled, with the passage of the centuries. Maybe they had, and I was observing replicas, but they seemed real, and the area they occupied so small. Outside Jerusalem, crossing invisible borders into the Palestinian Territories on the West Bank of the Jordan River, we entered the Arab town of Nazareth and the Church of the Nativity, the assumed birthplace of Jesus Christ. An Irish Catholic Butch Cassidy and the Baradine Catholic kid felt privileged to be taken to such a place about which we had been told since our infancy.

Our time in Jerusalem passed quickly. Bob took us around the Old City, stepping through doorways from the Arab quarters into the Jewish quarters, the Christian quarters, and the Armenian quarters, Arab and Israeli peacefully passing by each other. Our guides showed us a place where, in wars, Arabs and Israelis had shot at each other from a distance of a few metres, the walls still pock-marked from the gunfire. Coming from a country where a hostile force would be obliged to travel hundreds of kilometres across the open sea to wage war, I could barely believe it was possible for two countries to fight each other from across a street in a shared city.

Bob told Butch, Bob Sorby, and me not to bother coming to the scheduled official meetings and, instead, to explore this ancient city ourselves. We took advantage of a pleasant evening to walk from the foyer of the King David Hotel in search of a place to eat. Having ordered kebabs at a small café, we were surprised to be approached by two fit-looking young Aussie blokes wearing jeans. They explained they were from Melbourne, and suggested we not venture too much farther. It was clear they were from Mossad, Israel's national intelligence agency.

Bob told me of his long friendship with Shimon Peres, a former Israeli Labor prime minister who was now foreign minister in a power-sharing arrangement between Labor and the conservative Likud Party. Prime minister Yitzhak Shamir, a small, nuggety man, was our host.

Bob was not an admirer. But he reserved his animosity for Ariel Sharon, who had been considered responsible, as Israel's defence minister, for the 1982 massacre of Palestinians in two refugee camps in Lebanon.

Before leaving his beloved Jerusalem, Bob wanted to take me on a visit to the city's Western Wall, colloquially known as the Wailing Wall. At this Jewish holy place of prayer, a tradition had developed of visitors writing a wish on a small piece of paper, rolling it up, and inserting it into one of the many cracks in the wall's masonry. As we sat in the back of the car, Bob asked me for a pen. He wrote his wish: 'A historic third term.'

In the Australian Labor Party's long history, it had never won three successive elections. Under Bob's leadership, Labor had won the 1983 election, been re-elected in 1984, and was again facing an election in 1987. Bob had a chance of making Labor history. He rolled up his inscribed wish, walked towards the wall, where he placed a Jewish kippah on his head, and inserted the note while I quietly took a photo. Ten years later, I gave him the photo for his 68th birthday.

OUR PURPOSE IN VISITING DAVOS in Switzerland was for Bob to deliver an address to the annual World Economic Forum on the need in global trade talks to begin winding back farm subsidies to lift agricultural prices for efficient producers. Working on the speech proved less challenging than finding my way around this village high up in the Swiss Alps. Having decided to walk from our hotel to the venue, I became hopelessly lost, all snow-covered buildings looking remarkably similar to me. After two hours trudging through the ice and snow, telling myself not to panic as my hands turned blue, I made it to the venue to listen to Bob's erudite address.

More than two decades later, I visited the same venue, sensibly by courtesy of an official vehicle, three more times as Australia's trade minister, one of them with our son, Ben. There I was able to introduce Ben to former World Bank president Bob Zoellick, Thailand's prime minister, Yingluck Shinawatra, and president Barack Obama's trade representative, Mike Froman. But for all that notoriety, we rolled and played in the snow until my hands turned bluer than during my lost meanderings through the village in January 1987.

Our last stop before returning home was Egypt. Bob had wanted to pursue his interest in a Middle East peace plan with president Mubarak. We visited the Museum of Egyptian Antiquities, housing treasures from an ancient civilisation, and travelled several kilometres out of Cairo past a few paddocks and fields until suddenly, jutting into the sky, stood the Great Pyramid, several smaller ones, and the Sphinx. Compared with the Great Pyramid, the Sphinx seemed a little on the wee side, rising just over 20 metres.

Our visit to these 4,500-year-old monuments of a lost civilisation took place on the last day of our overseas tour. Cairo was dusty, the official car drivers carrying with them cloths to wipe away the most recent deposits. In the official order of precedence, the prime minister's travelling economic adviser and his speechwriter were a long way from the top. Stephen 'Millsie' Mills had taken up the role of speechwriter a couple of months after I started in the prime minister's office. So strict was the order of precedence that we were consigned to Car 13 in the official cavalcade, winding through the narrow streets of Cairo. That didn't bother us as much as the fact that Cars 8, 9, 10, 11, and 12 were empty.

Having inspected the pyramids, we stepped out of Car 13 onto the VIP jet to Australia without having showered. The smell of dust in our hair and on our skin was soon to mingle with cigar smoke, beer, and red wine. I'd brought my trusty guitar, and, soon, journalists, staffers, public servants, the prime ministerial doctor, security officers, and Bob and Hazel Hawke were singing 'Bye, bye Miss American Pie' as the good old boys and girls drank whiskey and rye, gin and tonic, beer and wine.

Singing wasn't the only way of passing time on the long flight home. By now, I'd gotten the hang of blackjack—so much so that I purchased a set of poker chips and a dealer's shoe, housing four packs of cards.

You'd think that, as a journalist, it would be a rare privilege to be invited to the front of the aircraft for a personal three-hour audience with the prime minister of Australia on the way home from an official overseas visit. At first, that's what journalists thought, too. One member of their brethren, Peter Logue, never needed persuading. If he was not proficiently upstaging my guitar performances on his piano accordion, he was playing blackjack with the prime minister and his staff. A couple of radio journalists were willing to give it a go. Butch and the Kid were certain starters. And then there was Bob, whose favourite word when playing mile-high blackjack was 'double'. Whatever the opening bet, Bob wanted to double it. We soon learned to halve our initial offering.

If a journalist was winning, he was obliged to stay until his luck ran out. If he was losing, he was welcome to try playing his way out of debt. Bob was very generous: a journalist's credit was good. Bob put me in charge of recovering journalists' debts back in Australia. Strangely, after several of these experiences on overseas trips, I found persuading journalists to join the prime minister at the front of the plane increasingly challenging.

Far from embracing me when I arrived home in Canberra from the Royal Australian Air Force base at Fairbairn, Cathy screwed up her nose at the look of my tousled hair and unshaven, grimy face, and the stench of sweat and alcohol mingled with Bob's cigar smoke.

Though tired, smelly, and a little drunk, I was cheery, for as we stepped off the plane onto the tarmac, we were greeted with the news that Sir Joh Bjelke-Petersen had announced his intention to become the conservative candidate for the prime ministership at the coming federal election.

At a rally in Wagga Wagga the day before we landed, Sir Joh announced: 'I am starting a bushfire today and it will go all over Australia.' His plan was to set up a new conservative party, depose John Howard as leader of the opposition, and take on Bob. Sir Joh was supported by former Treasury secretary John Stone, and his deputy, Des Moore, historian Geoffrey Blainey, National Farmers' Federation president Ian McLachlan, and the property-developing 'white-shoe brigade' on the Gold Coast. As a large crack appeared in the wall of conservative opposition to the Hawke government, I quietly thanked Sir Joh for helping Bob's wish in Jerusalem for a historic third term come true.

19

Resurgence

History, as written, credits the Joh-for-PM campaign with destroying John Howard's chances of winning the 1987 election. But there's a second explanation. By conveying the nation's predicament to the Australian people and making the necessary decisions to reduce government spending, Labor had already clawed back in the public opinion polls from well behind the Coalition in mid-1986 to running neck and neck by the end of the year. It's true, though, that Joh's campaign raged like a bushfire through the Howard campaign.

When I travelled to electorates around Australia with Bob, we usually returned to Canberra on Saturday nights. On Sundays, I spread the week's newspapers on our lounge-room floor and cut out the best quotes of Coalition members attacking each other. Sometimes the wealth of quotes was so great that it took half of Sunday just to compile the most vivid of them. I assembled them into a series of documents that I unimaginatively entitled *Quotable Quotes*.

Bob brandished *Quotable Quotes* in parliament with great relish, having heavily underlined and asterisked his personal favourites. After the second and third editions of *Quotable Quotes*s, I couldn't keep up with the vitriol flowing from the mouths of squabbling conservatives.

Meanwhile, the government had established the National Media Liaison Service, the initials of which were NMLS. They became known as the 'Animals'. Headed by Col 'Curly' Parkes, the Animals established a presence in each state, monitoring regional radio, television, and newspapers that hitherto had been inaccessible to us from Canberra.

The Animals took on the job of assembling the fourth, fifth, sixth, seventh, and eighth editions of *Quotable Quotes* based on my armfuls of clippings from the national media and their monitoring of state and local media.

Following early successes in Question Time, Bob waltzed into the chamber to exploit an attack by the leader of the National Party, Ian Sinclair, on his Coalition leadership partner, John Howard. This seemed strange, since Ian Sinclair had been supporting Howard against Sir Joh. But there it was in black and white, in the eighth edition of *Quotable Quotes*. Sinclair was bemused by Bob's withering critique. He made a personal explanation at the end of Question Time, denying he had ever uttered the words Bob had attributed to him.

Bob returned to his office and slammed the document on my desk. Upon re-checking with the Animals, it turned out that the attack on Howard had been launched not by Ian Sinclair but by an obscure member of the Queensland National Party. I was worried that our false accusation would dominate the television news bulletins that night. It didn't, because Joh's bushfire was spreading as he promised it would.

But I learned a valuable lesson in life: on important matters, never rely solely on information supplied by others, never use it before checking its authenticity, and never jump first and double-check later. While Bob continued to rely on me to provide quotes that were highly detrimental to the opposition, he instructed me to keep copies of all source documents with me as we travelled together. This was to prove physically demanding, as I carried around the best of *Quotable Quotes* and all supporting documents in two heavy briefcases up to, during, and beyond the 1987 election campaign.

WHILE BOB AND PAUL had been explaining the need for belt tightening, National and Liberal MPs in regional Australia were making extravagant new promises to their voters. With the help of the Animals, we listed these commitments. Paul Keating's senior economic adviser, Ken Henry—who later became Treasury secretary—worked with Treasury to estimate their cost. We attributed them to Howard, who had promised to cut taxes and return the budget to surplus while his MPs were promising more spending. A huge gap opened up between

Howard's promises of a budget surplus, lower taxes, and higher spending, which I called his $12 billion 'credibility gap'.

Although newspaper editorials began adopting the phrase of Howard's 'credibility gap', it was an obscure notion for everyday Australians. When one of Bob's political advisers remonstrated with me, demanding that I use more familiar language, I suggested simply calling it Howard's 'deficit'. The adviser liked that, so I changed Bob's Question Time briefing note from referring to Howard's 'credibility gap' to his 'deficit'. Bob had developed a lot of trust in me, and used the new terminology.

Following Question Time, Howard made a personal explanation, pointing out that, since the $12 billion figure included his promise to remove the budget deficit, it could not be correctly described as his 'deficit'. This time, Bob thundered into my cubbyhole, repeated the Howard explanation, correctly declared it legitimate, and shouted that I had 'fucked it up!' Guilty as charged, I pleaded. It was the lowest point of my career to date. I apologised profusely and, after the error with *Quotable Quotes,* promised it would never happen again. Under the intense, unrelenting pressure of a looming election campaign, was it a promise I was capable of keeping?

As Howard's credibility gap edged past $18 billion, Bob and Paul called on him to identify how he would fund the Coalition's mutually exclusive promises. Howard eventually released a tabulation of the promises he intended to keep, ruling out most of those made by his regional colleagues. But he was still a long way short of being able to fund his promised tax cuts while abolishing the capital-gains tax and fringe-benefits tax, and achieving a budget surplus.

During the course of these exchanges between the government and the opposition, the media received a leaked note from Howard to the previous opposition leader, Andrew Peacock, written during the 1984 election campaign. Howard had warned Peacock not to accumulate a set of election promises he couldn't fund, cautioning that people would start asking: 'Where's the money coming from?' In that note, Howard had unwittingly written the script for our television and radio advertisements for the final days of the 1987 election campaign.

AS A RESULT OF OUR COLLABORATION on Tasmanian forests, the
Hawke government and the conservation movement were getting on
much better. But, since it was now an election year, Bob was becoming
increasingly worried about being inundated with demands from
conservation groups across Australia to protect every imaginable natural
place. He felt that as soon as he protected one area, demands were made
for the government to protect other places that had never been raised
with him before. Bob said to me: 'Mate, I won't agree to the greenies
having an infinitely elastic agenda. I want you to settle with them an
agenda that we can achieve and, when we do, I want their support.'

As Bob himself wrote in his memoirs:

> I detailed Emerson to work closely with the lobby, particularly the
> Australian Conservation Foundation and the Wilderness Society in
> the lead up to the election. I told him there was to be no elastic agenda.
> Some of the environmentalists were unrealistic and never ending in
> their demands. As a result of Craig's good work, the specific areas
> of commitment were limited to Tasmanian forests, Kakadu, the wet
> tropics rainforest and Shelburne Bay in Queensland.

I organised a meeting with Bob and the key conservationists on 20
February 1987 to lock in that agenda. Representing the Wilderness
Society were Bob Brown and Jonathan West. Phillip Toyne and Joan
Staples came on behalf of the Australian Conservation Foundation. At
the meeting, Bob signalled his willingness to nominate the wet tropical
forests of North Queensland to the World Heritage List. Of course, the
conservationists were delighted with that undertaking. But of the four
environmental icons we had agreed to protect, the least well-known
proved the most difficult.

A Japanese company held leases for sand mining at Shelburne Bay
on Cape York. The sand was pure silica, and the company's plan was
to load it onto vessels and ship it off to Japan to be turned into glass.
This seemed a pretty low-value proposition for exploiting an Australian
wilderness area. The problem was that the Australian dollar had been
in free-fall, and treasurer Paul Keating was anxious about spooking
Japanese investors into judging that Australia was a place of high
sovereign risk.

By April 1987, the government formally resolved to nominate the wet tropical forests of North Queensland to the World Heritage List, fulfilling Bob's commitment to protecting the third icon. Only the fourth one—Shelburne Bay—still needed protecting. Paul persuaded the Japanese government that the rejection of silica mining at Shelburne Bay would not signal that Australia considered Japanese investment unwelcome. In announcing the protection of Shelburne Bay, the Hawke government fulfilled its pre-election environmental commitments.

Based on these undertakings, the conservation movement agreed to campaign for Labor at the election. The Australian Conservation Foundation recommended a vote for Labor in the House of Representatives; but with senior members of the Democrats on its council, it didn't advocate a vote for Labor in the Senate. The Wilderness Society went much further. It put television advertisements to air showing destructive clear-felling forestry operations in Tasmania, and urged voters to support the re-election of the Hawke government if they wanted the logging to stop.

HAVING BROUGHT DOWN A TOUGH BUDGET in August 1986, Bob, Paul, and the other economic ministers decided that a further round of spending cuts was necessary to help stabilise the economy ahead of the 1987 election. These new budget savings were to be announced in a special May statement. But some of Bob's ministers and personal staff members began advocating an early election to capitalise on the chaos within the opposition caused by the Joh-for-PM campaign. Paul, his staff, and I judged that our story of an economic crisis would ring hollow if the government opportunistically rushed off to an early election to take advantage of a divided opposition.

In deciding where to make the new spending cuts, Bob, Paul, Peter Walsh, John Dawkins, Ralph Willis, and other members of the Expenditure Review Committee met daily and well into the evenings. After one late-night meeting, we gathered in the carpeted area outside the cabinet room. As we stood in a semi-circle, discussing the day's work, John Dawkins, having read stories speculating about Bob calling an early election, turned to me and said: 'Why are you trying to talk Bob into an early election? It's a fucking stupid idea.'

I assured John: 'I'm not trying to talk Bob into any such thing.'

To my plea of innocence, John retorted: 'Well, you're fucking irrelevant then, aren't you?'

I was either stupid or irrelevant. John apologised the next day, and much later offered me the position of his chief of staff. He, like me, was exasperated with talk of a dash to the polls when serious policy work still needed to be done.

On 1 April, Bob publicly ruled out an early election. I drafted it into his media release. It read, in part:

> The world has cut more than $6 billion off the nation's income; that is, we are poorer to the tune of $1500 per Australian family ... We will not shirk our responsibilities in making the unpalatable, though necessary economic decisions: the May statement will be tough but fair.

Consistent with Bob's media release, we had decided that the theme of the May economic statement would be 'Restraint with Equity'. Liberal Party president John Elliott was an ally in the cause, querying on radio why millionaires received family payments that the country could no longer afford. We queried it, too, abolishing family payments for families with combined incomes above $50,000 a year.

We also abolished the unemployment benefit for 16- and 17-year-olds, and replaced it with a job-search allowance set at half the rate of unemployment benefit for all but the poorest families. At the same time, we increased financial assistance for school students, removing the incentive to leave school early and go on the dole. We cut defence spending, and sold part of the Australian embassy in Tokyo, which was situated on the most expensive real estate in the world. For good measure, we also sold the ambassador's residence in Paris.

Despite big overall spending reductions — the biggest on record — the public so warmed to the theme of 'Restraint with Equity' that, following the release of the May statement, the government's popularity rose sharply. Now we were genuinely contemplating going to the polls. It would be a mid-winter election, which was most unusual, since the conventional wisdom was that people casting their votes in the rain, wind, and cold would be grumpy and more inclined to vote against the government of the day. Nevertheless, Bob judged that the time was right, and he called an election for 11 July 1987. We had four weeks of campaigning to reassure the voting public that, in making large cuts in government spending, the Hawke government was placing Australia on the right track to economic recovery.

Before calling the election, Bob announced he had decided to appoint John Singleton Advertising to be the party's advertising agency for the campaign. His determination to appoint Singleton was met with anger, disbelief, and bewilderment by party officials and elders, since Singo had established the Workers Party in the mid-1970s, campaigning against the Whitlam government in 1975. But Bob liked Singo, and the Australian Made campaign had been a success. Singo's appointment was music to my ears, as we had become close friends and worked together well.

Within days of the election being called, Singo brought a songwriter, Terry Hannigan, to Canberra to unveil his proposed campaign song. Its chorus, 'Let's stick together; let's see it through', was to become our campaign slogan. The original song went:

> We're on our way, we're on the right track
> Australians have always been good at fighting back.
> With a little bit of strength and patience we'll see Australia right
> Nothing worth having ever happens overnight.
> Together, let's stick together
> Let's stick together; let's see it through.
> We've gotta keep on keeping on with that great Australian dream
> No one ever got anywhere changing horses in mid-stream.
> Together, let's stick together
> Let's stick together; let's see it through.

Bob, other advisers, Singo, and I gathered in the cabinet room in the Old Parliament House to sing along with Terry on his guitar. Graham 'Freudie' Freudenberg improved the lyrics by replacing the second 'let's stick together' with 'Australians together', his arm swishing in a theatrical loop, 'Australians together; let's see it through.' With that flourish, Bob, Singo, Terry, and staff sang the revised rendition with ever-increasing gusto. Never had the cabinet room, with its low ceiling, polished-wood furnishings, and slightly grimy 1970s high-backed, fabric chairs rocked liked it did that night, the air thick with smoke from Freudie's cigarettes and Bob's cigars. The 1987 election campaign song was settled.

That night, Bob asked me to accompany him throughout the election campaign. Loading my two briefcases with *Quotable Quotes* and supporting documents, a boy from Baradine nervously but eagerly prepared for the adventure of a lifetime.

20

Bob's wish

My first experience on the campaign trail was unnerving. A special campaign consultant to Bob, Richard Farmer, had asked me to arrange for Bob Brown to come out publicly at the start of the campaign in support of Labor. I told him this couldn't be done, since Brown and I had already agreed that he would make this statement during the course of the campaign, once the government's commitment to protect all four environmental icons had been announced. Farmer demanded that I instruct Brown to make the statement up front. I insisted that this would constitute a breach of trust on my part, and I was unwilling to raise the proposal with Brown.

At the first meeting at campaign headquarters, Farmer told the assembled gathering: 'Don't trust Craig Emerson, he is positively dangerous.' Although I was shaken and distressed when a member of the campaign committee told me of Farmer's statement, I decided not to confront him, since to do so would only cause more animosity and disharmony. But I realised that my perceived insubordination to seniors on the campaign committee and closeness to Bob meant that I could not afford to make any errors during the course of the month-long election campaign. The words 'positively dangerous' continued to intrude into my thoughts. I had never considered myself as a danger to anyone, other than to ants and sparrows in Baradine. Much later, Farmer and I resumed our friendship.

A couple of days into the campaign, Bob's daughter Ros visited the studio where he was filming the first set of campaign advertisements.

Bob suggested to Ros that they have their photo taken. They hammed it up, and the photographer snapped a great shot of father and daughter laughing and embracing. A couple of weeks later, the film crew presented Bob with a framed photo of the two. As Bob and I sat alone in the lounge room at Kirribilli House after the film crew left, Bob remarked to me, pointing to the photo he liked so much: 'That's the difference between 1984 and 1987, mate.' This time around, Bob was far more focussed, confident, and energetic than in the 1984 six-week campaign, when he'd been shattered by news of Ros's battle with heroin.

Wednesday 10 June 1987 was to be a low-key campaigning affair for the Labor side, but a much bigger day for John Howard, as he unveiled his long-awaited tax policy. It was my job to find a fixed-line telephone — since mobile phones weren't around yet — and ring Bob's senior economic adviser, Steve Sedgwick, for early advice from Paul Keating's staff about the opposition's policy.

We received their initial analysis, but a few days later ministerial offices discovered a gaping hole in Howard's costings. In their haste, the Liberals had twice counted cuts in payments to the states to fund their tax policy. Howard conceded the double-counting error, and his much-anticipated tax policy was in tatters. Paul Keating attacked Howard relentlessly, as only Paul could.

Our first electorate visit was to the seat of Rankin, held with a margin of just 0.7 per cent. If we could hold seats such as Rankin, we would win the election. Bob addressed the students at Browns Plains High School, telling them that the prospects for world peace were better than at any time since World War II, with a high likelihood that a nuclear arms treaty would be agreed upon by the United States and the Soviet Union before the end of the year. Eleven years later, I was elected to parliament as the member for Rankin.

Ahead of the election campaign, John Howard had promised to 'take a scalpel' to Medicare and 'pull it right apart'. In Melbourne, we assembled the state Labor premiers, who announced with Bob that if the Coalition were elected, they would consider a High Court challenge to Howard's decision to tear up the Medicare agreements with the states. The announcement highlighted to the public that the Liberals were intent on destroying Medicare, just as they had destroyed its predecessor, Medibank, when Malcolm Fraser was elected prime minister in 1975.

ALTHOUGH THE NEGATIVE CAMPAIGNING against Howard's Liberals was working, I was conscious that the media spotlight would eventually turn on Bob, as the public demanded he set out his plans for the next parliamentary term. Having severely cut spending in the August 1986 budget and again in the 1987 May statement, we couldn't credibly announce any major new spending programs.

On 19 June, Paul Keating, Peter Walsh, and social security minister Brian Howe met with Bob and advisers at Kirribilli House. What transpired at that meeting, and in the hours following it, inadvertently created the circumstances of Bob Hawke's much-lamented child-poverty pledge. Paul wanted to reduce the cost of Labor's family package that Bob was to announce at the campaign launch. The meeting agreed. Paul and Peter Walsh needed to leave in the early evening, so Bob left it to Brian Howe, his adviser Andrew Burbidge, Steve Sedgwick, and me to work out a less costly package.

The four of us retired to the study at Kirribilli House. In the original package was a family payment for all children under the age of six, regardless of their parents' incomes. Steve and I persuaded Brian to drop this expensive component. He and his adviser proposed that we use some of the savings to increase another proposed component of the families' package—a means-tested payment for children in poor families.

Brian's adviser informed us that this would take us a long way towards meeting the child-poverty benchmarks. Steve and I had never heard of these benchmarks, so we asked what they were. The adviser explained that they were estimates of the family payments needed to remove the financial need for children to live in poverty. If the means-tested payments already planned for the package were boosted by using some of the savings from abandoning the payment for all children under the age of six, we could say that by 1990 there would be no financial need for any Australian child to live in poverty. Good social policy was to coincide with good politics, or so we thought.

Having obtained the agreement of Bob and Paul to the revised, targeted families' package, Steve and I worked on a detailed policy document to be released at the campaign launch. On page 19 of the policy document, setting out the new family payments, we wrote: 'We pledge that by 1990 no child will need to live in poverty.' But by the time the speech was finalised, it read: 'We set ourselves this first goal: by 1990 no Australian child will be living in poverty.' Although expressed as a goal, the replacement of 'need to' with 'will' made the pledge unachievable.

The child-poverty pledge became an object of ridicule during the remainder of the election campaign and beyond. Bob later nominated the rewording, for which he took responsibility, as perhaps his greatest political mistake. Nevertheless, those enhanced payments to poor families, made through a new Family Allowance Supplement, helped alleviate child poverty in hundreds of thousands of families. Ironically, if there had been plenty of money to spend during the campaign, the child-poverty pledge might never have been made.

Following an unwisely extravagant campaign launch at the Sydney Opera House, to which Bob was transported by barge from Kirribilli House, we headed to Townsville to open the Great Barrier Reef Wonderland. It seemed that all the characters were there except Alice. I swear I saw the White Rabbit and the Mad Hatter. It was to be a joint opening with the Queensland government, involving none other than premier Joh Bjelke-Petersen.

We had been tipped off that Sir Joh would refuse to shake Bob's hand. As soon as Bob set eyes on Joh, he walked straight up to him in front of the cameras and extended his hand. Joh shook it — but said nothing. The event was becoming curiouser and curiouser. Joh had contracted laryngitis, and his internal enemy, National Party roads minister Russ Hinze, delivered the Queensland speech. Never one to let a chance go by, Russ, his blue eyes sparkling, gave the voiceless Joh a public bollocking. That night, the television news carried footage of Bob wandering through Wonderland, his arm around Joh's shoulder, silently thanking him for everything he had done for Labor through his ill-conceived and now-abandoned Joh-for-PM campaign.

Down the Queensland coast, at Amberley, outside Ipswich, Bob delivered a speech of reconciliation with Bill Hayden, whom he'd defeated for the Labor leadership in early 1983. Bill reciprocated generously, and Bob embraced Bill's wife, Dallas. Earlier that day,

Howard had launched his campaign in a low-key town hall affair that was more suited to the times than our glamorous Opera House launch.

FOLLOWING THE HAYDEN DINNER, I warned Bob that we were about to enter a black hole about which we'd spoken many times. It would be hard to maintain momentum during the looming second-last week of the campaign: the launch was done, and we had already announced our meagre policies. Our aim was to get through the black hole intact and hit the final week hard, pitching Labor's leadership and cohesion against the Coalition's disunity.

At BHP's invitation, Bob attended a luncheon with the company's board of directors. It was only slightly less curious than the event at the Great Barrier Reef Wonderland. Robert Holmes à Court was seated beside his enemies, BHP's CEO, Brian Loton, and chairman, Sir James Balderstone. Holmes à Court had launched a hostile takeover bid for BHP and had acquired sufficient shares to warrant a position on the board.

Despite all the pleasantries at the meeting, we learned later that the board had resolved to donate $100,000 to the Liberal Party and nothing to Labor. Holmes à Court advised the board that he had donated $200,000 to the Labor Party and nothing to the Liberals. Several years later, as director-general of the Queensland Department of Environment and Heritage, I negotiated with Robert Holmes à Court's widow, Janet, the acquisition of Diamantina Lakes pastoral station for dedication as a national park to support the dwindling bilby population in western Queensland.

As if to officially mark our entry into the black hole, on the Sunday morning of the second-last week, Bob stormed out of a pre-recorded interview with the ABC's *Four Corners* program. Later that morning, on the set for a live interview with the *Sunday* program, Bob composed himself. Everything was going well until one of the interviewers, Peter Bowers, stood up and unfolded a lengthy computer printout, purportedly listing Labor's 31 broken promises. Although most were repetitious, the imagery on the Sunday-night television news was terrible.

We flew to Adelaide to drive a foundation peg into the construction site for the Collins Class submarines. But it was a different type of

driving that appeared that evening on the National Nine News. Bob
had wanted to fit in a visit to see his Dad, Clem, whom he hoped would
be well enough to join us at the Hyatt Hotel in Melbourne on election
night. We'd arranged for the media bus to meet us at the next official
venue, but Jane Phelan of the Nine News team decided she wanted to
cover Bob's visit to his father. When she arrived at the aged-care facility,
Jane complained about the speed her vehicle had needed to travel to
keep up with us.

On the flight to Perth, Bob and I discussed the black hole yet again.
Political editor Paul Kelly had been complaining in *The Australian*
newspaper that, during the course of the election campaign, Bob was
conveying no sense of vision for Australia. We were flying to Perth to
announce the go-ahead of the Mt Channar iron-ore project to be partly
funded by Chinese investors. Several years earlier, Bob, at the urging
of Ross Garnaut, had raised with the Chinese government the idea of
China investing in Australian iron ore and steel production. But, upon
leaving Adelaide, we were advised that negotiations had not progressed
sufficiently for an announcement to be made during our Perth visit.
The black hole was getting blacker.

Bob decided on the plane to pen his own vision speech, responding
to Kelly's criticism. Titled 'Achievements, Alternatives and Prospects',
Bob's speech was never published. He gave me the hand-written speech
and asked me to brief the travelling media upon our arrival at Perth.
When we arrived at the hotel, Curly Parks contacted Butch to tell him
the National Nine News coverage was dreadful, comprising a protestor
launching himself onto Bob's car and Jane Phelan reporting on her
high-speed chase through suburban Adelaide, with television footage
of her car speedo hitting 130 km/h. Curly told Butch, who told me that
we'd lost the television news for the first time in the campaign.

The journalists weren't very interested in Bob's vision speech. In the
elevator on the way back to our hotel rooms, one of them asked me
what the news was like that evening. Glaring at Jane, I said it consisted
of a hurtling protestor, a car chase, and footage of a speedo exceeding
the speed limit. Stupidly, I repeated Curly's observation that we had
lost the television news for the first time in the campaign.

The media had never seen me annoyed like this. To make matters
worse, the following morning, Bob had an argument at a construction

site with a travelling radio journalist, with the journalist's colleagues all siding with him against Bob. Oh, for a beam of light!

At 5.00pm Perth time, I received a call from Steve Sedgwick to tell me there was a chance, after all, of the Mt Channar deal coming through in the next couple of hours, but he couldn't guarantee it. Ross Garnaut, as Australia's ambassador to China, was feverishly working with the Chinese authorities to finalise the agreement.

We were only an hour away from boarding our plane to fly back to eastern Australia. Would we gamble and tell the journalists not to go to the plane because there would be an announcement? If no announcement eventuated, the travelling media would hammer us for having delayed our departure for an undisclosed reason. Bob drew on his gambling instincts, and decided to stay in the hope that news of an agreement would come through. My mind went back to the trainer of Lightning telling Bob it 'will win'. This time, the gamble paid off. We announced the Mt Channar project, China's first overseas mining investment.

Yet we were not clear of the black hole. Sydney radio host and Howard supporter Alan Jones attacked Bob in an interview, causing him to announce a review of the government's 1985 tax-reform decision to limit interest deductions on investments in rental properties—so-called negative gearing. A schism opened up between Bob and the campaign headquarters, which defied Bob and backgrounded the media that Labor could easily lose the election. Paul knew the budget bottom-line outcome for 1986–87, a surprisingly small deficit, which he intended to announce on Sunday. Our plan was to exit the black hole, entering the last week of the campaign when we would refocus on economic management, leadership, and teamwork. But it seemed to be a case of Sunday too far away.

On the Saturday before the election, Mike Steketee, the chief political correspondent for the Fairfax-owned *Sydney Morning Herald*, had been scheduled for an interview with Bob at Kirribilli House. But Rupert Murdoch was in town, and Bob arranged to meet him at the same time and the same place. Bob's office had forgotten to re-schedule the Steketee interview.

That morning, Butch took a phone call from the butler at Kirrbilli House. He had a Mr Mike Steketee in the study and, given that the prime minister was meeting with Mr Murdoch in the lounge room, what should he do with Mr Steketee? Butch rang Mike on the phone in the study, apologised that Bob had an unforeseen commitment, rescheduled the interview, and the butler skilfully ushered Mike past the closed lounge-room doors and out the front door. A potentially disastrous meeting between News Limited's owner, Rupert Murdoch, the chief reporter for the rival news organisation, Fairfax, and the prime minister had been averted by a quick-thinking butler.

COUNT DOWN TO THE LAST WEEK of campaigning and, on Sunday, we were campaigning for John Brumby, the Labor member for Bendigo. Paul announced the budget deficit outcome: a whopping $800 million smaller than the budget-time estimate, made possible by larger receipts from two taxes that Howard had promised to abolish—the fringe-benefits tax and the capital-gains tax.

That night, at the Shamrock Hotel in Bendigo, we watched Pat Cash contest the Wimbledon tennis final. We invited the media into Bob's room for the last few games. When Cash scored the winning point, I leapt from my seat, obscuring the television shot of Bob doing the same. But at least we had footage of Bob watching the tennis. Howard hadn't bothered to stay up.

Monday's news bulletins were full of Cash and cash stories, the Wimbledon victory watched by Hawke, and the improved budget bottom line. Having failed to achieve lift-off for our vision speech in Perth a week earlier, we had been working with the prime minister's Canberra-based staff on a revamped version, replete with new microeconomic reform commitments. The so-called Ballarat Speech, delivered on 7 July 1987, set out a 12-point plan aimed at converting Australia from the Lucky Country to the Productive Country. It convinced the media that Labor was not just campaigning against John Howard, but had a vision for the country's future and a third-term policy agenda.

Joining Jeanette McHugh in the Sydney seat of Phillip on Tuesday morning, we were met with an environmental demonstration—in support of Labor. The conservation movement was making good on its commitments.

Singo's television advertisements featured a lady who became known as Whinging Wendy, standing in the kitchen, demanding that Mr Howard tell us where the money was coming from to fund his tax policy. It just didn't add up, she complained. Wendy Wood was the wife of Barry Wood, a Newtown rugby league forward. In the early 1980s, Singo had funded the revival of the Newtown Bluebags, a foundation Sydney rugby league club, re-naming them the Newtown Jets. Wendy's whinging voice penetrated the consciousness of Australian voters, reinforcing the year-long campaign we had been waging against Howard's bogus budget polices of lower taxes, higher spending, and a surplus.

Bidding farewell to Jeanette McHugh and the conservationists, we headed to Hobart. As we boarded the VIP jet, we heard that Liberal senator Michael Baume had been fielding calls on Hobart morning talkback radio when a caller, who gave his name as 'Robert', phoned in. Robert asked if he would receive the Liberals' promised $26-a-week tax cut starting from 1 February 1988, or as the spending cuts were phased in. Baume chanced his arm, answering that the tax cuts would be phased in with the spending cuts. Wrong. Howard had committed to starting the tax cuts on 1 February.

By the time we walked down the aircraft stairs at Hobart, an Animal had handed me the Baume transcript, ready for an impromptu press conference. On the plane, we rehearsed the line, and Bob delivered it perfectly, telling the gathered media: 'Senator Baume has let the cat out of the bag, and what a dirty, smelly creature it is.' We had exited the black hole.

On the Friday evening before polling day, a Morgan Poll was released, with Gary Morgan commenting that if the Liberals' resurgence continued, they would win the election. This put us all in a downbeat mood. That night, we thanked the staff and invited the media to Mietta's Restaurant in Melbourne. We feigned confidence, but were very nervous.

For polling day, the Electoral Commission had set up a computer in a room next to Bob's suite in the Hyatt Hotel. It included a device we called 'The Grim Reaper', which showed, at any time during the evening's vote counting, the seats that Labor was losing on one side and, on the other, the seats that Labor was gaining. Early in the evening,

The Grim Reaper was showing a loss of 16 seats and a gain of one. But the Reaper became less grim as the count proceeded, confirming by the end of the evening that Labor had won six seats and lost only two.

I was indescribably tired: no beers, no celebration, just bed. The next morning, I had breakfast with Bob and Hazel, and took a phone call from the United States. It was president Reagan congratulating Bob on his election victory. On the plane back to Canberra, Bob gave me a big hug. He had been granted the wish for a historic third term that he'd lodged in Jerusalem's Western Wall six months before.

21

Third-term blues

As the economic crisis began to pass, we were able to spend more time and money on social policy. In the early years of the government, expectations had been high among progressive voters that Labor would grant land rights to Aboriginal and Torres Strait Islander people. But Bob's interest in land rights was mugged by the reality of West Australian politics. The Labor premier, Brian Burke, had warned Bob that if he were to move on land rights, the mining industry would launch a well-funded campaign against him, warning city people that their backyards would not be safe from land claims.

Now, having won a new term, Bob was responsive to Bob Sorby's proposition that he had an opportunity to stamp his personal authority on the third-term agenda. We did some preliminary work on the idea of an agreement with Indigenous Australians. The departmental advice was that a treaty, such as New Zealand's Treaty of Waitangi with the Maori people, was impractical, but some sort of compact might be achievable.

We flew to Alice Springs with the new aboriginal affairs minister, Gerry Hand. Sorby and I incorrectly assumed that Bob would tell Gerry of his intentions on the flight. On Aboriginal Imparja radio, Bob proposed an agreement with Indigenous people for the 1988 Bicentenary of European settlement. Bob had written in a note he gave me:

> The government believes it is essential as we come to the Bicentenary
> year to recognise that two hundred years of European settlement comes

after forty thousand years of Aboriginal history. The government will explore how best to reflect that recognition and the obligations which this involves for the whole community.

Bob's statement was a shock to the interviewer and an even greater shock to Gerry. Bob briefed Gerry fully on the flight home. A national debate ensued, leading to a statement handed to Bob at the Barunga Festival near Katherine in the Northern Territory in 1988. The Barunga statement called for major changes, including Aboriginal and Torres Strait Islander self-determination, a national elected organisation to oversee Aboriginal and Islander affairs, and a national system of land rights. After a slow start, it appeared we were making some progress on reconciliation with Australia's first people.

WE WHITE INVADERS got a better sense of the country's Irish heritage during a visit to Ireland in October 1987. Starting in the United States, where Bob met with secretary of state George Shultz, we flew onto Vancouver for the Commonwealth Heads of Government meeting and then to Ireland. As we arrived in Dublin on a Sunday morning, Butch and I were greeted by our Irish hosts and invited to the hotel bar for a few cleansing pints of Guinness. Jetlagged, we travelled to a sporting ground to witness a mystifying hybrid of Australian Rules and Gaelic football that made so little sense to me I fell asleep. Following the official dinner hosted by Irish prime minister Charles Haughey, he, his ministers, and his staff retired with us to Bob's hotel suite for even more merriment and song.

We spent an inordinate amount of time working on the bilateral relationship at the Kitty O'Shea pub. But as we affirmed the warm friendship between Ireland and Australia, global stock markets began sliding. At a media conference at the Rock of Cashel in County Tipperary, journalists pressed Bob about rushing back to Australia to deal with a new economic crisis — the 1987 stock market crash. Bob explained that since the crash emanated from Wall Street, there was not much point in returning to Australia to try to fix it.

(In this stock market crash were sown the seeds of the 1991 Australian recession. An essential economic reform in modernising the

Australian economy had been the removal of many of the government regulations affecting the financial sector. Worried that the crash could inflict a recession on Australia, the Reserve Bank flooded money into the system to stimulate spending. But the crash didn't really hurt the economy much after all. In the brave new world of a deregulated financial system, the domestic and foreign banks on-lent the extra Reserve Bank money in an effort to capture or retain market share.

By early 1988, it was clear the economy was overheating, risking runaway inflation. The right policy response was for the Reserve Bank to increase interest rates. But the bank, supported by the government, delayed the necessary interest-rate rises. Only a succession of subsequent increases, culminating in punitive mortgage rates of 17.5 per cent, could cool it. If the Reserve Bank had increased interest rates earlier, before the economy had developed such a head of steam, the required interest-rate rises would have been much smaller. This was a big mistake. The very high interest rates cooled the economy so much that, in 1991, it plunged into recession. The government, the Reserve Bank, the Treasury, and the prime minister's department had all backed in the error of delaying interest-rate increases following the 1987 stock market crash.)

Next, we headed off to Geneva, where Bob was to argue for an end to the agricultural-subsidies war between Europe and the United States. Officials had scheduled an evening meeting for us to prepare a draft of Bob's speech, but Bob was keen for Butch and the Kid to accompany him to an evening of blackjack with Hazel and Sir Peter Abeles, across the border in France. To the understandable consternation of the public servants, the prime minister's trade adviser headed off for an evening at a casino instead of writing his speech for the next day.

Bob and Peter played well, and enjoyed good fortune. At one point in the heated private room, Hazel fanned herself unwittingly with a casino chip — more a rectangular plastic slab — whose redemption value exceeded $5,000. My 2 per cent of Bob's ultimate winnings made for a happy car ride back to Geneva, but an unhappy reception by officials, who handed Bob the draft trade speech that I was supposed to have prepared.

On to Belgrade, the capital of Yugoslavia, we flew, while the Caulfield Cup was being run back in Australia. I organised a sweep for the travelling party and media contingent. The legendary columnist for *The Courier-Mail*, Wallace 'Wally' Brown, had missed out on the opportunity to draw a horse in the sweep. He was unforgiving, and I described him as bitter and twisted. From that day, in good humour, I referred to Wally as 'Bitter' and he to me as 'Twisted'.

We travelled then to one of the world's most wonderful cities, the stone city of Dubrovnik in Croatia. Bob told Butch and me the story of the town reprobate who, centuries before, was staggering home from a big night out when he stumbled across a planned attack on the city under the cover of darkness. The reprobate raised the alarm, the city was saved, and he was hailed a hero. Bob suggested that Butch and I might emulate at least the first part of the reprobate's behaviour, which we faithfully did, sleeping it off most of the flight home.

By late November, we were back on the VIP aircraft for a visit to the Soviet Union. Under the leadership of Mikhail Gorbachev, the Soviet Union had begun a historic transformation, embracing the notions of *perestroika* (restructuring) and *glasnost* (openness) as it sought to modernise its old, inefficient, centrally planned economy.

As we flew into the stunning city of Leningrad in November 1987, we knew we were witnessing the making of history. More than forty years after the end of the Siege of Leningrad, during which more than one million people perished, the citizens of this beautiful city stood strong, and proud of their steely resistance to invasion. As a reminder to the world of Leningrad's profound influence over the art and culture of Europe and beyond, the Hermitage Museum displayed no fewer than three million works of art.

As grand as the deep cultural heritage of Leningrad was, if we ever needed any further reminder of how foreign this place was, the hotel breakfasts offered it. Bereft of Kellogg's Corn Flakes and Coco-Pops, our breakfast comprised cold-pressed meats, cheeses, pickles, and herrings. We gazed across the ice covering the River Neva with temperatures approaching 30 degrees below zero. *How far from Australia can we get?*, I wondered. A Russian punk-rock band played in the evenings at the hotel bar, a sure sign that Gorbachev's glasnost was catching on. Punk rock in Leningrad might have been one of the more dubious benefits of opening up to the West, but I felt that the process of restructuring the languishing, centrally planned Soviet economy by introducing private incentives for farm and factory production would be good for the people of the Soviet Union, at least in the longer term.

Bob and Gorbachev would have much to talk about at their meeting. Most of the travelling party was accommodated at a hotel in Moscow, but Bob and Hazel were put up at a state guesthouse outside the city proper. Bob wanted a few of us to come out for a discussion the night before his momentous meeting, but our attempt to gain entry to the guesthouse met with stern resistance from the Russian guards. After an hour or so, we were admitted.

Bob had been admiring the writings of a Russian economist who, in a rigorous and thoughtful analysis, described the Soviet economy as 'shit'. This unconventional economic language amused Bob, so much so that he kept saying it aloud, bursting into raucous laughter every time he repeated it. Bob asked me to stay back, and we talked about his impending meeting with Gorbachev until 2.00am, so excited was he to be standing at the threshold of a new era in human history.

Everyone in the travelling party — staff, public servants, security officers, Bob's doctor, and members of the travelling media contingent — had absorbed the enormity of the occasion of an Australian prime minister meeting the leader of the Soviet Union as he set along the course of reshaping his country and the world. Bob was to have about half an hour with Gorbachev, virtually one on one, with only Bob's foreign-policy adviser, John Bowan, and his Russian counterpart accompanying them. With great anticipation, the Australian media contingent awaited Bob's return. The allotted time passed, and news came that the meeting was continuing. Then it was extended further. Though anxious about deadlines back home, the Australian journalists seemed delighted just to be there, proud to be Australian and, dare I say it, just a little proud of their prime minister. Eventually, Bob returned, held a media conference, and everyone was happy to be a part of history.

Following an official dinner at the Kremlin, we met with other top-ranking Soviet officials, including foreign minister Eduard Shevardnadze, who later returned to his native Georgia to become its president. I was seated almost directly opposite Shevardnadze, and found myself staring at him. A strong and vigorous supporter of peace with the West and the democratisation of countries of the Soviet Union, Shevardnadze was one of the great figures of modern history. He became conscious of my fixed gaze, and began making eye contact with me, at first it seemed quizzically, but soon with apparent annoyance.

I pondered later that Shevardnadze was probably thinking: *Why is this crazy Australian staring at me?* Here was a man who had negotiated nuclear-arms-limitation treaties with the United States. Far away from Baradine, I had recently turned 33 years of age, and felt lucky just to be in the presence of such a person.

IN THE LAST WEEKS OF PARLIAMENT leading into Christmas 1987, tourism and sports minister John 'JJ' Brown was forced to defend himself against opposition allegations that he had shown favouritism in awarding a contract for an Expo 1988 pavilion. JJ had seen off the worst of the parliamentary attack, needing to survive only the last day of parliament ahead of the Christmas break. I had followed the debate for weeks, and, looking forward to the end of the session, clocked off after the final Question Time.

Tragically for JJ's career, there was to be one last opportunity for parliamentary scrutiny: the time allocated every parliamentary sitting day for Matters of Public Importance that immediately followed Question Time. It was during this debate that JJ inadvertently misled parliament over a detail in the awarding of the Expo contract. Had I tuned into the debate, I would have picked up on the misleading statement immediately, but we were already packing our bags for the Launceston Country Club in Tasmania.

Bob and Hazel had invited Cathy and me to join them for a few days of golf, fun, and general relaxation after a hectic year. A television news camera filmed our tee-off across a water hazard. Bob and I cleared the first hazard, but not the political sand trap down the third fairway. As usual, I was playing appallingly when Bob's office called me to advise that JJ's mislead was blatant and that the press gallery was demanding his dismissal.

A group of ministers assembled in Bob's office. Led by Richo, they advised me that JJ's position was untenable. I relayed the conversation to Bob in the middle of a fairway, and Bob, having sought to save JJ for weeks, sighed and said: 'Let him go.' JJ's ministerial career was over. I relayed the PM's decision to the assembled ministers, and Richo was promoted into the cabinet in JJ's place.

Later that day, Bob confided to Cathy and me that he had decided to appoint Bill Hayden to the position of governor-general in the coming bicentennial year. Bill had asked for it, explaining that, having been denied the prime ministership by Bob's successful challenge in early 1983, he wanted to reach the top elsewhere — as the Queen's representative in Australia. Bob swore us to secrecy, but if a betting market had been framed for candidates in the next Governor-General Stakes, I would have been tempted to put a few dollars on Bill Hayden, a staunch Republican, as the 100–1 outsider. In doing so, I would have confidently declared that, unlike Lightning, Hayden 'will win'.

Before Christmas, another minister resigned. To accommodate Senator Robert Ray's entry into the cabinet, Bob had agreed that the minister for community services, Chris Hurford, would be appointed to the position of Australian consul-general in New York. Labor held Hurford's seat of Adelaide by a slim margin of 1.9 per cent. A third-term government retaining such a marginal seat in a by-election was a near impossibility, but we were to make it even harder for ourselves.

During the campaign for the by-election to be held in early February 1988, the government-owned telecommunications provider, Telecom, announced it wanted to charge users for local telephone calls on the basis of time spent on the phone. Users who made short calls would get smaller phone bills, and those making long calls would pay more. From a strictly economic perspective, this user-pays proposal seemed sensible, but politically it was a disaster. I'd helped convince Bob that approving timed local telephone calls was a further test of his commitment to economic reform. Bob Sorby, on secondment from Bob's office for the New South Wales state election campaign, developed with me a form of words designed to get us through the by-election, while not totally shutting the door on timed local calls.

In the dying days of the by-election campaign, Bob and I were to fly in for a final day on the hustings. Using the agreed form of words on Telecom's proposal, Bob and our candidate, Don Farrell, successfully navigated through all the formal campaign events and media questioning. But as we were heading towards the VIP jet for departure, the media pack made one final request for a brief stand-up press conference. At the air base, a journalist asked, yet again, whether the prime minister would rule out timed local telephone calls. Bob, tired and annoyed, departed from the script to make a statement supportive of the principle.

The Liberals seized on Bob's statement, taking full advantage of the deep unpopularity of the proposal within the electorate, and we lost the by-election with a large swing against us of 8.4 per cent. On the Sunday after the by-election, we flew to Launceston for an electorate visit, where Butch arranged a press conference at which Bob was to perform a *mea culpa*.

Bob duly apologised for his poor campaign, but warned the new member for Adelaide, 'Mr Whitney', that he would hold the seat only until the next general election. The assembled media noticed the puzzlement on my face. *Who the hell is Mr Whitney?*, I wondered, since the newly elected Liberal was named Michael Pratt. On his innumerable flights on the VIP aircraft, Bob had been peering out the window at the Pratt & Whitney insignia on the engines.

Bob's prediction was right—Mr Pratt or Whitney was defeated at the 1990 election by Labor's Liz Harvey. But it took Don Farrell almost 20 years to recover from the searing experience of the Adelaide by-election loss, eventually entering the parliament in 2008. While in *mea culpa* mode, I rang Don's campaign director, an up-and-coming official from ALP headquarters, Gary Gray, and put Bob on to acknowledge that Gary and Don had run a good campaign, but we had buggered it up. I made my personal apology to Don in 2008 for setting back his parliamentary career by two decades. He forgave me, I think, and we became close friends and colleagues.

If the adelaide by-election debacle was a setback for Labor, even worse was to come. Immigration minister Mick Young also held the position of president of the ALP. One of many environmental battlegrounds for the government was the south-east forests of New South Wales, where the conservation movement opposed forestry operations by Japanese company Harris-Daishowa, which supplied woodchips for export to Japan. Nothing to do with Mick, you might think. As it happened, the New South Wales Labor Party secretary had received a cheque for $10,000 as a donation from Harris-Daishowa, but the donation had not been disclosed publicly, as required by law. The secretary erroneously told the media that Mick had given him the cheque with no accompanying letter. Later, when he found the letter, the secretary conceded that his recollection had been wrong and that Mick was not involved.

But the damage had been done. Mick could not immediately explain what had transpired at the New South Wales party office, since he did not know and could not reasonably have been expected to know. He walked around to the prime minister's office to tell us that the press gallery was demanding he hold a media conference to explain his actions. We implored him not to do so that day, since he would not be able to answer the media's questions about what had gone on. We suggested instead that he spend some time working out what had happened with the cheque, and then appear in front of the media to explain.

But Mick insisted on holding the press conference that day. He did so, but was unable to explain the sequence of events that had led to the donation's non-disclosure. The baying media immediately called for his resignation. An investigation by the Australian Federal Police soon cleared Mick of any wrongdoing, but he decided he'd had enough, and resigned.

Although the public perception was that the key reason for Mick's decision was that he had been stood down from the ministry twice before, in truth he did not want to put his wife, Mary, and their children, Michael and Janine, through more trauma. And he told his family he did not want to be a distraction for the Labor government, believing that no one person was bigger than the Labor cause.

Bob had spent a night at the Lodge with Mick, trying to talk him out of resigning, but to no avail. Mick had talked it over with his family on the weekend and had already made his decision. He announced his resignation just days after the Adelaide by-election. Mick had held the seat of Port Adelaide by the whopping margin of 16.3 per cent. While Labor subsequently retained the seat, we suffered a huge swing of 11.1 per cent against us.

Following these two bad by-election results, Bob's media critics wrote him off. He was fed up with the constant criticism. He had received an informal approach about his possible interest in being appointed director-general of the International Labour Organisation. At Melbourne's Hyatt Hotel, while we were travelling yet again, Bob raised the offer with me, and suggested I go to Geneva with him as his executive assistant. Cathy was willing to consider the idea, but Bob soon decided not to pursue it. We would, instead, try to extricate ourselves from the funk into which we had fallen.

22

All the president's friends

We entered another year, 1988, and another May economic statement reduced spending even further. It also announced the economic reforms foreshadowed in Bob's Ballarat speech during the election campaign, slashed tariffs, and gave notice that inefficient government business enterprises would be prepared for privatisation. This economic statement, delivered by Paul Keating, was pivotal in turning the nation away from an inward-looking Fortress Australia protected by high tariff walls to an open, competitive economy fully engaged with Asia.

Implementing the Ballarat commitments had required the formation of a special-purpose committee of cabinet, which we named the Structural Adjustment Committee. Obtaining grudging acquiescence from the trade union movement to tariff cuts was hard enough, but our proposals to open up government-owned enterprises to competition and to privatise some of them was met with fierce resistance. We had spent two years, including an election campaign, convincing the electorate that there was no alternative to large spending cuts to deal with the collapse in commodity prices. Now the two government-owned airlines, Qantas and Australian, were demanding taxpayer-funded equity injections.

Peter Walsh reserved special animosity for the airlines, having asked me to write for him, back in 1985, a paper setting out the arguments for the privatisation of selected government-owned enterprises. Now Bob was asking me to do the same. Keeping protected government airlines afloat would require the diversion of scarce taxpayers' funds from true Labor initiatives, such as reducing child poverty and supporting children from disadvantaged families to obtain a decent education. At no time did the ALP's union delegates or rank-and-file membership accept this trade-off. For them, it was an article of faith that a Labor government should never sell the family silver, even if the cost of keeping it exceeded the silver's value.

While members of the party's left were especially hostile to Bob's attempts at privatisation, they were much more impressed with his efforts to advance the cause of social justice. For many years, the term 'social justice' had come to be associated with left advocacy of wealth and inheritance taxes, to which the government was opposed. At a meeting of the Australian Labor Advisory Council, made up of relevant cabinet ministers and trade union leaders, an ex-communist union official, Laurie Carmichael, demanded that Bob get serious about social justice. Laurie was pragmatically open to reasoned argument, so Bob suggested that he work with me on preparing a social-justice statement. Bob appointed me as his social-policy adviser.

My suggestion to Laurie was that we call it a social-policy statement to avert any preconception that it would announce wealth or inheritance taxes. But Laurie and the parliamentary left, including Gerry Hand, Nick Bolkus, Robert Tickner, and Jeanette McHugh, insisted it be called a social-justice statement. If we were to do so, I said, we had to remove any suggestion that the government supported wealth taxes, inheritance taxes, and passive welfare. The left agreed, and Bob released Labor's first social-justice statement, *Towards a Fairer Australia: social justice under Labor*, in early May 1988.

With the social-justice statement and the May statement released, we travelled to the United States for a meeting with president Reagan and members of his administration. We assembled in the White House cabinet room, an ample but unpretentious space. Gathered around a large, polished wooden table that just as easily could have been dedicated to official dinners, we Australians met with selected members of the cabinet, including secretary of state George Shultz, and Treasury secretary James Baker III, and, of course, the president himself. In a photograph of Bob introducing me to president Reagan is James Baker and, in the background, a smiling national-security adviser, Colin Powell, who later became secretary of state to president George W. Bush.

Bob expressed Australia's gratitude for the president's efforts to maintain world peace through the signing of a treaty with Soviet president Gorbachev to eliminate nuclear weapons with a range of up to 5,500 kilometres. In response, the president said: 'Gorbachev is different. But the USSR is an adversary. The communist manifesto is to take over the world.' Reagan told us of his surprise at the warmth of people in the streets of Moscow towards him and his wife, Nancy.

Bob agreed that Gorbachev was different, for he wanted to reform the economy. The president said: 'Yes. He's the first Russian leader to agree to destroy weapons. They can't afford their military.'

Bob pressed the president on the US export-subsidy program, to which Reagan said we were 'all singing the same music'. The president revealed that he wanted the United States to get out of agricultural subsidies by the year 2000, but this had to be done slowly and with assistance to farmers, including through re-training programs. On export subsidies, he said: 'We want to try to make sure we don't interfere with you where your markets are.'

We discussed other issues, to which the president deferred to members of his cabinet. At the end of these exchanges, he sorted through a set of index cards he had been holding on his lap. He glanced at one after the other, saying: 'No. No. No.' I thought these briefing cards were probably the work of officials who'd collectively spent hundreds of hours on them; but it was the president's call, and he didn't consider the issues worth raising. So he invited us to lunch.

The room for our lunch was near the cabinet room where we'd just conducted the official business. When we were all settled, we agreed we had completed all the formalities, so the luncheon conversation became an exercise in exchanging jokes. The president opened with one that, out of deference to his memory, I will not re-tell, other than to say that there must be more conventional ways for a man to rid his body of a tapeworm. Bob followed with a joke no more refined than the president's. Next in line was James Baker III, who told a joke about a greengrocer trying to persuade a belligerent customer that he had no tomatoes that day. And so it went on, Australian, American, Australian, American ... I was at the end of the table, terrified that I would be required to tell a joke to the president of the United States that would make him laugh. Mercifully, the joke-telling petered out before it reached me.

UPON RETURNING TO AUSTRALIA, we were to be reminded that ALP national conferences are never easy for Labor governments. Delegates can make sure they're noticed by criticising the government, and prime ministers may struggle to win support for changes to the party's platform that they consider necessary for effective government. The June 1988 conference in Hobart was no different, but adding to the controversy surrounding it was an exposé by investigative journalist John Lyons published in *The Weekend Australian*.

At no stage had Lyons spoken to me, yet I featured prominently in the story, courtesy of others. Thus, 'Craig Emerson — described as Hawke's "surrogate son" — has made a big play to learn about horses since joining the staff. According to one source, he also likes to walk through the office shouting "Up the Mighty Bulldogs."' Lyons described me as 'a personable, bright man in his late 20s' who grew up in the western suburbs of Sydney. He wrote, to illustrate just how close the father-son type relationship was between Hawke and Emerson, that one observer had said: 'When Hawke is out of town and staying in a hotel he finds it difficult to go to sleep at night unless he knows that Craig Emerson is in the next room.' This was news to both Bob and me.

Lyons warned: 'Divisions are deepening — resentment is growing towards the new closeness between Hawke and Emerson.' In his memoirs, published in 1994, Bob confirmed this affinity: 'I was attracted by his intelligence and vivacious integrity; there was a boyish enthusiasm about everything he did.' Bob annotated my copy of his memoirs: 'Craig, you define what true friendship is. You know I think of you like a son but I also have an objective sense of your great worth as a human being.' If the allegation against me was that I was close to Bob, consistently loyal to him, then I plead guilty.

Our closeness was reaffirmed in August when John Howard told radio talkback hosts that he considered the rate of Asian immigration to be too high. Since the time of the Whitlam government, Labor had embraced a non-discriminatory immigration policy. Bob's anger with Howard's outburst was palpable. It was not as if Howard had chosen his words poorly. Rather, he repeated them over several days, hoping to lever a political advantage for himself and the Liberal Party.

Opening up a political front based on race was reprehensible, as far as Bob and his office were concerned. Bob drafted a resolution to be debated in both Houses reaffirming the parliament's commitment to a non-discriminatory policy. The resolution acknowledged that a Liberal government, under the leadership of Harold Holt, had been the first Australian government to adopt the principle of non-discrimination. Bob was leaving his office for the chamber when he turned to me, and, although immigration was not one of my policy responsibilities, said: 'Come with me, mate, and sit in the advisers' box. This is a historic day.'

I listened to Bob's passionate speech as he expressed his deep beliefs. Three Liberals crossed the floor to vote with Labor, including Philip Ruddock, who became immigration minister in the Howard government. It was a great day for decency and for an Australian prime minister committed to the noblest of principles. The parliamentary debate that day ended Howard's dalliance with what Bob described as 'playing the race card' in the political contest between the Liberal and Labor parties.

I never forgave Howard for his behaviour, injudiciously accusing him in a speech, fifteen years later, of 'not liking Asians'. My colleagues assumed this was a moment of madness. It probably was. But Howard's 1988 effort, backed up by his refusal in 1996 to condemn One Nation's founder, Pauline Hanson, for her racist, anti-Asian rants, plus his refusal to match Labor and put the One Nation Party last on how-to-vote cards, had made me intolerant of his intolerance. If we consider we have the right to judge others as if we were faultless, which many of us often do, we must at least judge them on their merits, not their race.

23

Tensions rising

During my time in Bob's office, Bob's relationship with Paul Keating seemed strong and friendly. Ahead of cabinet meetings, Bob and Paul talked and, whenever possible, backed the same policy position. When they met, Bob often referred to Paul as 'Paulie', and, on many occasions, Paul brought Bob a piece of classical music he thought Bob might enjoy. On the big issues, they were joint salesmen, doing the rounds of television and radio stations, selling the government's story and policies to the Australian people.

Communications between the two offices were good, too. Advisers such as Barry Hughes, Seamus Dawes, Ken Henry, and Tom Mockridge were approachable and friendly as we sought to solve common problems and reach positions that Bob and Paul could support. Often we were under pressure from political operators in the ministry to pursue populist courses of action or inaction, such as pork-barrelling marginal electorates, offering home owners cash payments to help them pay their mortgages, and shirking necessary decisions to reduce tariffs.

Labor's primary vote continued to slide. Voters objected strongly to rapidly rising mortgage interest rates, and they were tiring of the big changes to their lives being wrought by economic reform. As Bob reached the age of 60, well into his third term as prime minister, the press gallery began speculating about how long he would last as leader if Labor were elected a fourth time.

According to information that began filtering in from the press gallery following the August 1988 budget, Paul was briefing journalists that if Bob did not soon hand over the prime ministership to him, he would leave parliament. When Bob learned from Butch that Paul was telling the media he might resign, Bob decided to counter with a statement on the ABC's *7.30 Report* that nobody in the government was indispensable. This had the effect of diverting media attention from the budget that Paul had just delivered and onto the vexed issue of the leadership.

Having watched Bob's television appearance, Paul was infuriated, making his feelings known to Richo and other ministers. Richo arranged for Bob to appear the next evening on *A Current Affair* to praise Paul for his 'magnificent contribution', describing him as the world's best treasurer, and volunteering that his leadership ambitions were 'totally legitimate'.

The next afternoon, Bob and I were at his tailor's store in Sydney, where Bob was being measured up for some new suits. I received an anxious phone call from the prime minster's chief of staff, advising me that a *Canberra Times* journalist, Paul Malone, had been approached by someone with a recorded mobile-phone conversation between Paul and Richo. I wrote on the back of the tailor's business card the message Paul had delivered to Richo: 'Hawke is an envious, fucking little turd. If Hawke doesn't get out by the next election, I'm gone.' Richo reportedly told Paul: 'Don't worry about it. I've organised Hawke to go on *A Current Affair*.' He then said: 'By the way, I'm on a car phone.' Keating, conscious of how easily car-phone conversations on the old analogue system could be intercepted, hit the roof.

Malone did not purchase the full tape recording, and the remainder of the media, unsure whether it was a crime to publish the contents of intercepted mobile-phone conversations, never printed it. It was, however, authentic.

Having made my note on the business card, I briefed Bob on the contents of the phone conversation. Our two offices arranged for Bob and Paul to speak on a landline as soon as possible. We were scheduled to attend an ALP dinner arranged by the legendary Johnno Johnson at the New South Wales Parliament House. Upon arriving, we asked Johnno for a private room with a phone. Bob rang Paul, and they had a 45-minute conversation, during which they provided each other with the most detailed character analysis I have ever heard. Johnno repeatedly entered the room, unaware of the nature of the conversation, complaining that Bob was keeping 200 guests waiting. Each time, Butch and I ushered Johnno out of the room, explaining that Bob was involved in a very important telephone call.

As the exchanges proceeded, I knew the relationship between Bob and Paul could never be the same again. There was no shouting, no animation, but if there had been a friendship, it was over. At the end of the conversation, Bob and Paul agreed to meet face to face. That weekend I needed to go to the Lodge to meet with Bob. I could see through the side entrance to the kitchen that Bob and Paul were ensconced in conversation in the lounge room. This was the follow-up conversation and, of course, I let them be, wandering around the gardens until Paul left.

At no time did I know that this conversation led to a further meeting, with pre-arranged witnesses, at Kirribilli House, where Bob undertook to hand over the leadership to Paul after the 1990 election. When news of the Kirribilli agreement eventually leaked out, it explained for me how Bob and Paul had been able to restore a civil working relationship that took the government through the 1990 election.

Yet, for all practical purposes, the terrible falling-out between Paul and Bob did not obviously affect their ability to work together, or to be courteous or even warm towards each other. Nor did it affect the way I related to Paul's advisers.

On the Senate side of the new Parliament House was a grassy area that had originally been designed as a bowling green for senators. As finance minister, Peter Walsh railed against the bowling green ever being built, considering its upkeep to be a scandalous waste of taxpayers' money. Walsh had the support of ministerial staff and the press gallery, who by now had commandeered it and converted it into a lower-maintenance touch-football field. Each Friday at lunchtime, the more athletic staff members and journalists would meet for a friendly game of touch football, mixing the sides up randomly. Legends in our own minds, we shuffled up and down the makeshift field, mostly offside, not out of wilfulness but from an inability to retreat five metres at the play-the-ball.

From Bob's office, Peter Harris, who later became chairman of the Productivity Commission, joined me for the regular hit-outs, and, from

Paul's office, Tom Mockridge and Seamus Dawes strutted their equally questionable skills. At each lunchtime gathering, Tom Mockridge's routine instruction was: 'Stand outside me, Craig. I'll make you look good.' The truth was, no one could make me look good, but journalists remarked about the mateship between the Hawke and Keating advisers. It never occurred to us that it should be any other way. Bob and Paul were a fabulous duo, and it remains a source of great sadness to me that the old friendship between them has not been restored.

RICHO HAD BEEN A FREQUENT VISITOR to the Hawke office from as far back as I could remember. He and Paul were the only two who had the power and the relationships to be able to brush past the prime minister's chief of staff, who was responsible for keeping the daily schedule, and walk into Bob's office. But a different sort of relationship had developed between Bob and one of his senior colleagues. As the evening's commitments wound down, Kim Beazley, defence minister and leader of the House, would regularly visit Bob, the two of them with their feet up on the prime ministerial desk, chewing the fat. For Bob, it was a time of relaxation, and we rarely interrupted them through the blanket of cigar smoke they created as a cloak of privacy.

After the 1987 election, Cathy did not return to her job in Mick Young's office, instead taking up a position at IBM. But she never adapted to the corporate culture there, and applied for a position as Kim Beazley's adviser. Mick Young and Kim Beazley were close friends, and Mick obviously gave Cathy a good recommendation. When Beazley went missing from his office, Cathy was asked to ring me to ascertain whether he was with Bob. Invariably, I was able to confirm that, indeed, the two were ensconced in deep discussions about affairs of state. Through Beazley's late-evening visits to Bob's office, and my frequent visits to his to catch up with Cathy, we developed a deep respect and affection for each other.

Both were put to the test when, ahead of the 1990 federal election, Bob assigned me the task of phoning Kim to advise him that Bob had decided not to proceed with a defence department plan to move an armaments depot from an island in the Parramatta River to Jervis Bay. We were on our way to open the new Australian Conservation Foundation offices in the Melbourne suburb of Fitzroy, where Bob would make the announcement with Peter Garrett, who had been campaigning against the relocation of both the armaments depot and a longer-term proposal to relocate the navy from Sydney Harbour to Jervis Bay. 'You'd better ring Kim and let him know of our announcement', Bob instructed me. I phoned Kim in Perth, which was three hours behind the time in eastern Australia. After the phone rang several times, I heard: 'Helloooo', as an awakened defence minister answered.

'Kim, it's Craig.'

'Oh, g'day mate.'

'Kim, Bob's gonna announce today that we're not moving the armaments depot to Jervis Bay.'

'Oh. Okay, mate. Thanks for letting me know.'

'That went well', I thought, and I reported to Bob that all was good.

As we toured the new offices with Peter Garrett, my phone rang.

Now fully awake, Kim boomed: 'Mate, you can't do that!'

'It's too late', I advised him. 'Bob's on his feet making the announcement now.'

Well, he nearly was. I had carefully crafted the words with Bob the day before and settled them with Peter. Not only would the armaments depot not be relocated to Jervis Bay, but the government was also 'no longer disposed' to move the navy there either. The small audience of conservationists burst into rapturous applause. It seemed prudent for me to give Kim a wide berth for a while. He never raised the matter with me again.

24

The fifth icon

Keeping our commitments to protect the four icons—Tasmanian forests, Kakadu, the wet tropical forests of North Queensland, and Shelburne Bay—was proceeding according to plan when a fifth icon imposed itself on the government's agenda. An international treaty was being negotiated that would allow mining in Antarctica.

In early 1989, Cathy and I went on holidays to Thailand. Bob, meanwhile, had begun an official overseas trip, starting in Korea, where he and president Roh Tae-woo announced their intention to establish APEC—the Asia-Pacific Economic Cooperation Forum. Our plan was to hook up with Bob in Bangkok, after which Cathy would return home and I would join the travelling party for the rest of the official trip.

While in our modest Bangkok hotel, I had an idea to bring together everything we had done on the environment into a single statement, and add some new initiatives that didn't involve land-use conflicts or spending lots of money that we didn't have. Concern for the environment was rising around the world, as scientists published findings of a hole in the ozone layer above Antarctica, acid rain falling in Europe and North America, deforestation, loss of species, soil degradation, and global warming caused by the emission of greenhouse gases. At the backpackers' Vieng Tai Hotel, I began setting out subject headings for a comprehensive statement on the environment.

On the day of Bob's arrival, we took a taxi to the more salubrious hotel where he would be staying. As Bob and the official party entered the Oriental Hotel, I shouted 'Hey, Bob!' Bob turned and said: 'G'day, mate! Good to see you. Let's catch up for dinner.' We arranged to meet in the gardens on the edge of the Chao Phraya River.

I was so happy with the idea of having dinner on the lawns of this wonderful hotel, with its authors' lounge once host to novelists such as Somerset Maugham, Joseph Conrad, and Tennessee Williams, that in running across the lawn, I failed to see an embedded arc light. I smashed my shin into the metal casing, ripping my jeans and opening a gash from which blood flowed freely. As best as I could, I carried on a conversation with Bob and other staff as the blood continued to trickle from my wound. Bob explained his APEC success in Korea, an idea put to him by Ross Garnaut, but mainly I described to him the charm of a city that had hosted me for two years and which, for its extensive network of canals, had been called the Venice of the East.

The next day we met Thai prime minister Chatichai Choonhavan, who, in the course of conversation, volunteered that in its bid to build a steel mill in Thailand, BHP had chosen a local partner with no relevant expertise. The prime minister advised us that if BHP chose a better-credentialled partner, it would have an excellent chance of winning the tender. Bob asked me immediately to ring BHP's CEO, Brian Loton, to advise him of Chatichai's recommendation. Mr Loton did not seem to know much about the company's proposal. Following our return to Australia, I again contacted Mr Loton, who apparently had not acted on the Thai prime minister's advice.

As a reminder of looming economic trouble back home, Paul rang, very worried about a bad quarterly inflation figure that had just been released. He was adamant that we would need to lift interest rates again to cool an overheating economy. We were on our way to the 17.5 per cent interest rates that should have made any government unelectable a year later. We agreed we would meet, upon Bob's return to Australia, to decide on a course of further interest-rate rises.

At our next stop, New Delhi, Australia's high commission to India had organised a large, open-air, welcoming reception. As I wandered through the gardens, I was introduced to the New Zealand high commissioner to India. This tall, broad-shouldered diplomat told me of his conquest of Mt Everest many years before. I felt incredibly privileged to be chatting with Sir Edmund Hillary.

India's prime minister, Rajiv Gandhi, met with Bob and Hazel, where they discussed the possibility of Rajiv's young son, Rahul, attending school in Australia. Although Rajiv wanted this to happen, he was worried about security for his son. Two-and-a-half years later, a young female Tamil Tiger suicide bomber assassinated Rajiv; he was right to have been worried about security.

Back in Australia, while I considered my work on the environment worthy in its own right, it was to have another advantage. Geoff Walsh, who had returned to Australia from a stint at the International Labour Organisation to take up the position of Bob's chief political adviser, organised a meeting with Butch, Rod Cameron (the ALP's pollster), and me. Rod told us: 'Every time we talk about the environment, our vote goes up.'

Rod's polling confirmed that, with interest rates at punishing levels, swinging voters were unwilling to give Labor their number-one vote. However, they did not consider the Coalition, led by Andrew Peacock, to be superior economic managers. They were telling pollsters they were planning to vote for the protest party, the Australian Democrats, whose founder and former Liberal minister, Don Chipp, had pledged to 'keep the bastards honest'. Our task was to persuade voters to give their second-preference vote to Labor ahead of the Coalition. And since environmental issues had risen to rank as the second-highest concern among swinging voters, behind only the economy, a major effort on the environment seemed the best way of winning the 1990 election.

Richo's environmental adviser, Simon 'Baldo' Balderstone, and I wrote a joint briefing note for Bob and Richo, proposing an alliance between the conservation movement and Labor. Peter Garrett had recently been appointed president of the Australian Conservation Foundation, and Baldo and I recommended we work especially closely with Peter and Phillip Toyne, with whom we were both friends. We considered Peter and Phillip more pragmatic than the leadership of The Wilderness Society, which had, following Jonathan West's departure to undertake a PhD at Harvard University, become more absolutist in its demands.

In early March, I handed Bob a second brief, proposing a major statement on the environment for the middle of the year to cover the topics I had identified at the Vieng Tai Hotel while on holidays: soil degradation; a national tree-planting program; protecting endangered species; helping repair the hole in the ozone layer; responding to the greenhouse effect; and dealing with another new threat—international proposals to allow regulated mining in Antarctica. Bob enthusiastically welcomed the idea, and met with Richo and John Kerin to seek their cooperation. Richo was especially keen, and deployed Balderstone to work with me. Bob took the proposal to cabinet and, at my urging, asked his colleagues not to raise expectations about the statement that we might not be able to meet. At that point, a mischievous Kerin dubbed the project the 'World's Greatest Environment Statement', which quickly became known as WGES.

Mostly, the preparations for the statement went smoothly, our policy proposals being accepted by a special-purpose cabinet committee. Geoff Walsh then suggested we commission opinion polling to test alternative titles for it. My proposed title included the word 'cherish', and it came last. Most popular was *Our Country, Our Future*. Its centrepiece was to be a Decade of Landcare, including the planting of one billion trees, a policy based on a joint proposal of the Australian Conservation Foundation's Phillip Toyne and the director of the National Farmers' Federation, Rick Farley. After all the land-use conflicts, Bob welcomed the collaboration between farmers and conservationists, and was willing to dedicate taxpayers' funds to it.

But our work on responding to global warming caused by the greenhouse effect became the subject of a bitter cabinet dispute. Richo, supported by Kerin, wanted to include in the statement a Hawke government commitment to a 20 per cent reduction in Australia's greenhouse-gas emissions, conditional upon the response of other countries. Paul Keating and John Dawkins successfully opposed the Richardson position, leaving Richo livid. I wrote Bob a note about this while he was still in the cabinet room:

Richo has gone off in a rage. He's furious that Keating and Dawkins were allowed to prevail over him and Kerin [the energy portfolio minister] on the question of greenhouse emissions—the 20% target. He's saying the statement is gutted without it. Kerin has written him a note saying cabinet doesn't understand them and the problem. Suggest you say no final decision tonight—you need to think about it: with words for statement to be settled tomorrow with the concerned ministers. Sorry about this, but it's obviously important.

Bob called on me to broker a form of words that was acceptable to both Keating and Toyne. Having agreed to a new form of words, Paul called me to his office and said: 'Mate, you've gotta stop jamming green bits down these people's throats.'

In all the prior cabinet debates on environmental issues, Paul had been very supportive of Bob's position. Despite his growing frustrations with the conservation movement's demands, he was to be supportive again, this time on the vexed issue of mining in Antarctica.

On 24 March, an oil tanker, the *Exxon Valdez*, had struck a reef in Alaska, spilling hundreds of thousands of barrels of crude oil into the water and onto more than 2,000 kilometres of Arctic coastline, heightening public sensitivity to any proposal that could damage the world's frozen wilderness. At around this time, an international proposal emerged to allow mining in Antarctica, subject to strict environmental safeguards.

Bob and I were unaware that Australian government officials had been leading negotiations among the 19 members of the Antarctic Treaty for an agreement to allow regulated mining—the Convention on the Regulation of Antarctic Mineral Resource Activities. By mid-1988, officials of all member countries had agreed to the minerals convention.

When I read a cabinet submission in April 1989 recommending that Australia ratify the proposed convention, I was shocked that a proposition as momentous as this could have made it through the system without the prime minister or his office being aware of it. Bob had taken his bag of cabinet submissions to the Lodge for weekend reading, and was just as shocked. When he returned to his office on Monday, we concluded that the minerals convention had to be stopped and that Australia needed to change course.

Graham Richardson, as environment minister, and foreign minister Gareth Evans wanted Australia to ratify the convention, on the basis that it was better to have regulated mining rather than unregulated mining. But Paul Keating and Peter Cook opposed ratification. In late April, Paul wrote to Bob, urging him to defer cabinet consideration of

Gareth's submission and to consider, instead of the minerals convention, the establishment of Antarctica as a World Park. A week later, Cookie wrote to Bob in similar terms. In an ironic line-up, the environment minister supported the minerals convention, while the two most relevant economic ministers opposed it.

In Australia, Peter Garrett played a leading role in opposing the minerals convention. Internationally, fabled undersea naturalist Jacques Cousteau campaigned against the convention, and, influenced by Cousteau's campaign, French prime minister Michel Rocard began publicly expressing reservations about it. Bob and I decided to ring Rocard. We figured that with France on board, we might be able to mobilise a campaign against ratification among the member countries of the Antarctic Treaty.

Working from my briefing note, Bob opened with Rocard:

I am aware of your recent public statements expressing concerns about the Antarctic Minerals Convention. The government will be discussing the issue in cabinet on 22 May and it would be very useful for me to have as clear an understanding as possible of your thinking. I am opposed to mining in Antarctica and I am not persuaded that signing the Minerals Convention is the best course available to Australia to prevent it. I would like to explore with you possible courses of action that Australia and France might take together to protect the Antarctic environment. A preliminary chat now would be useful as a guide to my cabinet's consideration of the issue and as a forerunner to discussions when we meet in Paris on 19 June. If we wished to pursue some option other than signing the Draft Convention it would be important to know whether we would be standing alone. That may well be futile. But if Australia and France worked together we may be able to influence other countries with stakes in Antarctica, such as New Zealand and Norway. International public opinion on issues such as the greenhouse effect, ozone layer depletion and mining in Antarctica is intensifying so rapidly that there could be a real prospect of us getting a better outcome than the Minerals Convention. The Alaskan oil spell has had a considerable impact on public opinion.

Encouragingly, Rocard replied:

There is no disagreement between you and me. Ours is the first French government for some time that had a concern for the environment. Ecologists here in France say the convention would not stop mining. But I know if we don't ratify there could be problems: the better can be the enemy of the good. I want to say we will ratify but lay down a charter saying France accepts scientific research only, no mining. Is that okay with you?

Rocard's idea was to insert into the French legal instrument ratifying the minerals convention a so-called 'reservation', which would say that France opposed mining despite the convention itself allowing mining under particular circumstances.

Bob politely told him it was not okay, proposing instead that the two countries pursue a World Park.

Rocard said his English was not so good. 'Is cabinet hesitating on ratification?' he asked.

Bob said yes, the Australian cabinet was reluctant to ratify.

'Is that because you do not find the convention strict enough?' Rocard asked.

Bob explained: 'It doesn't ban mining. I am worried that, according to international law, we could not put a reservation to ban mining.'

Rocard queried: 'Can't we do that — put a reservation?'

Bob said that, according to international law, a country that made it clear it was opposed to mining could not sign a convention that allowed for mining.

He pressed Rocard: 'Are you open-minded about signing?'

Rocard assured Bob: 'Yes, absolutely. We are not ready to ratify without reservation.'

Encouraged by this confirmation, Bob said: 'Let's explore various options, including renegotiation, a new instrument, and a World Park. If you are advised that a reservation cannot be acceptable legally, would you be reluctant to pursue ratification?'

Rocard responded: 'Okay. That is our position.'

Bob predicted: 'That will be the view of our cabinet, I think. So we should explore other options together, assuming that advice about a reservation is correct, including a World Park.'

Rocard agreed: 'Okay, I will be waiting for your telex.'

With this conclusion to the conversation, Bob and I were confident we could get France on board for a campaign to stop the minerals convention from coming into force and to ban mining in Antarctica. But much persuasion would be needed, and many obstacles would need to be overcome. Bob's own department, which recommended ratification, advised him that a refusal to ratify might jeopardise Australia's relations with our strategic allies, the United States and Britain. At the cabinet meeting, Bob told his colleagues that he did not want any mining in Antarctica and did not support Australia ratifying the minerals convention. He said he wanted, instead, to pursue a World Park or a Wilderness Park. Most of Bob's colleagues humoured him, giving him no realistic chance of turning around the positions of so many countries that had pledged their support for the convention, but Paul and Cookie strongly supported Bob's position.

Following the cabinet meeting, I began drafting letters for Bob to send to the leaders of small European members of the Antarctic Treaty. Since these countries didn't have a big stake in Antarctica, we figured they were more likely to go along with our proposition that the minerals convention not come into force. Belgium and Italy quickly agreed with us. Now we had momentum. Soon, India joined the anti-mining campaign.

In June 1989, we embarked on an overseas visit that Bob had foreshadowed in his telephone discussion with Rocard. Bob, Hazel, and I met Jacques Cousteau for breakfast in Paris, and confirmed Australia's opposition to the minerals convention. The next day, Bob and I met with Rocard and his adviser in the gardens of the prime minister's office, where the four of us drafted a declaration opposing the minerals convention.

Following our garden meeting, we had lunch with France's president, Francois Mitterrand. Bob made his case to Mitterrand, but the president was evasive, saying he opposed mining in Antarctica, without committing himself to opposing the minerals convention. Anxious about Mitterrand's ambiguity, I slipped a note to Bob, advising that he should pin down the president. Bob asked Mitterrand straight out whether he would join us in opposing the minerals convention. Mitterrand agreed, explicitly stating that he would oppose ratification. At that moment, we had achieved our French mission.

Delighted with the outcome that had looked shaky for most of the luncheon meeting, we boarded a very fast train with the travelling media, on which we intended to announce the joint opposition of Australia and France to the minerals convention. But the very fast train slowed to a halt and broke down.

We used the time to gather the media around Bob's table to make the Antarctic announcement. But media questioning turned quickly to speculation back home that the government was considering applying a tax on imports of luxury goods. Bob entertained the questioning, refusing to rule out a luxury tax. Butch, realising that a possible luxury tax, instead of the Antarctic announcement, was shaping up as the main story from France, stepped in and closed down the media conference. It was the intervention by the prime minister's media adviser that dominated the news bulletins, followed by the luxury-tax story, with Antarctica running a poor third.

Butch, Geoff Walsh, and I were very annoyed with Bob for having fuelled speculation about a luxury tax when we had such a great story to tell about Antarctica. In a fit of pique, the three of us went to a bar on the Champs-Elysées near the Arc de Triomphe, and sat in the sun drinking pints of beer. Back at the hotel, Bob couldn't find us, and sent a message for us to come to his suite.

'What's wrong with you blokes?' he demanded.

'You fucked up the Antarctic announcement by talking about a luxury tax', I answered.

Butch and Geoff explained that, by responding to media questions about events in Australia, Bob had derailed the coverage of the overseas trip. We suggested that forthwith he refuse to comment on domestic stories while overseas. To stop us sulking, he agreed.

We flew to London to meet the Queen, Prince Charles, and Princess Diana. At Bob's first London media conference, he told the travelling journalists that he would confine his answers to questions about the trip. This, we had suggested, Bob should announce as the London Convention, which he did. It worked a treat; the journalists accepted the new discipline, advising their editors back home that the prime minister would not be speculating about domestic stories. Successive prime ministers have adopted the same practice, invoking the London Convention of whose genesis most would be unaware, but whose convenience remains unquestioned.

For our evening at the Mansion House, we were required to wear white ties and tails. We colonials were resplendent in our formal garb, but drew the line at top hats. Princess Diana was a striking figure, taller than I was, with gorgeous blue eyes. I struck up a short conversation with her, but she looked mournful, as if she didn't especially want to be there. That's probably because she didn't want to be there.

The following morning, Bob, Butch, and I attended an official reception at the House of Commons. Bob was introduced to dignitaries, while Butch and I waited in a corner near the luncheon table for a stand-up meal. An official of the parliament approached us, asking us to identify ourselves. We gave him our names, and explained we were the Australian prime minister's media and economic advisers.

'There's no place for you at the reception', the pompous official declared.

'That's alright', Butch said. 'We don't need to sit down. We'll just stand here and grab a sandwich.'

'Very well', the official agreed.

Minutes later, the official returned and announced: 'I'm afraid I am going to have to ask you to leave. You're not on the official reception list.'

Butch said: 'We're the prime minister's only advisers here. We can't leave.'

I added: 'We're happy to stand here in the corner.'

The official replied: 'No, I must insist you leave.'

We brushed past Bob to inform him we were being kicked out of the House of Commons, and left in rather a huff. It was not the first or last time we were to receive such exclusionary treatment. When we'd arrived at the air base for an official welcome at the start of our UK visit, we'd assembled in a small marquee with Bob. A British protocol officer approached me and inquired in an imperious tone: 'And you are?'

I dismissively answered: 'Craig.'

'Craig who?'

'Craig Emerson. Economic adviser to the Australian prime minister.'

The protocol officer checked his list and advised: 'You are not in the Royal Suite.'

Since I didn't know what the Royal Suite was, and had never aspired to be in it, I was not disappointed to be informed that I was out of it.

He directed: 'You are not in the Royal Suite. You are to assemble under the other marquee over there', pointing to an area around 10 metres away. I stepped over an imaginary line 'out of the Royal Suite', across no man's land, and into the commoners' area, where I was informed that the top dozen members of the travelling party on the protocol list were in the Royal Suite and the rest of us were not permitted to enter the exclusive marquee. To us ordinary Australians, they just looked like two tents of roughly equal-quality canvas.

So now, outside the House of Commons, from which we had been ejected, Butch told the driver who had the misfortune to transport us: 'That's what's wrong with this place. You people are so stuck up with your social classes that the country is fucked.'

The driver protested his innocence of the charge of elitism. I considered him not guilty. We asked him to take us to a pub where we could have a few bets on the Sport of Kings—the horse races, which were being held at Ascot on that day. We consumed copious quantities of warm ale, and lost all our money to the pub's resident bookie. We didn't manage to back a single winner or even a placegetter. Oh for *The Sportsman* and Bob's tips, though I doubt he would have been very close to the Pommy trainers.

We then returned to our hotel, where, literally bouncing off the walls, we angrily explained our shabby treatment to everyone who was willing to listen, and even more loudly to those who weren't. Now well into the evening, we moved on to a French restaurant, where I was interested in the duck for my main course. I asked the waiter to bring me the duck so that I could inspect it. My last memory was manhandling a whole, fresh, plucked duck. But by the time it arrived from the kitchen, apparently beautifully presented, I had fallen asleep at the table. Our visit to London coincided with a week of near-century heat. After an exhausting day of economic advice, I slept in my underpants with the air conditioning turned down to the minimum temperature, waking next day with a raging sore throat.

My opinion of British officialdom having taken a battering owing to my ejection from both the Royal Suite and the House of Commons, I embarked with jaded trepidation on the day's major engagement: a prime ministerial address to an audience of 600 business executives on

Australia as a favourable destination for British overseas investment. Bob jumped into his official vehicle, but a pompous official informed his two economic advisers, Rod Sims and me, that, since we were not in the Royal Suite—about which I was in no position to argue—we could not travel in the prime minister's cavalcade. Instead, we were to travel separately in a car generously provided by the British Foreign Office.

Although I judged it was probably futile, I asked the official whether Rod and I might be added to the Royal Suite just for the day, since most other members of the Royal Suite were not attending the economic function, enabling us to travel with our boss. This was impossible, the official explained, since membership of the Royal Suite had been settled by the protocol sections of the two prime ministers' departments before our departure from Australia, and they were immutable.

I had a sinking feeling that our exclusion from the prime minister's cavalcade would matter a lot. I was right. Rod and I soon realised that the vehicles transporting members of the Royal Suite were benefiting from controlled traffic lights that were turned green by an invisible magic wand at London's traffic-control centre to expedite the prime minister's journey. We in the Foreign Office vehicle were left to fight our way through heavy traffic—with Bob's speech in hand. Bob was obliged to wait 20 minutes at the venue, making him late for the 600 guests, until we breathlessly arrived with his speech. When we later explained the embarrassment to the pompous official, he showed no remorse and had no regret: the Royal Suite had been created for a good purpose, and it was his duty to police it.

The British treatment of those lowly Australians who were not in the Royal Suite made the Egyptian government's relegation of Millsie and me to Car 13 in the official convoy behind four empty vehicles appear thoroughly professional. At least we, in our little black caboose, like the prime minister, benefited from the magic wand in negotiating our way through Cairo's traffic chaos.

But we were to exact our revenge. Our final engagement was a morning at Lords watching the second Ashes Cricket Test between Australia and England. At an evening reception at Australia House ahead of the Test match, we met the Australian team and, as we were chatting to captain Alan Border, a beaming, moustachioed fast bowler,

Merv Hughes, joined us, carrying an enormous plate of seafood, including a whole lobster. This great Aussie tucker may have helped sustain Merv's energy levels; he took four wickets in the first innings. Happily, the segregation of Geoff Walsh, Butch, and me from the Royal Suite ensured we were unable to join Bob at the Lord's Pavilion to converse with members of the Marylebone Cricket Club. Instead, we watched Australia demolish the Poms from the outer on a brilliant, sunny day.

With our work done in England, our reunited official party travelled to Washington to meet president George Bush. At the White House, Geoff Walsh and I were late for the meeting with the president, because we had huddled under a staircase to get the cricket score. We were able to advise Bob that we had just won the Lord's Test. Bob was as thrilled as when I had told him, a couple of years earlier, that the horse he'd backed had won at odds of 33/1.

At the official meeting with president Bush, Bob put forward his case against ratifying the Antarctic minerals convention. The president told Bob he was relaxed about Bob promoting his position while in the US, but that he disagreed with us and supported ratification.

The next day, we met Democrat senator Al Gore, at Blair House, an official residence that accommodated visiting dignitaries. Bob opened the discussion by explaining his government's commitment to the environment, citing World Heritage Listings, research into the greenhouse effect, and our forthcoming statement on the environment. Gore responded by suggesting that, on the ozone layer and greenhouse-gas emissions: 'Australia could be in a position to exert leverage over the entire world's approach', since 'no one had taken the lead in advocating drastic action'.

He pointed out that Margaret Thatcher had been the closest to being such a leader to date. Gore argued that the Montreal protocol on protecting the ozone layer had been inadequate, and that in the next round of meetings, 'Australia's ability to focus attention and take the lead would shape views and action.'

On Antarctica, Gore explained: 'I had been inclined towards ratification of the minerals convention. Cousteau said how pleased he was with you. Greenpeace also supports your position. But other environmental groups are against your position. The World Resources

Institute is the largest NGO in the USA, and it is adamantly in favour of signing the minerals convention. They argue for signing and then proceeding to a stronger agreement. They want to avoid the risk of unregulated mining.'

Bob outlined Australia's position against regulated mining.

Gore asked: 'Couldn't Australia ratify and then veto mining?'

Bob explained, as he had done with Michel Rocard: 'No, not legally; a reservation would not be acceptable.'

Gore suggested: 'But don't put in a reservation, just veto any mining.'

Bob said: 'I won't accept any subterfuge.'

Gore then asked: 'What are the chances of your proposal succeeding?'

Bob advised Gore that India and France were already on board. Gore was surprised, saying: 'But France hasn't said it won't sign.'

Bob detailed the private talks he had recently had with Rocard and Mitterrand, quoting Mitterrand as saying: 'We will not ratify the convention.'

After lunch, Gore offered a new position: 'If some momentum develops and the world accepts your position, I will shift to you. My own preference is a tougher treaty that declares Antarctica an International Reserve, but it is hard to discard six years of work. Your position will have a big impact on the way the Senate reviews the matter. Please keep in touch. I will be heavily involved in the debate.'

Gore pointedly asked: 'If push comes to shove, will you let the convention become a dead letter?'

Bob said: 'Yes, I'm not going to be politically expedient. It is not likely that an individual company would explore in Antarctica without an international agreement. There will be an acceleration in public opinion against the minerals convention.'

Gore said that, upon reviewing the issue: 'If I decide to support Australia's position in the Senate, I will be in touch. Our objectives are exactly the same.'

If the Senate opposed the minerals convention, the United States would not be able to ratify it. We left the meeting more confident than ever that we could stop the minerals convention from coming into force, and prevent mining in Antarctica.

WHEN WE RETURNED TO AUSTRALIA, Bob asked me to invite Peter Garrett and his wife, Doris, to Kirribilli House for lunch to discuss the minerals convention. Peter arrived with Doris, his young children, and a cassette player. Under the veranda at Kirribilli House, Peter played us a track about Antarctica from Midnight Oil's forthcoming album. We assured Peter and Doris we would not waver from our commitment to oppose ratification of the minerals convention, and would continue our international campaign to persuade other Antarctic Treaty members to join us.

Several months later, Al Gore announced that he would oppose ratification of the minerals convention. Towards the end of the year, I received a phone call from Australia's chief negotiator, Alan Brown. Alan was at a meeting of the officials who had been negotiating the convention for more than six years. They were trying to salvage something from the wreckage. Alan said officials of other countries were proposing alternate language that would keep the minerals convention alive. Bob was in the room with me. I relayed Alan's message to Bob, and recommended he reject the proposed compromise. He did. The minerals convention was dead, and the Antarctic Treaty member countries agreed there would be no mining in Antarctica for at least 50 years.

Bob has ranked the campaign against mining in Antarctica as one of his greatest achievements. At the time he announced his intention to mobilise nations against the minerals convention, he was given no chance. But with a well-developed strategy and persistence, he prevailed.

Bob and I were proceeding against the advice of officials and the wishes of Britain and the United States. The support of Paul Keating was invaluable, as was the commitment and determination of Jacques Cousteau and Peter Garrett. If ever I had any misgivings about the benefits of the enormously long hours I was putting into my job as Bob Hawke's adviser, they dissolved that day.

Out of gratitude to Alan Brown, I drafted a letter of thanks for Bob's signature. Apparently, a prime minister praising a public servant in a personal letter breached all conventions in the Department of Foreign Affairs and Trade, but Alan, who had planned to retire, was promoted to the position of Australia's ambassador to France. No doubt he took the opportunity to reflect on the success of the Antarctic campaign with prime minister Rocard and Jacques Cousteau. The ban remains in force to this day—no mining is allowed in Antarctica.

25

Bulla-Shit and the Holy Trinity

Preventing mining in Antarctica was not the only purpose of our overseas trip in June 1989. From the United States, we flew back to Europe to meet German chancellor Helmut Kohl, a giant of a man.

Kohl told us how well Germany was getting on with the French, despite terrible hostilities between them spanning centuries. He predicted that by 2005, the military leaders of the two countries would be Franco-German-trained. He spoke of his plans for a single European market, a currency union, and a European central bank, assuring us it would not become a 'Fortress Europe' that excluded imports from Australia. Kohl said he never wanted to see another war in Europe. He suggested that the world was getting closer and more peaceful: 'Our young people on Eurail passes do not recognise borders.' Kohl recalled watching French refugees as a nine-year-old boy. 'It must never happen again', he lamented. Two years later, the Berlin Wall was down, and Germany had reunified.

When the official business was done, Butch and I joined some of the German officials for drinks at a bar in Bonn. As we moved into the wee hours of the morning, Butch had the good sense to make his way back to the state guesthouse—a schloss, half an hour by taxi from Bonn—where Bob and the travelling party were staying. As dawn broke, I realised I wouldn't have time to return to the schloss, pack my bags, and join the motorcade heading to the airport for our return trip to Australia.

Staying in the room adjacent to mine was a senior official from the prime minister's department, Dennis Richardson, who in later years was to be appointed director-general of ASIO, secretary of the Department of Foreign Affairs and Trade, and secretary of defence. I rang Dennis and asked if he would kindly go to my room, pack my bag, and bring it with him. Dennis found this a slightly strange request, but seemed cheerful enough in agreeing to do it. We met at the airport, where Dennis handed me my packed bag. I thanked him profusely, and he assured me it had not been a major inconvenience.

Mid-flight, I opened my bag for my toiletries so that I could freshen up. But I couldn't find my toiletries bag, so I asked Dennis where it might be. He hadn't checked the bathroom when packing my bag. It was probably not a wise move, but I remonstrated with Dennis about his neglecting to pack my toiletries. Dennis abandoned his well-disciplined graciousness, indignantly pointing out that it was not his job to pack my bags. Upon reflection, I considered he was right. When, 21 years later, I was appointed minister for trade, Dennis and I had one brief, polite conversation about the toiletries episode; but, beyond that, I judged it prudent not to raise the subject with him again.

On the flight home from Germany, Sandy Hollway organised a meeting between Bob and his main advisers: Geoff Walsh, Rod Sims, Sandy, and me. We were given copies of briefs from the prime minister's department on new economic-policy options. They included a 5 per cent consumption tax, cash payments to ease the burden of high mortgage interest rates on homeowners, and the proposed tax on imports of luxury goods.

As the group discussed each option, I remained silent. But as the discussion drew to a close, I offered my opinion: we should not do any of them, and instead stay the course. If we didn't have confidence in the economic direction we were taking, the Australian public would not have confidence in us. Bob accepted the advice, and we agreed to tough it out. We planned a series of major speeches in an effort to launch yet another political revival.

We put the finishing touches on the environment statement, and prepared for its launch. In Bangkok in January, I had started drafting the speech that Bob would give at the launch, writing: 'We have taken too much from the earth and given back too little.' Millsie added: 'It's time to say enough is enough.' Every evening television news bulletin carried footage of Bob uttering those two sentences, and of him and

Richo walking through a forest of eucalypts killed by salinity from excessive extraction of the Murray's waters for irrigation purposes.

In compliance with Bob's edict to avoid the conservation movement's 'infinitely elastic' agenda, I resisted requests for intervention into further land-use conflicts. But conflict over Kakadu would not go away.

In June 1987, when we had nominated Stage II of Kakadu National Park to the World Heritage List, we also gazetted as national park two-thirds of Stage III, which, as minister for resources and energy in 1987, Gareth Evans described as 'clapped-out buffalo country'. The remaining one-third of Stage III was to be a Conservation Zone, in which further mineral exploration could occur, subject to complying with strict environmental conditions. Cabinet also gave in-principle support to BHP's gold-mining project at Coronation Hill within Stage III. But now BHP was seeking approval to proceed with the Coronation Hill gold mine.

In a long meeting with Bob and me, Peter Garrett and Phillip Toyne demanded that the government at least defer any approval of Coronation Hill and scrap most of the Conservation Zone.

In my briefing note to Bob for the cabinet discussion, I wrote:

> I believe the best political decision is Richo's [to collapse the Conservation Zone]. It doesn't give the greenies their ultimate goal … but it would go close to giving us conservationists' agreement to direct second preferences to Labor. That one-or-so per cent would probably decide the election. The most rational decision would be not yet to collapse the Conservation Zone … This would not get conservationists' support.

I advised that, everything considered, Bob should not agree to collapse the Conservation Zone prematurely. Bob questioned me on my briefing note. I explained that I was concerned about the effects on business confidence of changing a definitive position we had announced two years earlier, but at the same time I could not guarantee that conservation groups would recommend a second-preference vote for Labor unless we agreed to collapse the Conservation Zone.

Bob accepted a request from Phillip Toyne for a phone conversation. It lasted 90 minutes. Phillip argued for collapsing the Conservation

Zone and incorporating the area into Kakadu National Park. Bob agreed with Phillip. Unfortunately, within a couple of days, Phillip's co-workers had leaked the conversation to the media.

The chairman of the BHP board, Sir Arvi Parbo, had been unsuccessfully seeking a meeting with Bob for weeks. Sir Arvi was insulted that Bob had found time for a lengthy discussion with the conservation movement's Phillip Toyne, and made his displeasure known publicly. Bob's cabinet colleagues were appalled, but he got his way in the cabinet room in late 1989, and only a small area of 46 square kilometres around Coronation Hill was excluded from the park. This caused enormous resentment among some of Bob's most senior cabinet colleagues, including John Dawkins and Peter Walsh, from which Bob's leadership would never recover.

After the 1990 election, an acrimonious cabinet debate about the future of the Coronation Hill gold mine further weakened Bob's leadership against a challenge from Paul. Bob advocated the rejection of the Coronation Hill gold mine, based on the Jaowyn people's belief that an ancestral being they knew as Bulla lived in that hill. When some of Bob's cabinet colleagues ridiculed this as 'Bulla-shit', Bob pointed out that Christians believed in the Holy Trinity of three gods in one, arguing that the Aboriginal people's beliefs were no less legitimate. Bob insisted on his position against mining at Coronation Hill, and cabinet acquiesced, but it marked a defining point in his later loss of the prime ministership.

WHILE WORKING on these controversial environmental issues, I was also obliged to discharge my responsibilities as the prime minister's microeconomics adviser. Those responsibilities were about to become more onerous.

The government needed to grapple with air-traffic congestion at Sydney's Kingsford-Smith Airport, and had to decide whether to support or oppose a proposal to build a third runway. Local residents, fed up with aircraft noise, were bitterly opposed to the third runway. So were their elected representatives. Richo opposed the third runway, preferring that a new airport be built at Badgery's Creek, west of Sydney, instead. Working with Richo's office on environmental matters was easy; his staff members were always happy to see me.

As I walked past the open area of Richo's office to meet with Baldo and the others, I would say hello to a quiet, young staffer. I considered myself lucky when I got a peep out of him. The only time I could get him excited was when I was in the office to discuss the third runway. He had definite views on that, which were best described as unbridled hostility. It turned out he had his eye on a state seat directly under the flight path. Somewhere along the way, Morris Iemma lost his shyness and became a very effective premier of New South Wales.

The Department of Transport had done a comparison of the costs and benefits of the third runway and Badgery's Creek. My PhD thesis had included several chapters on cost-benefit analysis, helping equip me with the knowledge to scrutinise the department's work. Under plausible assumptions, the difference between the third runway and Badgery's Creek was not huge; sure, the third runway was superior, but Badgery's Creek wasn't too far behind. Based on my analysis, I supported Badgery's Creek.

Richo didn't care how I had reached my conclusion; he was just happy that I opposed the third runway. Bob accepted my advice, and went so far as to have a private meeting with the New South Wales premier, Nick Greiner, who strongly supported the third runway. With just the three of us in the room, Bob revealed to Nick that he supported the early construction of an airport at Badgery's Creek, and opposed the third runway. Nick calmly said he had a different view, but that the state government would work with the federal government to fund and build the necessary infrastructure for connecting the Badgery's Creek airport to the city centre.

Learning of Bob's decision, transport minister Ralph Willis urgently sought a meeting with him. Again, there were just the three of us in the room. Bob asked me to explain my analysis. Ralph, who was a gentle soul, exploded. Bob and I were taken aback. His department's analysis, he shouted, showed the third runway as clearly superior. I agreed, but explained that the department had used the most optimistic assumptions about the third runway, and the most pessimistic assumptions about Badgery's Creek. Ralph asked me to work with his department over the weekend. I did so, and after discussing the assumptions, and testing and re-testing the numbers, it became clear to me that the gap in favour of the third runway, though not as big as the department had been claiming, was nevertheless large.

In one of the most difficult professional decisions I have ever made, I walked into Bob's office alone on Monday morning to tell him: 'Bob, I've changed my recommendation about Sydney airport. Based on the work I did with the Transport Department over the weekend, I now support the third runway.'

After I explained the revised analysis to Bob, he said, to his great credit: 'Okay, mate, if that's your best objective assessment, I'll have a fresh look at it.'

Richo wrote in his 1994 book, *Whatever It Takes*, that he'd gained assurances from both Bob and Paul that they opposed the third runway: 'But a funny thing happened on the way to the forum, and to this day I have no idea what it was.' Richo, now you know.

Later in October, we travelled to Kuala Lumpur for the Commonwealth Heads of Government meeting. When I returned home to our house in the Canberran suburb of O'Connor, I found our small dining room decorated with streamers and balloons. Cathy told me the best news I could ever have received: we were going to have a baby! Of all the dumb and smart things I had done, none seemed smarter than helping to create a new life. We were thrilled. I felt I had been given the greatest imaginable gift from a wonderful woman who, to that moment and beyond, had given me the happiest days of my life.

26

Winning ugly

When comedian Austen Tayshus was asked what he wanted for Christmas, he replied: 'Nuclear war, so as to remove the threat of it.' It was a little like that when mortgage interest rates hit 17.5 per cent. By late 1989, voters were coming to the conclusion that Labor's economic strategy was not working. Internal party polling showed large swings against us in marginal seats, and party pollsters and strategists gave us little chance of winning the 1990 election.

Our environmental credentials seemed to be one of our very few political assets, along with the restored professional relationship between the great persuaders, Hawke and Keating. Also working in our favour was a change of Liberal Party leadership, from John Howard back to Andrew Peacock. Bob remarked to me in later years that if Howard had been opposition leader in the 1990 election, we might well have lost.

After the Christmas break, I began working with Geoff Walsh on an election strategy. We would make a series of inexpensive announcements for a fourth term, including support for childcare in a social-justice statement, and the release of statements on education and training, women, roads, drugs and law and order, industrial relations, and health. In the final week of the campaign, we would issue a progress report on implementation of the 1989 environment statement. In contrast with our heavily negative 1987 election campaign, this strategy would give us something positive to say twice a week. In a note I prepared titled 'Possible Program of Policy Announcements', I wrote:

Relying on finding holes in the Liberals' policies and waiting for their gaffes would be far from adequate. Our proposal for a series of discrete policy statements through the campaign is designed to provide impetus so that we are doing the agenda setting—which itself should help dissipate any feeling that the government is tired and has run out of ideas.

Geoff and I discussed the note with Bob at Kirribilli House, and he accepted it. We had recommended that the first announcement be an economic statement from Paul. In order to reinforce our responsible approach to the budget, we pre-determined a modest spending limit of less than $350 million in the first year of a new term, and had each of our proposed policies costed by the Department of Finance. We would announce the spending limit at the outset, together with the savings decisions we had made to fund it, reassuring the public that the total of our pre-election spending commitments was affordable. As each new initiative was announced during the course of the campaign, Peter Walsh would issue a signed certificate as finance minister, authenticating the costings.

We knew the situation in Victoria was dire. The state bank was in trouble because of risky business-lending practices by its merchant-banking affiliate, Tricontinental. We fully expected this to become public during the campaign. To make matters worse, the Victorian tram workers' union had embarked on a month-long tram strike, causing immense inconvenience to Melbourne commuters.

Western Australia was no better. In a scandal that was to become known as WA Inc, the state Labor government had provided loans and financial guarantees to business mates whose companies were now failing, creating huge losses for taxpayers. Although WA Inc did not involve the Hawke government, the spillover onto the Labor Party's reputation as a financial manager meant we faced an electoral wipeout in the west.

Signs had been emerging that the national economy, battered by high interest rates, was beginning to slow. Several major Australian corporations had collapsed, and in late January, following discussions between Paul and Reserve Bank governor Bernie Fraser, the board of the Reserve Bank made its first interest-rate cut in more than two years.

Although the level of interest rates remained very high, the direction was now downward, and more interest-rate reductions looked likely.

Before Paul's press conference on the interest-rate cut, we had been tipped off that the Liberals were planning a campaign theme that a vote for Hawke was a vote for Keating, since it was unlikely that Bob would see out a full fourth term. The Australian public viewed opposition leader Andrew Peacock as superficial, a bit of a show pony, not up to running the Australian economy. Butch developed the antidote to the Liberals' campaign message, which Paul agreed to apply. At the press conference, a journalist asked what the treasurer had to say about Liberal claims that a vote for Hawke was a vote for Keating. Paul replied: 'A vote for Andrew Peacock is a vote for Andrew Peacock.' The Liberals, aware of Peacock's weak electoral image, never used their freshly minted slogan again.

AN ELECTION WAS IN THE AIR, and the time had come for the Liberals to unveil their much-heralded health policy. As in 1987, the Liberals were convinced they could dismantle Medicare, save money, and use the proceeds to fund tax cuts. This was the third time they had set out to destroy the very popular Medicare and, yet again, they couldn't make the numbers add up. Thousands of Australians would be worse off. Liberal health spokesman Peter Shack was directed by the Liberal leadership team to convene a press conference to admit the opposition's health-policy failure.

Shack opened his press conference with the admission: 'Now, I want to say to you, with all of the frankness that I can muster, the Liberal and National parties do not have a particularly good track record on health, and you don't need me to remind you of our last period in government.' He went on to concede: 'We have laboured under a misapprehension that there was a billion dollars to be got out of Medicare. There is not.' And finally: 'You might accuse us of a lot of things, but one of the things I don't think we're guilty of is learning from our past mistakes.'

With those admissions, our electoral stocks began rising. Bob agreed to hold a media conference in the so-called Blue Room of the ministerial wing in Parliament House. Geoff, Butch, and I agreed that the 'grab' for that evening's television news should be Bob saying: 'Just don't get sick under the Liberals.' The three of us walked into Bob's office and briefed him accordingly. He agreed this was the killer line that would cut through into the lounge rooms of viewing Australians — or so we thought.

Rather than stand up at the back of the Blue Room, we joined other advisers to watch the full media conference on a monitor in the chief of staff's office. Bob gave a long, technical exposition of the consequences of the Liberals' failed health policy and of the superiority of Medicare. As he rattled off one statistic after another, we waited for the killer line.

'Say it, Bob. Say: "Just don't get sick under the Liberals", I urged into the monitor, as if he could hear.

Not once in his lengthy opening statement did Bob utter the killer line. Then I deduced he was being clever, waiting for questions so that he could drop the line as if he'd just thought of it. 'Impromptu is best', I reasoned.

Now Bob was getting really cagey, not using the killer line in response to the first question, or the second, or the third. As a Hollowman would, I got that sinking feeling when questioning turned to other subjects such as the election date. Our last, vain hope was that Bob would use the killer line in his summing up at the end of the media conference. But there was no summing up. It just finished.

Obviously pleased with himself, Bob waltzed across the corridor to greet us. 'That went well', he declared. One or two junior advisers agreed. Geoff and Butch looked as dark as they did when Bob had entertained speculation about a luxury tax while we were trying to promote French agreement to a mining ban in Antarctica. I couldn't contain myself.

'It was disastrous. You fucked it up', I blurted, surprising myself, and the prime minister even more so.

'What was wrong with it?' Bob asked.

'You only had one line to deliver — "Just don't get sick under the Liberals" — and you didn't say it once in half an hour.'

It was as if someone had farted. The room began emptying, advisers silently returning to their workstations. I confessed to colleagues: 'I think I've upset Bob.' Later, I overheard him saying to an adviser: 'I think I've upset Craig.' Although Bob and I were close, I would be of no value to him in the coming election campaign if I played the part of a loyal yes-man. No damage was done, and perhaps a little good.

Before deciding on an election date, we travelled to New Zealand to review and renew the Closer Economic Relations agreement between our two countries, and to spend a day at the Auckland Commonwealth Games. At the games stadium, Bob joined the Queen in an exclusive area—no doubt the Royal Suite. Mercifully, this time we were not members of the suite. Geoff Walsh, Butch, and I sat in the open stands behind the dignitaries.

A Mexican wave started, progressing around the stadium until it reached the royal enclosure, where it died for a lack of enthusiasm on the part of the Queen, Bob, and other dignitaries to arise, throw up their hands, and chuck drink cups and other possessions into the air. Geoff, Butch, and I energetically took part in the booing of the Queen and Bob for failing to join in the fun. We continued with this ritual for several rounds of the stadium, but then decided it was time to leave for our hotel.

As we walked through the car park, we recognised a young Aboriginal girl walking barefooted towards us. We congratulated Cathy Freeman on having just won a gold medal as a member of the Australian women's 100 metres relay team. With a beaming smile, this bright 16-year-old girl said: 'Thanks very much', and walked by.

IN A THREE-HOUR BRIEFING of Bob and staff on the latest polling, Rod Cameron and Margie Gibbs advised that we would certainly lose a swag of seats in Victoria, but could still win an election if everything went our way. But it quickly became clear that not everything would go our way.

We had worked with the finance minister, Peter Walsh, his office, and his department on a fully costed list of spending initiatives that would be announced during the campaign. Peter Walsh's adviser, David Cox, came around to inform us that a finance department official had misdialled, accidentally faxing the complete score sheet of election promises, with dollar amounts against each, to radio station 2CC in the press gallery instead of to the finance minister's office. Not quite knowing what to make of the document sitting curled up, unsolicited, in the fax machine's in-tray, a radio journalist gave it to a young Tony

Wright, who at the time was writing for *The Canberra Times*. We told *The Canberra Times* that the document was just an early working draft. We decided, nervously, that we should not be diverted by this horrible departmental error.

Bob and I sat together in his office. Bob had in front of him the document to authorise the dissolution of the parliament for an election on 24 March 1990. He wasn't sure. We sat in silence. Bob asked: 'What do you reckon?' I said: 'Go on, sign it. It's not going to get any better for us if we wait.' Bob signed the instrument. The election campaign was on.

27

Sticking with the plan

The 1990 election campaign started badly. In the early evening of the first day, a group of charitable organisations had assembled at Parliament House for a long-planned conference, followed by drinks. I had been at the drinks function that Bob was scheduled to attend, and foolishly reported to him as he arrived that the head of the Brotherhood of St Laurence, Archbishop Peter Hollingworth, had condemned the government for failing to eliminate child poverty within three years. Bob sought out Hollingworth and berated him. A boom microphone picked up Bob's tirade, which featured in the next day's media coverage.

On the same day, an auditor's report was released, revealing that Tricontinental had amassed losses of $1.5 billion, for which Victorian taxpayers would be expected to foot much of the bill. To cap off a day from hell, a puzzling, murky story aired on the ABC about the National Crime Authority investigating Liberal Party president John Elliott. It did not come from us, but it looked like the consequence of Labor Party dirty tricks.

At a media conference the following day, Bob grabbed and removed a clutch of microphones that journalists had attached to his lectern, leaving no room for his notes. An angry prime minister appeared on the television news bulletins.

On a much brighter note, within days of the election being called, the Australian Conservation Foundation announced it was recommending a second-preference vote for Labor. The Wilderness Society had already made the same recommendation. The second-preference strategy was locked into place, the culmination of years of work and collaboration.

Meanwhile, protesting airline pilots were determined to defeat the Hawke government for opposing their exorbitant wage claims. They had been taking industrial action for months. If the government gave in to the pilots' demands, the long-standing agreement with the trade union movement to moderate its wage claims in return for such worker benefits as Medicare and family payments for low-income earners would collapse, and Australia would face a wages explosion and the return of high inflation.

Bob's close friend Sir Peter Abeles ran Ansett Airlines. Peter was resolute in resisting the pilots' wage demands, bringing in foreign pilots to replace them. Relations between Bob and the pilots hit a new low when Peter persuaded Bob that the uniforms they were wearing during protest action were not theirs but the property of Ansett Airlines. Bob publicly accused the pilots of stealing their uniforms.

Everywhere we went on the campaign trail, we were met by protesting pilots and their wives. They displayed placards bearing statements such as: 'Hazel has one, Bob is one.' They even began jostling Bob and Hazel as we visited the wet tropical forests of North Queensland. After more than a week of this concerted protest activity, we reached an agreement with the travelling media: they would no longer put footage of the striking pilots to air, having already given it extensive coverage.

Frustratingly, the story about the National Crime Authority and John Elliott would not go away. Every time a journalist questioned Bob about it, he offered comments that kicked it along. Geoff Walsh and I were travelling with Bob. I pointed out that we had wasted more than a week of the campaign distracted by matters that would not determine its outcome. Bob listened, dropped the Elliott matter, and began releasing the policy initiatives that Geoff and I had outlined at Kirribilli House. Each morning, Geoff, Butch, and I met Bob for breakfast, armed with the day's media release. Bob trusted us, and each announcement went smoothly.

In the evening after we released Labor's childcare policy, we were to gather for dinner with several members of the travelling media party. Bob was waiting for me so that we could join the group. But I was on the phone, hearing out Gerry Hand, who was incensed by our announcement that a re-elected Hawke government would extend childcare subsidies to the private sector. Bob was hurrying me off the phone, but I let Gerry take out his anger on me — such was the role of staffers.

OUR ECONOMIC MESSAGE was about diversifying the Australian economy from its heavy reliance on primary-commodity exports to one that relied on the creative talents of its people. We argued that Australia needed to make the transition from the Lucky Country, blessed with rich endowments of fertile land and minerals, to the Clever Country.

The major announcement at the campaign launch was the establishment of 50 Cooperative Research Centres, risky ventures that would push Australia to the frontiers of applied scientific research. This was the brainchild of Bob's chief scientist, Professor Ralph Slatyer. When Ralph first advised Bob and me of the price tag months earlier, I thought we wouldn't be able to afford it. But Bob, a classmate of Ralph's at Perth Modern School, was attracted to the proposal, and we found the necessary budget savings to fund it.

As the campaign proceeded, we released our remaining costed policies, complete with certificates signed by Peter Walsh, according to our pre-determined schedule. But we ran into a problem when we decided not to release a policy for more funding of the National Crime Authority, concerned that this would revive the John Elliott story that had derailed the early part of our campaign.

Instead of the final tally of campaign commitments equalling the pre-announced total, we were going to end up under-spending by $20 million. We thought this would look inelegant. Our final major scheduled announcement for the campaign was to be on the environment, so Bob gave me the authority to decide which environmental initiative our surplus $20 million would be spent on. To this day, researchers on climate change are probably oblivious as to how they received a promise of $20 million in the closing days of the 1990 election campaign.

Having been with Bob every day of the 1987 election campaign, I knew how gruelling a month on the campaign trail could be. But I had promised Bob that I would spend the entire 1990 campaign travelling with him. My brother, Lance, was marrying for a third time. He understood when I told him I could not be at the wedding.

Cathy attended for both of us. Bob later invited Lance to join us at the Randwick races. We had a fabulous time that Lance never forgot.

Geoff Walsh and I cemented a lifelong friendship during that campaign. Geoff, a Victorian, was more pessimistic about our prospects than I was. But we shared a commitment to implementing our program of announcements, briefing Bob each morning at breakfast, and ensuring he had most evenings off. After a rocky start, Bob remained cheerful and disciplined throughout.

Singo met up with us from time to time with his partner, Liz Hayes, previewing the most gorgeous television advertisements on the environment. With soaring pictures of Tasmania's tall trees, stunning images of the Great Barrier Reef, and sweeping vistas of Kakadu, these television advertisements appealed directly to Democrat, Green, and Independent voters, urging them to give their preference vote to Labor.

Singo's advertisements helped persuade a sufficient number of undecided voters to give their second-preference vote to Labor, providing us with a small advantage over the Coalition. Despite only 39 per cent of voters giving their first-preference vote to Labor, and despite losing a staggering nine seats in Victoria, we won the election.

IN THE DAYS following our election victory, Singo proposed a celebratory dinner at Eliza's, a Sydney restaurant he co-owned. Bob, exhausted like the rest of us, was hesitant, but I persuaded him to go. However, when a cowgirl rode a horse onto the restaurant floor, I knew I had pulled the wrong rein. The food arrived, followed by speeches, whereupon Bob thanked everyone except Geoff Walsh, Butch, and me. Geoff and I walked out in disgust. By evening's end, Bob was asking where I was, to be told I had left early. I stayed with Singo and Liz Hayes.

Following my return to Canberra several days later, I turned up at Geoff's house. Geoff told me Bob's work on the new ministry was going badly; there was very little renewal, and he was allowing the factions to decide the line-up. While I was there, Bob rang Geoff asking whether he'd seen me. Geoff said he hadn't, but if I got in touch he'd ask me to ring Bob. A couple of hours later, I rang Bob for a very tough conversation. He had won a fourth term, and I thought he should take control of the policy agenda and the ministerial line-up. I said: 'The country's going down the tube, and the ministry is to be selected on factional patronage, not on the basis of Australia's best interests.'

Although Bob rejected many of my contentions, he said: 'Well, instead of criticising from the sidelines, why don't you come in here and help me?'

When I arrived at the office the next day, Butch asked how the ministerial reshuffle was going. I explained that the factions were totally dictating the ministerial line-up. The right faction wanted to dump Ralph Willis, a cabinet minister. I thought Bob should stamp his authority on the composition of the ministry by insisting that Ralph be retained and that newcomers Simon Crean, Northern Territory senator Bob Collins, and independent Bob McMullan be included in the ministry. Butch and I agreed that he would go into Bob's office and tell him the word was all around the press gallery that the factions were determining the ministry. Butch told Bob the media would tear him to pieces for failing to exercise his authority.

I was with Bob when Butch came into the office to report the press gallery's intentions. Bob was furious that he was to be so maligned by the media after winning the election. He explained to me that Ralph Willis had been his research officer at the ACTU, and he was unhappy about the prospect of him being dumped from the ministry. Bob said: 'I can't let it happen.' I agreed, and I argued for the inclusion of Crean, Collins, and McMullan.

Unfortunately for the left faction, they were the next grouping through the door to deliver their list of nominees to the ministry. Bob blew up. He told them they had to make room for Crean. They pointed out that Crean was of the right faction, to which Bob said he didn't fucking care. Their ears still ringing, the left-faction leaders left the room. Late that night, they asked to meet Bob at the Lodge, where they agreed to forego one ministerial position for Crean as long as the next ministerial vacancy went to the left.

Bob's insistence on retaining Ralph Willis in the ministry and including Bob Collins meant there wasn't room for both Allan Griffiths from Victoria and Ross Free from New South Wales. Richo reports in *Whatever it Takes* that he had rung Bob Collins 'at the beginning of that crazy day to tell him he was "fucked",' before ringing him again 'at the end of the day to tell him he was "unfucked" because of Hawke's

LEFT: Eileen Beatrice Emerson, my grandmother on my father's side, circa 1910

BELOW: My father, Ernest Victor Emerson, at the age of 20

LEFT: Me and my brother, Lance, at the age of six and ten respectively

BELOW: At St John's Convent School, at the age of eight

ABOVE: Bachelor of Economics Honours graduation with my parents, Marge and Ern, 1997

RIGHT: With resources and energy minister, senator Peter Walsh, Beijing, 1984

LEFT: With Bob Hawke, Barrie Cassidy, and Bob Sorby on our flight back to Canberra after the 1987 election victory

BELOW: With Bob Hawke in Dubrovnik, 1987

ABOVE: Bob Hawke introduces me to US President Ronald Reagan, 1988

BELOW: With Jacques Cousteau, and Bob and Hazel Hawke, 1989

ABOVE: My farewell from Bob Hawke's office, 1990

RIGHT: In training for the Parliamentary Rugby World Cup, 2003

ABOVE: With Kevin Rudd, Wayne Swan, and Julia Gillard, at Question Time in the House of Representatives, 2009

BELOW: Meeting President Barack Obama, 2011

ABOVE: Delivering speech, 2012

BELOW: At the World Economic Forum, Davos, Switzerland, 2012

support and the generosity of Ross Free, who had decided to make the sacrifice'.

We were unable to get McMullan up, but retaining Ralph Willis and successfully pushing for both Collins and Crean was a good result.

Now came the task of allocating portfolios. Mostly, this wasn't difficult. But one big problem was that Richo was interested in the communications portfolio, and he deserved to be rewarded for his performance as environment minister. No one in the office thought it a good idea to give Richo responsibility for communications; we were worried that, as a political fixer, he would be more interested in doing deals with media moguls than undertaking much-needed economic reform of Australia's television, radio, and telecommunications industries.

Bob met with Richo and offered him the social security portfolio. Richo was hardly over the moon, but grudgingly accepted it. Bob had already offered the other leader of the right faction, Senator Robert Ray, the defence portfolio. Everything else fitted into place, and Bob was about to settle on the line-up with a sense of satisfaction.

The next day, Bob put it to me that he might switch Richo and Ray. He spoke to Richo, and told him he could do better than social security, and that defence was his if he wanted it. Richo was delighted. All that was left was to ring Ray and inform him that he was to take on social security instead of defence. Ray refused. He insisted that Bob stick to his original offer. Bob was obliged to ring Richo back to tell him he was staying in social security. Richo was apoplectic. When Bob put the phone down, he turned to me and said: 'What have I done?' Bob had made Richo an enemy for the remainder of his time in parliament.

This mattered because, although Richo was but one caucus member, he had devoted years to organising and doing favours for a large number of members of the New South Wales right faction. Many owed their careers to him. Few could advance without his active support, or at least his acquiescence. Richo had mobilised support from New South Wales right MPs for Bob's successful challenge against Bill Hayden in 1983, and was capable of mobilising support for Paul to challenge Bob for the prime ministership. On that day, Bob knew this was now inevitable.

When it occurred, in 1991, Bob held no grudges against Richo. He told me that the New South Wales right was very tribal, and that since Paul was a member of the tribe and he was not, it was only a matter of time before the tribe elevated Paul to the leadership.

28

Birth and rebirth

Tired after more than six years as a staffer, and with a baby on the way, I decided the time to move on was fast approaching. We were scheduled to travel to Gallipoli to commemorate the 75th anniversary of the ANZAC landing. Butch said to me: 'You will be the first Australian to quit at Gallipoli.'

In the normal spirit of bipartisanship prevailing on such occasions, the new opposition leader, John Hewson, and his wife, Carolyn, accompanied us on the RAAF flight, joining us for the usual sing-alongs.

We traversed the Dardanelles on a specially commissioned ferry, waking at 2.00am in preparation for the dawn service. Accompanying us at Gallipoli was a large group of ANZAC veterans, now in their nineties. It was an enormous honour to witness a Turkish veteran being led by his carers towards an Aussie veteran. As they approached, nobody could be sure of their reactions. These two old men threw their arms around each other, embracing in forgiveness, friendship, and respect. Of course, I cried.

Officials had arranged a mid-morning meeting between Margaret Thatcher and Bob in a wooden cabin on the former battlefields. It was a small, single room furnished with a few chairs and a table, and through its windows we could see open grass and a few rosemary bushes. A great deal of blood had been spilled on these hallowed lands. Accompanying Bob were Sandy Hollway, John Bowan, and I. Accompanying Margaret was just her chief press secretary, Bernard Ingham.

At that meeting, my most useful contribution was to pour a glass of water for Margaret. She and Bob began discussing our countries' positions ahead of an international meeting on climate change. Bob asked me when the meeting was to take place. My guess was wrong, and Bernard nominated the correct date. I had not distinguished myself, but my mind was elsewhere, and Bob did not seem to mind.

BACK IN AUSTRALIA, my interests were shifting to life outside the prime minister's office and the approaching birth of our first baby. We knew we were having a boy, but as the due date arrived and passed, the doctor told us the birth had to be induced.

Cathy and I arrived at Canberra Hospital on the shores of Lake Burley Griffin at 8.00am on Saturday 30 June 1990, expecting to greet our baby a few hours later. Cathy wore a singlet of my dad's that I'd recovered and retained following his death 12 years prior. The hospital staff administered the solution that was used to induce labour, but after several hours, nothing much had happened.

Just before noon, Bob rang me on my mobile phone. After asking how Cathy was going, he passed on the Saturday race-day information he'd extracted from his friendly trainers, and I gave him the tips from a subscription service I'd joined.

Cathy was obliged to squat on a birthing-room floor, and I squatted with her as she received injections of morphine and then pethidine. In perhaps the most regrettable statement I've ever made, I turned to Cathy and said: 'I don't know how much longer I can do this.' If she hadn't been so full of painkillers, she surely would have punched me.

Through the afternoon, the nurses monitored the baby's heart rate. At one stage, we couldn't find a heartbeat for what seemed like more than a minute. The baby was not coming out, and I could sense the nurse was worried. She telephoned Cathy's obstetrician, who gave her instructions. Still the baby was not coming. He was fighting, his heartbeat weakening. Finally, the obstetrician relented, came to the hospital, and arranged an emergency caesarean section. It was now 4.00am.

Cathy was taken into an operating theatre as I waited anxiously. Within just a few minutes, a trolley appeared bearing our baby, wrapped in aluminium foil for warmth. The little boy looked at me, and I held his tiny hand. He had cuts on his forehead where he had fought for 20 hours to enter the world. I cried with joy. The nurses took this little miracle to his mother who, having been administered a general anaesthetic following an earlier cocktail of all available pain relief, had not yet seen him. I wrote on a note his weight and time of birth, and the words: 'A strong, brave little boy.' We named him Benjamin.

I phoned Cathy's family, my brother, Lance, and my boss, Bob, to tell them of the arrival of our boy, baby Benjamin.

In preparation for this new phase of our lives, Cathy and I discussed where we should live. From the age of 21, inspired by Gough Whitlam's efforts to modernise and internationalise Australia, the protest movement, and the sheer excitement of the mid-1970s, I had contemplated a career in politics. But I lacked the confidence to attend a Labor Party branch meeting. Everyone would know the procedures, and I would know nothing, I thought. I would embarrass myself. So I had never participated in student politics or joined Young Labor.

Now, at 35 years of age, having worked for and become close to a prime minister, helping make big changes for the country and living a fast-paced professional life, I could not see myself returning to academia. Bob had been encouraging me to become a politician. Having worked for Bob for four years, I was no longer active in the centre-left faction of the party. And I opposed the left's economic-policy prescriptions of industry protection and government-run business enterprises. The Hawke–Keating model of an open, competitive economy was fully consistent with my training in economics. I wanted to join the right of the party.

Cathy and I were interested in living in Sydney as a great city and as a location from which I could pursue my political ambitions. I sought Singo's guidance. He was close to an investment banker, Malcolm Turnbull, and asked if I was interested in working with him. I was. Singo put us in contact, and Turnbull arranged to meet me at the offices of Whitlam Turnbull & Co. After our discussion, I returned to Canberra. A fax arrived from Turnbull, proposing that we meet again to discuss the terms of a job offer.

Bob had suggested I get some advice from Richo about the ALP in New South Wales. Richo told me I would likely end up contesting a preselection against a local councillor or mayor in his sixties. My rival would have stacked the local branches with supporters, and I would probably be defeated in a rank-and-file ballot. Since there was no central committee vote in the New South Wales system, no one from on high could help me. In Queensland, however, a central electoral college had 50 per cent of the vote, with the rank-and-file membership accounting for the other 50 per cent. If I could win the support of the electoral college, I would be on my way. Based on this advice, I somewhat reluctantly turned down Turnbull's offer, and we decided to move to Queensland.

Many months prior to being elected premier of Queensland, Wayne Goss and his personal adviser, Kevin Rudd, had met with Bob, Geoff Walsh, and me in Bob's office. Rudd and I maintained contact thereafter. We later met in the bar of Canberra's Hyatt Hotel, where I expressed an interest in moving to Queensland. Rudd offered to speak to the environment minister, Pat Comben, who had been looking for a director-general to lead his department.

However, on the night before I was to fly to Brisbane for my formal interview with the minister, our new son, Ben, developed a high fever from an infection he had contracted. We took him to Canberra Hospital, and didn't leave for home until 2.00am. My interview went badly; I had little to say about departmental restructuring, which was the minister's main interest.

Minister Comben announced he intended to re-advertise the position. More than a month passed, and I was offered a re-interview. Ahead of it, I asked Sandy Hollway, who was an experienced senior official in the prime minister's department, for advice. We prepared a chart depicting a proposed departmental structure; I learned that 'KPIs' was short for Key Performance Indicators; Sandy taught me some more public service acronyms; I proficiently displayed my newly acquired knowledge in my re-interview; and I got the job. Rudd had supported me throughout this process, and I am sure was instrumental in my appointment. We took a European vacation, I finished up in Bob's office, and we moved to Brisbane in November 1990.

Before heading for Europe, I had one, final, private discussion with Bob, during which he indicated he was considering going into business and was preparing to hand over the prime ministership to Paul. I was half-expecting Bob to announce his intentions while we were away.

At four months of age, Ben had covered enormous distances from Australia to England, touring London, Paris, and southern France. We had unwittingly destroyed the little boy's sleeping pattern, and he cried constantly in the back of the car we had hired to drive through Europe. Sleep-deprived, we gave up the car and took a train from Toulouse through Italy to Rome. While visiting the Vatican, I filled a small film canister with water, and asked Cathy to hold baby Ben while I poured water onto his forehead, reciting: 'I baptise you in the name of the Father and of the Son and of the Holy Ghost.' Once a Catholic, always a Catholic; but not every Catholic father gets to baptise his son at the Vatican.

When we returned to Australia, Bob told me he had changed his mind about handing over to Paul. *This is going to end badly*, I thought to myself. The economy was heading towards recession. Storm clouds were gathering. I was departing for a new life at the right time. Upon leaving Canberra, I wrote Paul a letter thanking him and his advisers for treating me so well and for all the good work we had done together. In response, Paul wrote:

I can quite easily respond by saying how much I enjoyed your company over the years, always finding you both cheerful and helpful. What I have always appreciated is your belief in longer run rational policies — and knew I could always rely on this instinct in critical discussions. When things get tough, many people look for the quick and easy option — ones you understood do not serve anyone well in the longer term. Had we fallen for these in 1987 and 1989, I believe we could have kissed both elections goodbye. On the big ones you never dropped the ball once — a tribute one could only pay to a few around here. [...] You have spent long enough here. Too long dulls everything — the instinct and the appreciation. I am pleased you have taken the job in Queensland — a place which could use your skills and strengths. Certainly the environment movement owes you one. Craig, best wishes for the future for Cathy and your bub! Warm regards, Paul Keating.

At my farewell in the prime minister's office, Bob said:

I really find it impossible to convey adequately the contribution that you've made, Craig, not just to me, to the government, but to this country. You're a very fine economist and your professionalism was there for all to see. What was important is that you're no academic economist. You were always there to make a very serious and relevant contribution to a continuous range of economic discussions and decision making that we went through. But even more important was the sense of realism with which you tackled specific microeconomic problems. And I suppose when the history of this government is written, it's going to be a conclusion of any objective writer that the way in which we were able to deal with the environmental movement was one of the distinguishing features of our success. The simple truth is, that as far as I'm concerned, we couldn't have done it without you, Craig. But it wasn't just the environment. As well as being an economic adviser, an environmental adviser, you were also very much a political adviser. Your contribution reached a most effective peak in the last election campaign. We went into that campaign not favourites. Every day had to be a winning day, every contribution had to be a winning contribution. The truth is that no prime minister has ever had a travelling trio — of you, Butch and Geoff, and Grunter, out in advance — of the quality, commitment and intelligence of that group. So my friends, you can see that Craig has been to me very special — and there's a particular bond and affection between us. It's a relationship which is based upon the joy I have had from the first day I really saw him, a vibrant enthusiasm and commitment that he wanted to be part of making this a better government and through that, a better country. So it is for all those reasons, Craig, that I want to convey to you the grateful attitude and the love and affection that I have for what you have done.

It was an indescribable honour and privilege working for Australia's greatest prime minister. Here was a man who believed deeply in the brotherhood of man, an internationalist who considered every human being equal, who abhorred discrimination on the basis of race, colour, or religion.

In his union days, Bob worked with union officials who had been denied the opportunity of a good education, but whom Bob considered to be among the most intelligent people he had ever met. He told us of these experiences time and time again. They drove him in his determination that his government would provide financial support for parents struggling to keep their children at school. It led directly to his infamous child-poverty pledge, which changed the lives of millions of poor families and contributed to increasing the proportion of children completing high school from one-third to more than two-thirds.

In pursuing his ideals, Bob was a pragmatist, never confusing ends with means. He copped plenty of criticism from the media and the party's left wing for associating at black-tie dinners with the likes of Kerry Packer, Peter Abeles, and Alan Bond. Yet by gaining the confidence of the business community, Bob was able to win four elections and, with Paul and their cabinet colleagues, change Australia for the better, setting it up to enjoy the benefits of the Asian Century.

As in his union days, Bob was a relentless advocate. He and Paul formed a formidable team in explaining honestly to the Australian people the challenges confronting the country, and in enlisting their support when implementing necessary but often painful changes. When the political pressure to deviate from the right story and the right policies became almost unbearable, Bob and Paul refused to buckle.

At a personal level, although I was exhausted by the unrelenting pressure and workload, I was grateful throughout for how well Bob had treated us staff members. He valued us — the advisers, steno-secretaries, personal assistants, drivers, and security personnel. Otherwise, we would not have been there. Never did he belittle a staff member for providing ill-considered advice or opinions. As would an advocate in a courtroom, Bob assessed competing arguments, and if the weight of argument suggested he should change his opinion, he did.

Most of all, Bob had a great sense of fun. While we were having a break, or when work was over for the day, it was time for play. The thrills and spills of betting on horses, the tales of woe, the sing-alongs with the travelling media on official overseas visits — all provided the levity to balance the grind of governing the country. Whether it was lawn bowls before Question Time at the Old Parliament House, cups of tea to chill for a while afterwards, or the buzzer summoning me into the PM's suite to listen to a mid-week horse race on which I had placed a bet at his instruction, the day's work was interspersed with periods of frivolity and hilarity. No histrionics, bad moods, or cutting remarks—just enormous respect for staff members, who returned it with devoted loyalty.

29

Alfalfa and recycled toilet paper

Before leaving Canberra, we had a picnic in a park with Kim Beazley, Mick Young, and veterans affairs minister Ben Humphreys. Through our friendship with Sally Loane, a Canberra journalist, we had come to know former Australian Wallabies captain Mark Loane, an ophthalmologist living in Brisbane. Mark persuaded us to look for a house near his apartment in the leafy suburb of St Lucia, which was close to the Queensland University campus where we could go running on Saturday afternoons. We bought an old-style Queenslander with a veranda and high ceilings in the adjacent suburb of Toowong.

My arrival as director-general of the Department of Environment and Heritage aroused great curiosity within the conservation movement, so we decided to throw a Christmas party for them as a way of introducing ourselves. As we were shopping for food, Cathy held up a handful of alfalfa, derisorily asking: 'They eat this, don't they?' During the party, a conservationist emerged from the bathroom, complaining we had not provided recycled toilet paper. The new chapter in our lives was to be as colourful as the last.

Environment minister Pat Comben, a British naturalist with greying hair, a beard, and a lisp, warmed to me, dubbing me 'Sir Humphrey', from the British television series *Yes, Prime Minister*. Pat and his wife were avid bird-watchers. At our first evening barbecue in their backyard, Pat pointed to a bird nestled in a tree. Offering me a hint, he asked: 'What sort of owl is that, Sir Humphrey?' More in hope than in wisdom, I speculated: 'A Hooty Hoot Owl?' By now, the environment minister and the Queensland conservation movement were becoming suspicious that I was not going to be Australia's David Attenborough.

Had they known of my attempts to protect baby Ben from a green tree snake—which I only later learned was harmless—at our new tropical home, their worst fears would have been confirmed. As Cathy, Ben, and I returned one steaming-hot afternoon to our Toowong Queenslander house and edged towards the carport beneath the back veranda, a snake measuring well over a metre slithered across the carport's concrete floor into a small, unweeded garden bed. The only useful plant in the tiny space was a pawpaw tree entangled with a vine climbing up to the plastic meshing that enclosed the veranda.

Worried about the snake emerging and biting Ben, I tried to frighten it out into the open with repeated thrusts of a pitchfork. Cathy watched from the veranda, cradling Ben, as I thrashed around in vain, certain that the snake had entered the dry grassy area and that it had not left it. 'I'll have to burn it out', I told Cathy, drawing on my experience of lighting fires and extinguishing them with Lance and Kimmy Meyers in the paddock behind our house at Baradine. Cathy didn't think this was such a good idea, especially on a blisteringly hot Queensland summer's day. 'The dead vine goes up the pawpaw tree and onto the plastic webbing', she observed. 'Don't you at least think you should get the hose?'

A sensible idea, I thought. I dragged a running hose onto the lawn next to where the action was to occur. Then I poured half a can of mower fuel into the garden bed. But I hadn't brought matches with me, so I fetched some from inside. When I returned to the garden bed, I threw in a lighted match, and it exploded in flames. The fire raced up the dead vine entwining the pawpaw tree, igniting a good many metres of the plastic webbing. Cathy retreated inside with Ben, rolling her eyes at her pyromaniacal husband, as I doused the fire with the handy hose I had at the ready. The venomous snake never emerged. I suspect it was long gone, wondering from afar what all the fuss was about.

Despite such transgressions, I took my day job very seriously. Wayne Goss had led Labor to victory in Queensland in 1989 after the party had spent 32 years in opposition. At just 38 years of age, he was a young and fit new premier, a sharp contrast with the ageing Sir Joh Bjelke-Petersen who had thrown a pall of corruption over the Sunshine State that, following revelations in an ABC *Four Corners* program of endemic police corruption, had been recast as the Moonlight State.

An inquiry headed by Tony Fitzgerald uncovered widespread corruption within the National Party government. Four ministers were jailed. Sir Joh himself was charged with perjury in relation to a $100,000 cash donation from a developer, but the trial resulted in a hung jury. Its foreman, Luke Shaw, who had vetoed a guilty verdict, was later found to be a member of the Young Nationals. Despite the controversy, no retrial was ordered, owing to Sir Joh's age.

Much of the Goss government's early energy was devoted to rebuilding the state's institutions. Pat Comben did not trust his department. Although it contained many professional officers, Pat thought years of National Party political appointees had compromised the department's integrity. He wanted a clean-out. My approach was to utilise the talents of officers in the best way possible, rather than dismissing them on suspicion. But, having come from a Labor prime minister's office, I was not trusted by certain sections of the department.

Bjelke-Petersen had demonstrated his lack of interest in the environment through his road-building activities in the Daintree rainforest. Environmentally sensitive crown land and leasehold land had been handed over to National Party supporters as private freehold. So, too, had valuable coastal areas. He actively opposed coal-mining companies spending money on mine-site rehabilitation; pollution controls were virtually non-existent; and the enforcement division within the department was chronically under-staffed and demoralised.

Goss had made a large number of pre-election environmental commitments. The area of Queensland devoted to national parks was to be doubled within three years, and a hierarchy of protected areas — some allowing controlled, limited uses such as tourism and grazing — was to be designed, legislated, and implemented. The state's first legislation to regulate pollution was to be written and enacted. Coastal-protection legislation was to be prepared. A management plan was to be developed for the Queensland wet tropical forests that the Hawke government had nominated to the World Heritage list. And the government would need to respond to an inquiry it had established into logging on Fraser Island, chaired by the same Tony Fitzgerald. It was an audaciously ambitious first-term agenda for a party that had not experienced government in more than three decades.

As we made progress on each of these tasks, requests flowed weekly from the premier's office for television stories depicting the premier in environmentally attractive settings. Working with Pat Comben's press secretary, who dubbed these weekly events 'hastily cobbled-together shams', we delivered, with unwavering regularity, brilliant television images of our environmentally sensitive premier.

But managing environmental issues in the frontier state did not always go to plan. Long before my appointment as director-general, the previous government had approved the establishment of an industrial-waste incinerator in suburban Brisbane. Included in the waste for incineration were body parts from amputations, together with bandages and other horrible medical waste. As a newly appointed departmental head from a southern state, I was not even aware of the existence of this waste facility, much less of its odious throughput.

Imagine my surprise, then, when the minister's media adviser informed me at around noon on a Friday that Queensland's daily newspaper, *The Courier-Mail*, had contacted her for comment on a departmental briefing note it had obtained describing the waste facility as belching toxic, carcinogenic smoke into the urban air, creating a serious health threat to the people of Brisbane.

It transpired that the brief was, in fact, a document prepared by a junior officer who had never passed it onto a superior in the department, but had decided to leak it to the Queensland Greens, who forwarded it onto the newspaper. Nevertheless, the shock revelation was being readied for a splash across the front page of the top-selling Saturday edition. The minister, his policy adviser (Damian McGreevy, who the minister had dubbed 'Bernard' from the *Yes, Prime Minister* TV series), his media adviser, and I were desperate, scrambling to contain the damage, mindful that premier Goss would not be impressed. That was until we received good news: there were unconfirmed reports that the Queen Mother had died.

'Hooray!' Bernard and I exclaimed to the minister and his media adviser. 'This will knock the incinerator story off the front page', the media adviser delightedly pronounced. Life was a cabaret again. Two hours later, the bad news came through: speculation about the Queen Mother's passing was wrong; she was in fine health.

'Bugger!' Bernard lamented. Through my years with Bob Hawke, I had learned that problems rarely turned out to be as disastrous as initially feared. Comforted by this knowledge, I rose early on Saturday to retrieve *The Courier-Mail* from our front lawn. Splashed across the front page was the banner headline: 'Brisbane's Wittenoom', a reference to the West Australian town near which asbestos had been mined, causing deadly mesothelioma. Defying all my experiences in the prime minister's office, this imaginatively hysterical front-page splash greatly exceeded my worst expectations. We never forgave the Queen Mother.

Of course, this was not to be the end of the matter. The National Party's environment spokesman, Doug Slack, referred me to the Criminal Justice Commission for my failure as director-general of the environment department to regulate the waste incinerator. He didn't refer the minister, just me. With my background as a Hawke adviser, the National Party obviously considered me fair game. After making an initial assessment, the commission cleared me of any wrongdoing.

Slack had previously referred me to the Criminal Justice Commission for allegedly using my office resources to establish a public-discussion series that I called 2020 Vision. With my co-convenor, Fleur Kingham, now president of the Queensland land court, and long-time partner of the then-premier's principal private secretary, David Barbagallo, we invited high-profile speakers to public forums at which they would present their visions for the year 2020. Speakers included Bob Hawke, Wayne Goss, deputy leader of the federal Liberal Party Michael Wooldridge, Peter Garrett, Rick Farley, and Malcolm Turnbull. Futuristic thinking, it seemed, was anathema to the Queensland Nationals. Certainly, Michael Wooldridge told me of the enormous pressure they had placed on him to withdraw from his forum—pressure he resisted.

The commission sought from me documents relating to the 2020 Vision series, then spent more than two months on the case before advising me informally that I was likely to be cleared. When I inquired as to when the letter clearing me might arrive, I was told it would be before Christmas. Each day leading up to Christmas, I waited for the letter. On the last working day before the break, I phoned the commission, to be told that the relevant officer had already gone on holidays. Upon my return to work, after a stressful holiday period, a letter clearing me of all allegations was sitting on my desk.

IN REFERRALS to the Criminal Justice Commission, I jagged the trifecta out of a totally innocuous phone call. On a Saturday morning on a summer's day, I received a phone call from Wayne Goss's media adviser, Dennis Atkins, who had been a friend since my days in Bob Hawke's office, when he was — and still is — a senior journalist in the press gallery. Atkins and David Barbagallo had been planning to visit Starcke Station, a property on Cape York that the government had decided to purchase and turn into a national park.

Barbagallo's brother was to transport them around the local area to identify a picturesque location for the premier's announcement of the Starcke purchase. Before Atkins and Barbagallo arrived at Cooktown, Barbagallo's brother and his party drove into the adjacent Cape Melville National Park, leaving his four-wheel-drive vehicle with two rifles in the back, and venturing along a dirt track. (It was against the law to take firearms into national parks.) Coming across the unoccupied vehicle, a park ranger confiscated it, leaving the passengers to walk out of the park. They had done so, before meeting up with Atkins and Barbagallo at Cooktown.

Barbagello and Atkins were heading to the Cooktown police station to report the confiscation of the vehicle when Atkins phoned me. He did not ask me for any help, instead seeking clarity on the powers of national park rangers to confiscate vehicles. I told the adviser I was unsure of the full powers of park rangers. That was the end of the conversation, other than Atkins saying he would phone me back to let me know how they went with the police.

Nevertheless, I thought I should be aware of what had transpired and of the powers of park rangers to seize vehicles, so I phoned the far-northern regional director of the National Parks and Wildlife Service to inquire about park rangers' powers. I made it clear that I was not seeking any assistance or intervention. The regional director had already been advised of the vehicle's confiscation, and was concerned that the National Parks and Wildlife Service was legally exposed, since park rangers had no power to confiscate vehicles and leave the occupants to make their way back to civilisation. He told me he had already begun making arrangements to assist Barbagallo's brother with alternative transport in order to minimise the department's legal liability.

Having finished at the police station, Atkins phoned me back to tell me that everything was under control and that they did not need any help. I phoned the regional director to tell him that the group had their own transport, and that no assistance was required. This, I thought, was the end of the matter.

However, based on the telephone call from Atkins asking about the legal powers of park rangers, the National Party, informed by the park ranger, made a formal complaint to the Criminal Justice Commission, attaching an anonymous letter that alleged 'corrupt intervention' on my part. The commission conducted a two-month initial assessment, followed by a full-blown commission of inquiry that lasted a further six months.

The National Party worked closely with a friendly journalist at *The Sunday Mail* (who was later appointed to a senior position in the incoming National Party government). Whenever it appeared that the commission of inquiry was running out of steam after finding no basis to the allegations, a fresh set of accusations appeared in *The Sunday Mail*, and the inquiry was extended. The ABC's *Four Corners* program devoted an entire episode to the alleged corrupt conspiracy.

Towards the end of the inquiry, the allegations became even more bizarre. We even made the pages of *Playboy* magazine. In a story titled 'Cape Fear', *Playboy* suggested we were part of a smuggling ring, illegally bringing guns and drugs from Papua New Guinea to sell on the Australian black market, while *The Sunday Mail* claimed we were involved in smuggling foxtail palm seeds from Cape Melville National Park. Apparently, these palm seeds fetched $2 each when sold to nurseries, since they spawned a species of palm tree that was especially decorative and durable. It was illegal to remove foxtail palm seeds from Cape Melville National Park, the only place where they grew in the wild.

One night, as I was lying in bed, trying to sleep, I was struck with fear. At the front of our house were several palm trees. By now, I had learned to identify the unique variety of palm whose seeds I had allegedly been smuggling, since its fronds did, indeed, resemble a fox's tail. I rushed out the front door, thanking my lucky stars that none of our palm trees was of the foxtail variety.

As *The Sunday Mail*'s centre-page spreads on the so-called 'Foxtail Palm Affair' continued to level fresh allegations, including that I had personally instructed the regional director to charter a plane to fly the premier's advisers out of the area, the Criminal Justice Commission called me to appear at a secret hearing, where I was to be interrogated under oath. The commission deemed this necessary, despite the lengthy recorded interviews I had done with commission officers.

The so-called 'star chamber' was a small, sterile room with pale, wooden walls and matching Spartan furniture. I sat at a bench with a microphone in front of me. Positioned at two benches diagonally across from me were the presiding commissioner and counsel assisting. This unusual positioning seemed designed to unnerve the witness; as I faced the commissioner to respond to his questions, the counsel assisting asked follow-up questions from the side, or made observations during the course of my answers. I could not look at both inquisitors at the same time.

At the hearings, the commissioner's line of questioning was reasonable, asking me what had happened and putting each of the allegations to me for a response. But when I produced a printed Telstra telephone bill, listing all the calls I had made that month to prove I had phoned the regional director only twice, at 8.34am and 9.36am, counsel assisting argued this proved nothing, since I could have left the house, gone to a public telephone booth, and made further calls to instruct the regional director to intervene, as had been alleged. The presiding commissioner asked me whether I was willing to hand over the telephone bill, which I gladly did. I explained that I had two witnesses to my phone calls, who would provide evidence if required.

Following the secret hearing, I rang the presiding commissioner. I said: 'You've had months to gather your evidence. I've got my witnesses, so let's go to court right now. The counsel assisting obviously thinks I'm guilty of something with his claim that I might have gone out to a public telephone booth to make improper phone calls.'

The commissioner said: 'We are not trying to fit you up. We have an obligation to deal with all the allegations. Otherwise, the inquiry will not be seen to have been complete.'

I countered: 'The allegations will keep coming through *The Sunday Mail*. As soon as you follow up and dismiss one, another will be made, just to keep the inquiry going. I want to go to court.'

The commissioner said it was in everyone's interests that each allegation be thoroughly investigated. That night, when I got home, I punched a hole through the plasterboard wall. The protracted inquiry process taught me two valuable lessons.

First, I found I could handle each twist and turn in the saga, but not knowing when it would end had a corrosive effect on my ability to cope. Much later, I advised a parliamentary colleague and friend, Craig Thompson, when allegations of impropriety were being made against him, to prepare to enter a dark tunnel whose length he would not know. He needed to condition himself to the inevitability that the process would be protracted and that it would be in the interests of his accusers to draw it out for as long as possible. My decision to support Craig, arguing that he should not be judged by the opposition or the parliament but by a court of law, was based on my experience with the Criminal Justice Commission.

My second lesson was that, when allegations are made against you, the phone falls silent. Week after week, Cathy and I received no phone calls from friends. Only a couple stuck with us by coming to visit. Our friends no doubt assumed our phone was being tapped, and they were probably right. From this lesson, I have made it a practice when a friend or colleague is in trouble, either through allegations against them or for a gaffe they might have made, to visit them or at least phone or text them to offer support.

Ten months after the two phone calls to me from the premier's media adviser, the Criminal Justice Commission released its 337-page *Report of An Investigation Into the Cape Melville Incident*. It found no criminality or official misconduct by any of us, concluding that the allegations of a conspiracy or improper interference were 'entirely without foundation'. It went so far as to point out that this was the third unsubstantiated allegation against me. Based on the National Party's track record of trying to destroy my reputation, the report recommended that legislation be enacted to make it a criminal offence to circulate to the media referrals of public officials to the commission before giving it an opportunity to conduct an initial assessment of their veracity.

In settlement of a defamation action I had initiated against *The Sunday Mail*, the newspaper's editor offered to print a story written by me but published under my journalistic tormentor's by-line. It was a very well-written piece reporting on my exoneration by the Criminal Justice Commission.

AS THESE VARIOUS Criminal Justice Commission investigations into National Party allegations against me took their meandering course, I tried to concentrate on implementing the Goss government's environmental agenda. A colleague and friend, Ross Rolfe, the director of the National Parks and Wildlife Service, worked with me on establishing a Cape York Wilderness Zone. Our plan was to purchase large pastoral leases on Cape York, combine them with existing national parks, including Starcke, and develop a land-use plan that protected the region's environmental values while allowing Aboriginal usage for tourism and cattle-raising in agreed areas. We worked closely with the Cape York Land Council's Noel Pearson, and made good progress.

Our plan reached a crucial stage that required Ross and me to charter a plane to Coen on Cape York, where we met with representatives of the various Aboriginal groups that claimed a traditional connection to the land. Before taking the flight, we had advised premier Goss that we were close to reaching agreement. But the meeting at Coen was not going well. A white legal adviser had been urging the traditional owners to reject our proposal, warning that we were not to be trusted. They weren't saying no; they just weren't saying anything.

I could sense a looming disaster if we returned to Brisbane to advise the premier that the negotiations had stalled. We joined the group sitting just 20 metres away from us, whereupon an amazing turn of events followed: the men delegated the decision to a group of women elders. Now we were talking. We quickly reached agreement, and headed for our chartered plane. As we drove towards the airstrip, I asked Ross whether we should wait for Noel Pearson and his colleagues, who had asked me for a lift back to Cairns. Ross said Noel had told him to go on ahead.

'But didn't Noel mean he would come a little later and join us on board?', I asked.

Ross reassured me: 'No, they must have their own chartered plane coming to pick them up later.'

I pressed: 'Are you sure? I think Noel just meant to wait a half an hour or so for them to join us.'

'No, no. He's happy for us to go ahead.'

We took off in the chartered flight with several empty seats and travelled back to Cairns, where we had agreed to meet Noel and friends for dinner. The evening wore on with no sign of Noel. Abandoning the idea of dinner, we waited at our hotel. Eventually, a distraught Noel Pearson arrived, looking rather ill.

'Why didn't you fellas wait for us?' he asked.

Noel explained that they had arrived at the airport, to be told that we had flown back to Cairns. They had not arranged a flight, but hurriedly did so. By the time it arrived from Cairns, a nasty tropical thunderstorm had developed. Their tiny four-seater was tossed savagely in the turbulence as lightning flashed and the skies opened. We could have lost the Cape York Wilderness Zone that night, but Noel took the misunderstanding in remarkably good humour.

As the 1995 state election approached, Goss decided to make the Cape York Wilderness Zone the first announcement of the election campaign. He sent us a message that in the draft policy document we were to state that if the pastoralists refused to sell their land, the government would compulsorily acquire it. Ross and I considered this unnecessarily provocative, since the pastoralists had already agreed to sell the land to the department, but we reluctantly added the statement. Immediately following the calling of the election, Goss took a flight to Cape York to announce the Wilderness Zone. The reaction was swift and boisterous. Landowners and residents of Cape York rose up in protest at the threat of compulsory acquisition.

At the election, the Goss government went within one seat of losing government. But, as if this wasn't bad enough, a court challenge to the result in the Townsville-based seat of Mundingburra, which Labor had retained by a handful of votes, resulted in the court directing a re-election for that seat. By that time, I had completed five years as director-general of the environment department, and Goss had asked me to establish and head the South East Queensland Transit Authority to plan for the region's transport needs. Having done that, I telephoned Goss and offered to join his personal staff, soon working on the Mundingburra campaign.

In what was to become known as 'the long, hot summer of

Mundingburra', I encouraged the conservation movement, with which
Labor had a good relationship, to work against the Queensland Greens,
whose leader, Drew Hutton, had formed an alliance with the National
Party. The conservationists agreed, campaigning for a vote for Labor
ahead of the Greens candidate. But it wasn't enough, and Labor lost the
re-election and government to the Nationals, who scrapped the Cape
York Wilderness Zone.

Following his resignation from state parliament, Goss described
his government's acquisition of two large Cape York properties for
dedication as national parks—Starcke and Silver Plains—as among
his finest achievements. If the Queensland Greens had not supported
the National Party in key seats, he could have added the Cape York
Wilderness Zone to the list.

By the time I left the environment department, we had indeed
doubled the area of national parks in Queensland; stopped logging on
Fraser Island and secured its nomination to the World Heritage List;
added to the World Heritage List the Queensland section of what is
now known as the Gondwana Rainforests of Australia, straddling the
border with New South Wales; put in place a management plan for the
Wet Tropics of Queensland World Heritage Area; ended all native-
forest logging in Queensland; established a hierarchy of conservation
areas; and enacted the state's first effective anti-pollution legislation.

30

Struggle against the machine

Cathy and I married in 1991. Family, friends, and our toddler son, Ben, joined Labor luminaries, including Bob Hawke, Kim Beazley, and Mick Young, at a reception in Bungendore outside Canberra. But we struggled to gain acceptance from a closed political system in Queensland.

A tight group — led by Wayne Goss, his chief of staff, Kevin Rudd, ALP campaign director Wayne Swan, and Australian Workers' Union secretary Bill Ludwig — effectively decided who would advance through the party ranks and who would not. I had asked Hawke to have a word with Ludwig, which he did. Bob identified me as a future Labor leader, and asked Ludwig to support me in my ambitions for a federal seat.

Having been pivotal to my appointment as director-general of the environment department, Rudd and I became close family friends, visiting each other's homes regularly. Cathy obtained a job in the newly created cabinet office, reporting to Rudd, who had shifted from Goss's personal staff to take up the position of director-general. As a trained economist and a policy adviser to cabinet ministers Mick Young and Kim Beazley, Cathy won the position on her own merits, despite National Party efforts to smear her under parliamentary privilege as having received favoured treatment by virtue of being married to me.

As we got to know other party members and factional players, some offered to support my federal ambitions. Soon, rumours began circulating about the intention of the minister for veterans' affairs, Ben Humphreys, to resign from parliament. My supporters had some influence in ALP branches within Humphreys' seat of Griffith, but it was also the seat in which Rudd lived. He had confided in me his interest in a political career in Canberra, while maintaining a public position that he remained interested in returning to the Department of Foreign Affairs and Trade, from which he had been seconded into Goss's office.

Nevertheless, I phoned Humphreys to ask about the possibility of him supporting me as his successor. Humphreys said I should talk to Wayne Swan. Since Swan had already told me that Rudd was his top priority for a move to federal parliament, I met with my supporters, who were keen to press on, thanked them, and told them I was withdrawing my interest.

Word had obviously gotten back to Rudd about my inquiry. Our friendship ended at that moment, and he declared me *persona non grata* to factional organisers who worked for him in the cabinet office and in ministerial offices. One especially vicious group began sending anonymous faxes to *The Sunday Mail* journalist who had run the foxtail palm campaign against Goss's staff and me, alleging all sorts of scandalous behaviour on my part. Following the journalist's experience with that saga, and in light of the anonymity of the authors of faxes, she never wrote a story about them. I knew my adversaries well. They pretended to be supporters, but one of their group had fallen out with them and informed me in quintessential Queensland ALP vernacular that Rudd's people were 'rat-fucking' me. It felt like it, too, though we maintained pleasantries.

If I had been wiser and more patient, I would not have made the telephone call to Ben Humphreys. Rudd never forgot it and was bent on revenge, so much so that he stored it up for use in a spiteful conversation with me 15 years later when, as prime minister, he was advising me of my position as the last member of his first ministry.

Bill Ludwig, however, remained a firm supporter, and we became close friends, sharing Christmas holidays on the Gold Coast with Bill's son, Joseph, his daughter, Carmen, and our families. Queensland's population growth continued to outpace that of the other states, creating the inevitability of a new federal seat, with most analysts predicting it would be located on Brisbane's southern outskirts. Ludwig advised Cathy and me to move there from our Queenslander house in Toowong. We bought a house in the young, expanding suburb of Calamvale.

Here we were gifted our second miracle, a boy we named Thomas. He arrived as a ball of muscle, arms waving and fists clenched, seemingly protesting about not being consulted over the timing of leaving his mother's womb. Tom was pure blonde and, belying first impressions, he was a contented boy with a wonderfully placid disposition, a great friend and companion to his older brother, Ben. As little boys, they played in the mud that passed for our lawn during the daily summer Queensland tropical downpours, and were horrified as they grabbed cane toads from the pool filter box in the descending darkness, mistaken in their belief that they were rescuing their missing pet guinea pigs.

AS A RELATIVE NEWCOMER to Queensland, I would need to meet and persuade, one by one, several hundred ALP branch members, whom I did not know, to support my candidacy. This involved learning about them, helping them when they needed help—whether in their working or personal lives, in disputes with their neighbours about overhanging tree branches, or in arguments with each other over their own political ambitions—conducting street stalls each Saturday for ALP state and local government candidates, hand-delivering thousands of pamphlets into suburban letterboxes, and sweeping floors after fundraising events.

Any hope that I could rely on my four years as an adviser to Bob Hawke as a selling point was quickly dashed when a couple of supportive, hard-headed local ALP members reviewed an introductory letter I had drafted. My draft ran for two pages. Those wily locals put red lines through most of it, including references to my prime ministerial adviser's role. The redraft said, up front, that some day I would like to win preselection for a federal seat, but, in the meantime, I was keen to listen to their opinions and learn of their problems, and wanted to work to help local branch members and candidates. It is said that all politics is local. My redrafted, half-page letter was a testament to this truth.

Having visited branch members at their party meetings and in their homes for several years in an area spanning three existing federal electorates, I was surprised when the electoral commission defied the pundits and created the new Queensland seat on the Sunshine Coast, north of Brisbane. The assessment of Ludwig and local supporters was that I might have had sufficient votes to successfully challenge the sitting Member of Parliament for the south-side seat of Forde. But this was at the height of the affirmative-action debate within the Australian Labor Party, and it would not have been a good look for me to challenge one of the party's few female MPs. We quickly abandoned the idea, and Cathy supported the alternative option of me travelling regularly to the Sunshine Coast to make myself known to ALP members in the new seat of Longman.

The branch members were concentrated on Bribie Island. Through frequent visits, and with the backing of the local female state MP, I gained strong support for preselection as the Labor candidate for the seat. But Wayne Swan was in favour of his electorate secretary, a woman, who had not been visiting local branch members. I was asked to withdraw from the contest, which I reluctantly did. It turned out to be just as well—the Liberals won Longman at the 1996 election with a margin of 10 per cent. It was back to working with branch members in our local area for a tilt at preselection for the following federal election.

Out of work, with Cathy at home, too, I formed a small business with a friend and colleague from Goss's office, Raymond Garrand. We each contributed $1,000 towards the partnership, registering our business as Eco Managers, designing and purchasing letterhead and business cards, and acquiring a personal computer and a laptop. We won contracts with Korea Zinc, which was establishing a zinc refinery in Townsville, talked seven national and multinational gas companies into establishing and funding a Queensland Gas Industry Taskforce, which, of course, we would advise, and participated in a team bidding for a gas pipeline that was for sale. We adopted the practice of keeping overheads to a minimum so that if we were not making money, we were not losing it either.

As the High Court brought its hearings into the Wik native-title case to a close, I noticed a report in a small news item that one of the judges had asked why native title could not coexist with private ownership if the use of the land had not effectively precluded some traditional practices, such as hunting. All the official advice and most of the private legal opinion was that private ownership automatically extinguished native title, and that the Wik case would fail.

Based on my chance reading of that newspaper story, which also suggested the High Court's judgement would be brought down in December 1996, I proposed to Raymond that we ask a legal-counsel friend to be ready to write a summary of the judgement and what it meant for corporations if, by chance, the legal experts were wrong. We reasoned that if the High Court ruled in favour of the Wik people, major corporations would be scrambling for advice to their CEOs and boards just as their companies began closing down for Christmas. The High Court brought down its decision two days before Christmas, ruling that, in particular circumstances, native title was not extinguished by private ownership. We had our legal counsel's four-page brief within a day. We set a price of $200 for a copy of the brief, and faxed just about every major corporation in Australia. We made enough money to pay for our Christmas vacations with our families, and had some left over.

By the time of my preselection, Eco Managers had developed a reputation for expertise in the energy sector and in environmental management. Clients were rolling in. While it was sad to leave the company, the experience of running a small business, including the need in the early days to raid the coin jar at home for lunch money, later helped me in my appointment as minister for small business after the 2007 election.

It was while we were running our small business that our third miracle arrived. On my only weekend home from 'the long, hot summer of Mundingburra' in January 1996, Cathy fell pregnant. In October, our gorgeous daughter, Laura, was born. A friend told me we would be having a girl with my Celtic colouring, that she would be my 'brown-eyed girl'. Baby Laura was, indeed, my brown-eyed girl and, as she grew up, we learned to sing Van Morrison's classic together.

CATHY AND I enjoyed many wonderful times with our growing family and with each other, catching tadpoles and throwing boomerangs in a nearby park, acquiring a clinically insane Jack Russell puppy named Chester, holidaying at the beach, and visiting the children's grandparents in Canberra and my home town of Baradine. But the pursuit of a parliamentary career ensured my mind was never very far away from politics. Indeed, within days of Laura's birth, an organiser from the right-wing grouping within the Labor Party, of which we were members, approached Cathy. A decision had been made by the ALP state conference to add a women's delegate to its numbers. The vote was shaping up to be extremely tight, and our group's candidate would need every vote she could get.

Cathy was still in hospital with Laura, recovering from her caesarean operation. The candidate was a close friend of Cathy's. I drove Cathy to the venue for the stand-up ballot, piloting the trolley supporting the intravenous drip as Cathy walked from the car to the queue of women waiting to vote. As they saw Cathy lining up, the women vacated the queue. Cathy voted, and returned immediately to the hospital. Her friend won by one vote.

During the new term of parliament, another redistribution of Queensland's electorates was likely, because the state's continuing strong population growth had created bulging disparities in the sizes of various seats.

An opportunity looked like it might open up for me when the sitting Labor Member for Rankin announced he would not recontest the seat at the next election. But when Wayne Goss publicly indicated his interest in the seat, it looked like curtains for my parliamentary ambitions.

I concluded that if I withdrew, I would not get another chance, so I decided to make my intentions known. I announced that I, too, would be a preselection candidate for the seat of Rankin, pitting myself against the much-loved former premier who had led Labor from the wilderness to government just eight years prior. Mutual friends demanded that I withdraw from the contest, branding me disrespectful for standing in the way of Goss's transition from state to federal parliament, where he was being touted as a future leader. Although I had good support in the local branches, so did Goss, since his former state seat of Logan was wholly within the federal seat of Rankin.

When the results of the redistribution were announced, again, despite the pundits' predictions, the new seat was drawn not on the south side, but west of Brisbane, adjacent to the city of Ipswich. Although Pauline Hanson had won the Ipswich-based seat of Oxley at the 1996 election, it was with the word 'Liberal' beside her name on the ballot paper. Despite being dumped by the Liberal Party for her racist pronouncements during the 1996 election campaign, the decision came too late for fresh ballot papers to be issued, which would have identified Hanson as an independent candidate.

I visited Ipswich in the days following the release of the new boundaries, willing to take on Hanson at the election. Again, Cathy supported my new proposal to contest Labor Party preselection for the seat, which, if I were successful, would involve us moving to Ipswich. While this would require a lot of fast work getting to know the local ALP members, there was no obvious Labor candidate for the seat.

Since a central panel of the Labor Party was empowered with 50 per cent of the preselection vote, I asked Bill Ludwig for a meeting. He told me to come to his city office on a Saturday afternoon. I took along a folder of documents and a set of arguments supporting my case for being preselected for the seat of Oxley. It being a Saturday, just the two of us were in the building. Ludwig, as usual, sat behind his desk and I, as usual, sat in one of the chairs facing him. *This is it*, I thought. *My effort here will determine whether or not I have a political future.*

I opened my folder containing positive statements Bob Hawke had made about me, Paul Keating's farewell letter to me, and a photo of my Dad as an ex-serviceman. As I began my well-rehearsed presentation, Ludwig stopped me in my tracks. With both thumbs in the air, Ludwig said: 'You're my union's candidate for Rankin.' I was astonished. While I still needed to win a rank-and-file ballot for the other 50 per cent of the vote, I would compete in the race for Rankin with the support of the powerful Australian Workers' Union.

'What about Wayne?' I asked, knowing Goss intended to nominate for Rankin.

Ludwig explained bluntly: 'You can't beat Pauline Hanson, but Goss can.'

'Will you explain to Wayne?' I asked.

Ludwig said he would arrange for the state secretary of the Labor Party to talk to Goss in the next couple of days. 'You don't need to say anything', he said.

I told only Cathy of this shock development. As the week wore on, the state member for the seat of Woodridge that was located wholly within the redrawn federal seat of Rankin demanded that I publicly announce my intention to contest the Rankin preselection. He was a mortal enemy of Goss's, but a close friend of Ludwig's. On Thursday, I arranged to see Goss. Again, it was just the two of us. We made a cup of tea as I prepared to explain the reasoning behind Ludwig's decision to support me for Rankin and Goss for Oxley. As I started my explanation, Goss interrupted: 'Are you telling me you're the AWU's candidate for Rankin?'

'Yes', I replied, realising at that moment that no one had advised him of Ludwig's decision. Ludwig had not relayed his decision to the ALP state secretary. We awkwardly finished our tea, and agreed that neither of us would make a public statement. The next day, the state member for Woodridge contacted me again. He was clearly aware of Ludwig's support for me. He demanded that I clarify my intentions to him: was I running or not? I confirmed I was running. He promptly leaked the news to *The Courier-Mail*, which broke the story that Goss would not have a smooth pathway to Canberra, since his former adviser, Craig Emerson, was contesting the Rankin preselection.

For several weeks, *The Courier-Mail* ran stories about the contest between Goss and me, quoting 'the Emerson camp' and 'the Goss camp'. The journalists phoned me when seeking information from 'the Emerson camp', and I suspected the member for Woodridge was a source, too, since the stories claimed I had strong support within the branches that he and his allies controlled. But who were in the Goss camp? A close confidant of Kevin Rudd's told me he had first-hand knowledge that Rudd was the anonymous spokesman for 'the Goss camp'.

Under the new boundaries, the seat of Oxley had been extended to within one kilometre of Goss's home. Goss announced his interest in nominating for Oxley, but he was diagnosed with a brain tumour shortly thereafter. After some years, we spoke again, but the friendship was never restored.

The remainder of my pathway to preselection was anything but smooth. Women were encouraged to contest the Rankin preselection under the ALP's affirmative-action program, especially since men, including Swan and Rudd, were assured of preselection in other winnable seats. Three women ran against me, urging branch members to support them because they were women. Ludwig told me I needed to win the rank-and-file preselection well, since he was under pressure from within the central panel to support a female candidate. Ludwig had gotten me to the starting gate, but I had to win the race by the length of the straight.

I had been working in the branches for five years, and branch members, especially women, resented being told they had an obligation to vote for a woman. In the end, I gained 75 per cent of the rank-and-file vote. Since Rankin was one of only two seats that Labor had retained following the 1996 electoral wipeout, I was, in all likelihood, headed for Canberra.

Ludwig later wanted my guts for garters for voting for Simon Crean in a leadership challenge by Kim Beazley. While we fell out spectacularly at that time over my support for the leader, the truth is that I would not have been able to contest the preselection for Rankin without Ludwig's backing. But even at this very early stage of my political career, I was accumulating enemies from within my own party, just for seeking preselection. Many more were to join them.

31

Back to Canberra

My return to Canberra was as an elected representative, but all my memories and experiences were as a staffer working for Bob Hawke. Although I was now 44 years of age, my overwhelming sense was that I had graduated from being a fresh-faced ministerial adviser to being the parliamentary representative of 80,000 people with their own needs, anxieties, and aspirations. It was at this time that I looked upon democracy with awe. What an amazing system.

At our induction, the parliamentary officials allowed us to walk past the advisers' box in the House of Representatives and onto the green carpet, a stroll that was strictly forbidden for anyone other than MPs and attendants. At first, I found it unnerving crossing that imaginary line. The chief opposition whip, Leo Macleay, allocated Kevin Rudd and me favoured rooms—a signal, he told me, of the high hopes the leadership of the parliamentary Labor Party had for us. Opposition leader Kim Beazley and shadow treasurer Simon Crean knew me well from the Hawke days, and gave me every encouragement to progress through the ranks.

As newcomers, Rudd and I could not yet occupy opposition frontbench positions; we needed to earn our stripes. The appropriate launching pad for our parliamentary careers would be as chairs of the relevant caucus committees: in Rudd's case, the foreign affairs committee; in mine, the economics committee. Competition for these positions was intense. The left faction had nominated as its candidate for chair of the economics committee the same backbencher whose protectionist views I had criticised to Bob Hawke's delight, just before joining his office. There was competition, too, within my own right faction for the position. Then, as if by magic, the left relinquished its claim to the position, the other candidate from the right withdrew after being informed I had majority support, and I was elected unopposed. Beazley had quietly made his support for my chairmanship of the committee known to factional leaders, and they made it happen.

Since the 1998 election had been fought over the introduction of a goods and services tax (GST), Labor set itself on a course through the Senate-inquiry processes of demonstrating the unfairness of the tax and the dubiousness of its purported economic benefits. As an active opponent of the GST when the Hawke government had considered it in 1985, I was well versed in the arguments for and against the tax. Most engaged among the group of backbenchers appointed to work with Crean and my recruiter to the ALP, senator Stephen Conroy (then a shadow minister, who was to chair the Senate inquiry), were Julia Gillard and a fellow economist, David Cox, whom I'd met many years earlier when Peter Walsh had unsuccessfully tried to convince Cox's then boss, the South Australian minister for minerals and energy, of the merits of the Resource Rent Tax.

In the House of Representatives, I gave almost 100 speeches on the GST, seeking to hone my speaking skills by relying progressively less on notes and more on ad-libbing. After around the 50th speech railing against the complexity and unfairness of the GST, I began sounding repetitious. It occurred to me that a little theatre might be useful. The standing orders governing the conduct of debate in the House permitted the limited use of props to illustrate a debating point.

Under the so-called 'new tax system for a new century', fresh milk for human consumption was to be GST-free, but milk for consumption by pets would attract the GST. So I took into the House a cardboard cutout of a cat, a glass, a saucer, and a cup of milk. During my speech, I poured some of the milk into a glass and drank it GST-free, then poured the remainder into the saucer for my cardboard cat, and challenged the taxman to tax me on the portion of the milk I had purchased for my kitty. The ever-combative Mark Latham, who I later supported for the party leadership, was unamused by my performance, dubbing me 'Catman'.

Undeterred by Latham's derision, I mocked treasurer Costello's claim that the GST was a 'streamlined new tax system' by taking into the House copies of the legislation and regulations, which measured more than a metre in height, together with a set of scales, which the documents tipped at 7.3 kilograms. Simon Crean got into the act, bringing into Question Time mixed salads, teddy bears, children's pyjamas, and any other prop that might illustrate the GST's complexity. I worked with Crean's advisers — chief of staff Phil Tardif and economic adviser Chris Fry — on each stunt, to the point where we named ourselves *Stunts 'R' Us*. After delivering some of my more colourful speeches, I wrote a media release that Crean's office distributed to both the press gallery and to caucus members. When Latham finally worked out how to use emails, he sent one to Crean's office with an instruction that he be removed from the distribution list for 'Emerson's infantile stunts'.

At the height of the GST debate, Kim Beazley needed to miss Question Time in order to deliver a speech to the national congress of the Australian Council of Trade Unions. In his absence, for the discussion on a Matters of Public Importance immediately following Question Time, Beazley instructed chief opposition whip Macleay to arrange for me to move the motion triggering the debate and speak to it, and for Rudd to second the motion and speak after me. Macleay phoned me to arrange the paperwork for submission to the Speaker. Macleay then phoned Rudd, who asked whether he was to move the motion or second it. Macleay told Rudd he would be seconding it. Rudd said he wanted time to consider it. Macleay said that was fine, but Rudd couldn't assume he would ever be put on the speaking list again. Rudd seconded it.

LACHLAN MURDOCH, son of media mogul Rupert, invited Kim Beazley to bring his most promising backbenchers to dinner at his Sydney harbourside residence. Beazley chose Tanya Plibersek, Julia Gillard, Nicola Roxon, and me. Along with shadow communications minister Stephen Smith, who had portfolio responsibility for media policy, we boarded a VIP aircraft to accompany Beazley for a convivial night with Murdoch and his wife, Sarah. Rudd complained bitterly to Beazley about not being included.

As I walked along the corridor from the caucus room with Beazley one day in late 1999, he asked me to come into his office. He closed the doors and said: 'Mate, when we win the election, I'll serve a term and then, a year or so into the next term, I'll hand over to you. You're a younger version of Tony Blair.' As an ambitious political novice, I wanted to hear what I heard and, as an experienced politician, Beazley no doubt told me what he thought I wanted to hear. Of course, I was delighted, and thanked Beazley profusely for his confidence in me.

On the other hand, despite the two of us sharing the same Labor values, my relationship with Wayne Swan had never been warm. But at a dinner for members of the right faction in Canberra's Civic Centre, ahead of the resumption of parliament in February 2001, we seemed to get on well. Could this be a fresh start? At that time, the successor organisation to Queensland's Criminal Justice Commission had established a commission of inquiry into the practice within the Queensland branch of the Labor Party of falsely enrolling members in order to maximise votes in internal party ballots. False enrolment is a crime.

While the independent commission of inquiry was underway in Queensland, the Liberal government in Canberra decided to take full political advantage by establishing its own parliamentary inquiry. Its chair was a South Australian backbencher, Christopher Pyne. By now, two of the factional organisers who had been close to both Bill Ludwig and Kevin Rudd—one of them having been employed as Rudd's personal assistant in the cabinet office—had fallen out with the party, and were cooperating with Pyne's inquiry. Pyne asked one of them under parliamentary privilege whether, as the Member for Rankin, I would have benefited from false enrolments in the state seat of Springwood. 'Yes', the witness replied, I could have so benefited.

That night, I was mentioned on ABC television as a possible beneficiary of alleged criminal behaviour. Pyne and his star witness had clearly rehearsed the evidence ahead of the exchange at the day's hearings, since Pyne would not have known where the Queensland state seat of Springwood was located, and the witness had obviously told him it was within my seat of Rankin. It was not; it was wholly located in an adjacent Liberal-held seat.

Swan and I adjourned to the Canberra bar favoured at the time by parliamentarians and staff members from both sides of politics, the Holy Grail. To our delight, one of the patrons that night was Pyne. Cordially at first, I pointed out to Pyne that the seat of Springwood was not in Rankin, and that he had conspired with his star witness to smear me under parliamentary privilege. Pyne replied by inviting me to appear before his inquiry, where I could argue my case. I told him there was no case to argue; it was not a matter of opinion, but of fact, that the state seat of Springwood was wholly outside the boundaries of Rankin.

Realising that Pyne was not interested in correcting the record and had no misgivings about using parliamentary privilege to impugn my reputation, I called him a 'slimy Liberal cu*t'. He asked me to repeat my statement. I did. Then he called over several Liberal staffers. Again, Pyne invited me to repeat my statement. I did. An amused Swan was within earshot and joined the conversation, advising Pyne: 'What comes around goes around.'

A little worse for wear, we turned up for Question Time at 2.00pm the following afternoon. To a packed House, Pyne made a statement urging the Speaker to refer Swan and me to the parliamentary privileges committee for seeking to intimidate him as chair of a parliamentary committee. Amid the following uproar, one of our shadow ministers and a St Patrick's College old boy, Martin Ferguson, was ejected from the House for describing Pyne as a 'poonce', causing the press gallery to consult the Macquarie Dictionary. The allegations led the evening television news bulletins, photographs of the Holy Grail were splashed across the front pages of the next morning's newspapers, and the Speaker requested from the Holy Grail's proprietor any closed-circuit television footage of the exchange.

In his office, the Speaker explained to me that he needed to investigate the claims thoroughly, but didn't think there was anything to the allegations that would breach parliamentary rules. Disturbingly, although he was under no obligation to do so, the Holy Grail's proprietor supplied the footage to the Speaker. Unsurprisingly, the footage recorded general bar-room din, but no individual conversations. It certainly did not show me shoulder-charging Pyne, though I must admit, from my days as a rugby league forward, that the thought had crossed my muddled mind.

I was exonerated, but not before Kim Beazley told Bob Hawke that anyone who aspired to be on the frontbench should not go to the Holy Grail. I did not consider it prudent to tell Beazley that, by this test, he would struggle to fill even ten of the 30 shadow ministry positions.

AS PARLIAMENT MOVED through an election year, I had a sense of foreboding that promising to roll back the GST and to block the proposed partial sale of the government-owned telecommunications giant, Telstra, would not be sufficient for Labor to win government. Yet Labor had won a by-election in the affluent Brisbane seat of Ryan with a huge swing of 10 per cent, small business was complaining angrily about the GST paperwork burden, and petrol prices were soaring. Simon Crean, senator Peter 'Cookie' Cook, and I agreed to form a petrol-price task force as a campaigning vehicle. Although it had wide membership, Julia Gillard and I did most of the work and all the report-writing.

In a second by-election, in the Victorian seat of Aston, the Liberals campaigned hard and hung on, limiting the swing to less than 6 per cent. This gave Howard and the Coalition heart. Bob Hawke invited me to dinner at his house in August, where he expressed his confidence that Labor was about to form government. Standing in the kitchen, I said: 'I don't think so, Bob.'

'What do you mean?' he asked.

'Look at Labor's primary vote. It has been falling for months. People are signalling they are going to vote Democrat as a protest about the sale of Telstra. They should be coming directly to us, but they're not.'

That trend continued until one of Howard's ministers, Ian Macfarlane, arranged a fundraising function in Toowoomba in his electorate, with treasurer Peter Costello as guest of honour. Disgruntled branch members began leaking documents to a conduit to me that revealed the Queensland branch of the Liberal Party had instructed Macfarlane's local branch to prepare its GST returns in such a manner as to avoid paying GST. In attacking the arrangement, we argued in parliament that the government expected everyday Australians to pay the GST, but did not consider that the Liberal Party had an obligation to do so.

Day after day, Beazley and Crean—and, sometimes, I from the

backbench — attacked the government and Macfarlane over the scandal. Documents continued to arrive. It was getting to the point where members of the press gallery were calling on Howard to sack his minister.

While Macfarlane was on the ropes, a Norwegian freighter named *Tampa* responded to a mayday call from Australian authorities to rescue more than 400 asylum-seekers from a distressed Indonesian fishing boat. The Howard government instructed the captain of the *Tampa* not to enter Australian waters. When he defied these instructions, Howard ordered Australian troops to board the vessel. A standoff developed between the troops and the *Tampa*'s captain, who refused to leave Australian waters. In response, the government rushed a bill into the parliament empowering it to remove the *Tampa* forcibly from Australian waters. A section of the bill prevented any criminal proceedings from being launched against any Australian official for removing the *Tampa* or for returning asylum-seekers to it. They would be legally free to engage in otherwise criminal conduct, including assault and even murder.

The Australian public, encouraged by Liberal and National Party politicians, regarded asylum-seekers with great suspicion. Obviously, the Howard government was counting on the Labor caucus rejecting the odious provision. Along with many colleagues, I spoke against it at the caucus meeting, becoming teary during my remarks, since I knew we were about to make a decision that would cost us the election but which, as a party with a moral conscience, we were obliged to make. When I sat down, Julia, who also opposed the bill, sympathetically said: 'You're an emotional little critter, Emmo.' Yes, I was emotional, and I was proud of my party.

As predicted, the Australian people erupted with anger when they heard the Coalition claims that Labor was threatening national security. Government MP Peter Slipper appeared on the news bulletins at the doors of Parliament House with the politically deadly accusation: 'Labor MPs are traitors to their country.' Not one Coalition MP expressed any concerns about the fascist provision in the legislation, and my expectations about the public reaction were fulfilled when I returned to Queensland that weekend.

On the streets and in the main shopping centre at Woodridge, the electorate's poorest suburb, but host to a large multicultural community, one local resident after another told me that Labor was a disgrace. A Labor-supporting woman on the footpath outside my office typified the local reaction. When I tried to explain Labor's position, she put her hand up towards my face and said: 'No, I don't want to hear your excuses', and walked away.

In subsequent discussions with the government, the Labor leadership was able to secure the removal of the offending provision. Labor agreed to pass the amended bill, but, of course, the left in the community, including many ALP members, then accused Labor of racism and of a lack of empathy with asylum-seekers.

Just before the election campaign, a stricken Indonesian wooden vessel carrying asylum-seekers sank north of Christmas Island. Howard and his ministers accused the asylum-seekers of having endangered their children's lives by scuttling the vessel and throwing their children overboard, obliging the navy to rescue them. The government produced photographs that it claimed proved asylum-seekers had deliberately thrown their children into the water, using the pretence to great political advantage. When grainy photographs emerged in the dying days of the election campaign showing asylum-seekers had not, in fact, done so, the public was reminded of Labor's unpopular position on the border-protection bill.

As I had predicted, Labor was smashed in the election. The left, right, and centre of the Australian community condemned Labor for its position on the *Tampa* legislation, each for entirely different reasons, but it is not clear how we could have handled it differently if we wished to remain a party of conscience and morality. Only after the election did the government admit what it had known beforehand—that asylum-seekers had not thrown their children into the water.

32

Five fresh faces

During the election campaign, Simon Crean suggested he and I meet at a Brisbane café on his next visit to Queensland. If Labor lost the election, it was widely anticipated that Beazley would stand down, vacating the leadership for Crean. We discussed the case for generational change. The Beazley shadow ministry contained many ministers from the Keating government, and Crean wanted to freshen it up with new faces. Crean sought my opinion. The five I suggested were Julia Gillard, Nicola Roxon, Kevin Rudd, David Cox, and me.

At around 8.00am the Sunday after polling day, Crean phoned me. 'What do you think should happen?' he asked.

'You should be leader, Jenny Macklin should be deputy leader, and I should be shadow treasurer', I replied.

No doubt taken aback by my forthright answer, Crean responded by saying that giving me the shadow treasurer's position would be a bold move, but might be a clear symbol of his commitment to generational change. He would think about it and get back to me. He told me he wanted to promote Rudd as well, but that, based on the number of caucus members elected from Queensland and New South Wales, Queensland was not entitled to any new frontbench positions.

The New South Wales right had agreed to forego one position to help solve this dilemma, which had become known as 'the Queensland problem': Crean's plan was to allocate the New South Wales position to Rudd, and for the former veterans' affairs minister in the Keating government, Con Sciacca, to make way for me.

When Bill Ludwig learned of Crean's intentions, he told me I would have to wait. Bill was a loyal man, and his first loyalty was to his close friend Sciacca. Crean told Ludwig he was intent on promoting me to the frontbench. Ludwig, in turn, refused to support the retention on the frontbench of another Queenslander, Arch Bevis, if Sciacca was to be demoted. Both Sciacca and Bevis were furious about their relegation, and both blamed me for it. No amount of explaining that I could not possibly have replaced both of them would satisfy them. Bevis and I eventually reconciled, but Sciacca and I didn't for as long as he was in parliament. I had a new enemy within the caucus. Such is the arithmetic of politics. If you are ambitious—and no MP lacks ambition—you will make enemies.

Crean appointed me shadow minister for innovation, industry, trade, and tourism, reasonably deciding it was too risky to throw me into the shadow Treasury from the backbench. When Crean phoned me with the news, I was delighted; it was a mega-portfolio, a key shadow-cabinet position. But then he added that Dr Stephen Martin, a Speaker of the House in the Keating government, would share the portfolio with me as shadow minister for trade and tourism, and that he, too, would be of cabinet rank.

Although Steve and I light-heartedly dubbed ourselves 'Doc 1' and 'Doc 2', there was no way this arrangement could work. It was no launching pad for the leadership, while Rudd, as shadow foreign minister, and Julia, as shadow minister for immigration and population policy, had won portfolios that were in the news daily. Rudd was in heavy demand as Labor's spokesman in dealing with international terrorism during the aftermath of the World Trade Center bombings, the war in Afghanistan, and the looming war in Iraq. Julia's task was to develop a robust asylum-seeker policy, which she accomplished with great skill and dexterity.

Innovation, industry, trade, and tourism—indeed, all matters economic—occupied almost none of the parliament's time, and garnered even less of the media's interest. In any event, although Crean didn't know it, Cathy and I were about to go through a very difficult time in our lives.

PRESELECTION FOR A WINNABLE SEAT in parliament is an ultra-competitive exercise, requiring an enormous dedication of time and energy. My long and difficult quest for preselection had taken its toll on our marriage. And as a parliamentarian, even when you are not officially working, your mind is on work, planning your next move towards advancement, anticipating the manoeuvres of those—mostly from within your own party—who are determined to thwart your progress.

Although I found enough time to be a good father, I found none to be a good husband. Cathy was left at home to prepare the meals, wash the clothes, pay the bills, keep the house clean and tidy, get the children to bed, attend to them when they woke during the night, and do it all again the next day. And the next. She would have appreciated some thanks, some interest in and discussion of her day, some flowers. It's no excuse, but when I was little, Mum asked Dad why he never bought her flowers. He responded: 'You can't eat flowers.' It was a reflection of his years as a prisoner of war, during which the daily task of securing an adequate supply of food dominated prisoners' minds. I inherited the prejudice against giving flowers as gifts from my father.

As I saw it, Cathy and I were engaged in a joint venture to put me into federal parliament, taking it for granted that, as the daughter of a South Australian state minister and deputy premier, she understood we were both making sacrifices for a noble cause. Now, reflecting on my attitude, it was outrageous: the exploitation of a beautiful woman's loyalty and devotion to our children and to me. But living through the task and anxiety of gaining preselection, I could not find the time even to reflect on my priorities and my lack of support for my wife, let alone consider changing them.

Looking back now on my state of being then, I was physically and emotionally exhausted, self-absorbed, focussed on career advancement, and blind to Cathy's world of motherhood, her needs and aspirations, her friendships with neighbours, and the support she was giving me. While I loved my children, I let my wife down, viewing her as a support for my ambitions but not as the wonderful woman she was then and is now.

Our lives increasingly grew apart. In Canberra, I formed a close friendship with Julia Gillard that, over time, developed into a romantic relationship. Cathy asked me to leave the family home. We agreed to separate, but that we would spare our three children any rancour, vowing not to blame or criticise each other in their presence. Despite the sadness that arose from a broken marriage, we kept that vow, sharing time with them and staying in close touch as parents of three wonderful children.

Inevitably, stories began emerging that I had walked out on my wife and children. I am confident they did not come from the Coalition. Indeed, I am grateful to the Liberal and National parties for the restraint they showed in refraining from highlighting the fact that two of Crean's five fresh faces were in a romantic relationship.

When I told Bob Hawke, he cautioned me that it would damage my leadership aspirations. Bob was soon to have dinner with Kim Beazley, and gave him the news. Beazley was horrified. If ever I had legitimate claims to the leadership—and many dispute that I did—they quickly dissolved. Voters would never accept as leader a man who had walked out on his wife, leaving her alone to raise his children. It didn't matter that, in fact, we continued to raise our children as loving parents. Such is politics, and I do not consider myself to have been treated badly by either the media or the Coalition.

Julia and I bought a house in Canberra, and stayed together for three years. We shared good times and hard times. Julia's star was rising, because she was performing extremely well in a difficult portfolio. Crean described her as 'the star turn' of the shadow ministry. Almost every Friday evening, my three children stayed over, and I took them to sport on Saturdays. Cathy and I got together for the children's birthdays and for Christmas. While there were difficulties all round, the children knew that their mum and dad loved them and cared for them.

WITH 2002 DRAWING TO A CLOSE, the opposition needed to develop a position on the Bush administration's threat to invade Iraq. As shadow foreign minister, Rudd devised a complex formulation setting out the conditions under which Labor would support Australia joining the United States in an invasion. Using the Rudd formulation, Crean was trying to straddle the pro-American camp in the parliamentary Labor Party and the no-war camp in the broader party.

Rudd was dissatisfied with Crean's performance, one of our colleagues telling me Rudd had asked to meet with him to discuss 'regime change'. According to my colleague, Rudd wasn't referring to removing Saddam Hussein, but to replacing Crean with himself. A little more than a year after Crean had used his leadership to insist on Rudd's elevation to the frontbench, Rudd wanted to displace him.

Crean went on to deliver a faltering exposition of Labor's position at an anti-war rally in Brisbane. His polling figures were deteriorating, and Kim Beazley had made it known that he was interested in making a comeback for the leadership. Dubbed 'the Glimmer Twins', Wayne Swan and Stephen Smith led a campaign against Crean. Julia and I had spent Easter with Crean, bushwalking in Tasmania, reaffirming our loyalty to him.

Bill Ludwig had no time for Crean, however, and was a great admirer of Beazley. When Crean spoke at a dinner ahead of the Queensland state ALP conference, Ludwig and his supporters gave him a frosty reception. Ludwig had inculcated in all members of the AWU faction the principle that it always supported the leader, yet I was the only one within the faction still supporting Crean. At one defining moment at the conference venue, I saw Ludwig crossing an open courtyard alone. I contemplated approaching him to explain my position, but decided against it. *Why should I have to explain that I am supporting the leader?* I asked myself. That, after all, had been the faction's position for as long as I could remember.

Perhaps if I had had a frank discussion with Ludwig, our friendship and my parliamentary career might have taken a different course. But I didn't, instead clashing with Swan on Sunday current-affairs television over our opposing positions on the leadership.

My view was, and remained so throughout my time in parliament, that if a leader was not performing satisfactorily, he or she deserved the respect of being afforded a private discussion with a delegation of senior colleagues, during which the delegation would explain the situation, giving the leader time to improve, and offering him or her a final opportunity of a dignified exit if the required improvement did not eventuate. Surely a caucus had that responsibility to its elected leader. But rarely did this happen, partly because members of any such delegation would not want to jeopardise their positions if the leader survived and turned vengeful. Anonymous backgrounding against a leader was always easier. To their credit, at least Swan, Smith, and my friend Stephen Conroy challenged Crean from the front, rather than stabbing him in the back.

Although Crean easily won the subsequent ballot against Beazley, his leadership was weakened. In an awkward post-ballot television interview on ABC's *Lateline* program, Con Sciacca, representing the Beazley forces, was seated in one corner of the ABC's small Parliament House studio, and I was seated a couple of metres away, separated only by a curtain, facing another camera. In the darkness, Sciacca and I could hear but not see each other.

Upon entering the studio, I had reached into my pocket and turned off my mobile phone. Or so I thought. Midway through my response to Sciacca's remarks, my mobile rang. *How could that be?* I puzzled, fumbling in my trouser pocket to silence the ringing while I tried to remain coherent. *There, it's off now*, I sighed inwardly with relief, without missing a beat in my reply to the host, Tony Jones. But Jones asked a follow-up question and, to my astonishment, the mobile rang again. Terminating the interview, Jones said: 'I'll let you get that call.'

My diligence in turning off the mobile phone ahead of the interview had gone unrewarded. So diligent had I been that I turned it off once on the way to the studio and once again upon entry—or, more accurately, my last act had been to turn it back on. Meanwhile, Beazley's key supporters had gathered in the office of one of our Queensland colleagues, Bernie Ripoll. As they watched Sciacca and me representing our two sides in the ballot, Ripoll chanced his arm that my mobile was in my pocket and turned on. His luck was in. My fumbling attempts to keep my gaze on the television camera while killing the ring tone were a source of great hilarity among our colleagues.

Crean's standing in the community did not improve in the months following the Beazley challenge. My close friends, including senator Joseph Ludwig, with whom I had bought an apartment soon after arriving in Canberra, advised me that if I wanted to be leader one day, I should stick my head up above the parapet.

John Howard had always refused to repudiate One Nation leader Pauline Hanson's anti-Asian pronouncements, and had a poor personal track record on the issue, dating back to his 1988 statement that there was too much Asian immigration. Now he was committed to finalising a free-trade agreement with the United States, whereas I, as shadow trade minister, was sceptical about the benefits to Australia of bilateral trade deals, much preferring global agreements. I felt that, by discriminating in favour of the United States, the proposed deal effectively discriminated against our major Asian trading partners, including China. Accordingly, in a speech at Monash University, I accused Howard again of discriminating against Asians, as he had done in 1988. 'Labor frontbencher calls Howard a racist', screamed the headlines and television bulletins. I hadn't, but that didn't seem to matter.

US trade representative Robert Zoellick had responsibility for trade in the Bush administration, and was visiting Australia to meet prime minister Howard and his trade minister, Mark Vaile. As was customary, Zoellick also arranged a meeting with the opposition leader. According to convention, the meeting would include the shadow minister for trade. Not this time. Zoellick refused to meet with Crean if I attended. Crean said to me: 'This is bad for me, but even worse for you.' Zoellick met with Crean and his staff, during which Crean explained that I was pro-trade and that my remarks were not a criticism of the US administration. He suggested to Zoellick that at least we have a telephone conversation.

In the afternoon of the following Saturday, Zoellick phoned me before leaving Australia. He told me his media adviser had briefed him that my speech had accused the Bush administration of racism. Zoellick pointed out that George Bush's secretary of state, Condoleezza Rice, was a black American. I explained that I had made no such accusation, that I had not accused Howard of racism, and that my concerns related to the economics of bilateral deals at the expense of multilateral negotiations. We ended the conversation on sufficiently cordial terms such that, at the World Economic Forum in Davos almost a decade later, I was able to share a meal with Zoellick, who had recently retired as president of the World Bank, and to introduce him to my son Ben.

At a personal level, I got on well with Tony Abbott. But the role of any opposition is to expose weaknesses in government ministers. Following the Beazley challenge, Crean offered me the shadow industrial relations portfolio. I had sought it, since Abbott would be my counterpart, enabling me not only to broaden my experience but also to raise my profile.

In the early period after Pauline Hanson's formation of the One Nation Party, the Liberals had assessed that she was taking more votes from Labor than from the Coalition. But as the One Nation phenomenon gathered momentum, it became clear that Hanson was doing more harm to the Coalition. Abbott formed a group with the Orwellian title 'Australians for Honest Politics', which funded a challenge to the legality of One Nation's registration as a political party. Information gathered during that case was later used against Hanson in a criminal case; she was jailed, but the conviction was overturned on appeal.

Although Abbott and his co-founders refused to reveal who had funded the legal case, leaks about it began flowing to me from conservative forces in Queensland, and I pursued Abbott inside and outside parliament. Ahead of a television interview with Laurie Oakes on the *Sunday* program, another network invited me into the studio to watch Abbott respond to my allegations on its program. Off air, as he prepared for the interview, Abbott said: 'Dear God, I wish this blessed thing would go away.'

My interview with Oakes was vicious. Oakes was incensed that I was pursuing Abbott. My argument was simple: if Abbott was truly for honest politics, why did he continue to conceal the identity of the donors to his slush fund? Was it an associated entity of the Liberal Party and therefore subject to the disclosure laws governing political donations? During the course of the interview, I could get out only half sentences before Oakes interrupted. It was a knock-down, drag-out brawl. Not long after, Crean came under pressure from within the caucus for allowing me to attack Abbott over his pursuit of Hanson. I wasn't defending Hanson, but I wanted to expose Abbott's hypocrisy.

BEAZLEY'S SUPPORTERS honoured their undertaking to give Crean clear air, but, try as he might, he could not improve his public image. Towards the end of 2003, I came to the conclusion that Crean's position was irretrievable. As a close personal friend and key supporter, I resolved to visit him and personally advise him to step down. I had organised dinner with Laurie Oakes to try to repair our damaged relationship, and told him off the record of my thinking. Oakes offered to talk to Crean privately as well. However, while Oakes and I were discussing the leadership crisis at Canberra's Aubergine Restaurant, I was unaware that three senior colleagues—John Faulkner, Robert Ray, and Martin Ferguson—were meeting with Crean at his rented accommodation, telling him that his leadership was terminal. They were going about a leadership change the right way but, outrageously, someone had leaked their planned visit to ABC television, and it was reported on the evening news.

Crean's key supporters met with him in his office before Question Time to advise him that he had lost the support of a majority of the shadow cabinet and that he needed to resign the leadership. I hugged him on the way out. But it was dignified. While he made preparations for Question Time, he asked me to lead the discussion of the day's Matter of Public Importance. When Question Time was over, Crean asked me to accompany him to his office. I reminded him of my obligation to speak in the House. He said: 'Okay, come to my office as soon as you've finished. I want to get this bloke up', nodding towards Mark Latham.

Concentrating on a policy debate for an hour while the leadership of the parliamentary Labor Party was in crisis was not easy, but I managed to get through it without any stumbles. By the time I returned to Crean's office, a group of supporters—including Julia Gillard, Laurie Brereton, Kim Carr, and Mark Latham—were there. The group was intent on denying Beazley a return to the leadership, by installing the volatile Latham as leader instead. My view was that Beazley was the best option and that, having kept his pledge of no destabilisation following the first challenge, he deserved another go at leading the party. But I was torn between my friendship with and loyalty to the group that had formed around Crean and my personal preference for Beazley.

Latham announced he would contest the leadership, and began phoning caucus members. Beazley's supporters then made a terrible mistake: they argued that Beazley should return to the leadership to 'save the furniture'. Latham, by contrast, was pledging to do everything possible to win the election. Beazley, too, considered the election winnable, and was willing to throw everything at achieving victory. But marginal-seat holders were interpreting the message from Beazley's supporters as meaning that he could not save them, but could save their colleagues in safer seats. Unsurprisingly, a large number of marginal-seat holders pledged their votes to Latham.

When Latham phoned me, I promised him my vote. Julia had also persuaded a large number of women to vote for Latham. At this stage, Wayne Swan asked to meet me, and we had a brief discussion. Bill Ludwig had been a strong critic of me from the day I voted for Crean against Beazley, including leading a walkout of AWU delegates during the ALP national conference when I presented the industrial relations platform for debate. Swan said: 'If you vote for Kim, I will try to smooth your relationship with Bill. I can't guarantee anything, but I think he'll be okay.' I thanked Swan, but explained that I had committed my vote to Latham.

The Monday night before the ballot, Julia advised me that Latham was ahead by one or two votes. On Tuesday mornings, a group of parliamentarians from all parties routinely gathered on the Senate playing fields for a game of touch football. It turned out that a fellow player and close friend, Robert McClelland, was having the same misgivings as I was. Our offices were adjacent. As we walked back to them to shower ahead of the decisive caucus meeting, McClelland asked me to join him in his office for one more chat.

He put a proposition to me: although we had both pledged our vote to Latham, we would both vote for Beazley. We would show our completed ballot papers to each other and confirm to others that we had voted for Beazley. I told McClelland I could not vote for Beazley, having told Latham and our friends that I would vote for him, but I would be willing to say McClelland had voted for Latham when, in fact, he had voted for Beazley. McClelland, still in his grass-stained football shorts, thanked me, and said he would think about it as he headed to the shower.

Shortly before the caucus meeting, McClelland phoned me and asked me to sit with him in his room until the start of caucus, so that Beazley supporters would put no more pressure on him. As I sat down, he told me he had spoken to a former St George rugby league forward, Robert Stone, who urged him to vote for Latham. McClelland said: 'I can't let Simon down. I'm voting for Latham.' We walked together to the caucus room, and both voted for Latham. Having marked my ballot paper, I walked past Latham and showed it to him, with a number one written beside his name. Almost two years later, after having resigned from parliament in January 2005, Latham published *The Latham Diaries*, a scathing book about his time in politics, reserving special animosity for me, questioning whether I had voted for him when he knew I had. As it happened, he had won the leadership ballot by a single vote.

If voting for Crean against Beazley had jeopardised my parliamentary career with my Queensland right-faction colleagues, voting for Latham against Beazley had put it in mortal danger. Upon hearing the result of the ballot during a meeting of union colleagues, Bill Ludwig exploded, pinning Latham's victory by one vote on me. My only hope of remaining on the front bench after the coming election would be if Latham pulled off a miraculous victory. In his betting days, Bob Hawke had successfully backed a few 33/1 chances, but I didn't fancy mine in having backed Latham.

33

Fasten your seatbelts

Following his victory in the caucus leadership ballot, Latham summoned his key supporters to his office. I was not invited. As Latham worked on his shadow ministry over the ensuing days, I arranged a meeting with his key organiser, Laurie Brereton. I put the suggestion to Brereton, more in hope than in expectation, that I be appointed shadow treasurer. It was a brief discussion. Brereton explained that Latham had one 'star turn', Julia, and that he didn't need any more, but that he would pass on my request. Latham phoned me with his decision: 'Emmo, you're a victim of your own success. I need to keep you in industrial relations because of the rapport you've built up with the union movement.'

Although I was a little disappointed about being judged as lacking merit for the shadow Treasury position, I had greatly enjoyed industrial relations and my work with comrades in the union movement. My time in the portfolio had brought me closer to ACTU secretary Greg Combet. And whereas Bill Ludwig had ruled me disloyal for refusing to vote down a Labor leader, the secretary of the Shop Assistants' Union, Joe de Bruyn, understood my motives in supporting Crean. Combet, de Bruyn, and other senior union officials worked with me on a flexible industrial relations policy that nevertheless protected vulnerable workers.

We had settled Labor's industrial relations policy between us, but Greg wanted to ensure that Latham was personally committed to it. Latham suggested dinner at Chairman and Yip, a famous Canberra restaurant, where Greg and I took him through the policy. The tablecloth was made of butcher's paper, and Latham used a felt pen to write notes on each feature of the policy as Greg and I explained it. It was a pleasant dinner, and Greg was satisfied that Latham, having understood the policy, was likely to implement it if we won government.

Many months later, Latham began publicly criticising a feature of the policy that enabled bargaining between unions and multiple employers. These multi-employer agreements were designed to deal with situations such as those that occurred in the hospitality industry, where one hotel might be receptive to a union's claim for a wage rise for its members, but feared that rival hotels that did not come to the party would use the advantage of lower wages to win market share. I sought to raise Latham's public criticism of the multi-employer agreement provisions with him as we left a shadow cabinet meeting. He turned away and headed to the Members' Dining Room for dinner, refusing to discuss it with me.

Alarmed that Latham was repudiating a policy to which he'd agreed at our dinner, I advised Greg that we had a problem. Greg sought a meeting with Latham. We joined him in the leader's office, and, to our surprise, Latham pulled out the annotated butcher's paper from a drawer in his desk where he had stowed it. He found the notes he had scribbled about multi-employer agreements, asserting somehow that this proved we had not discussed it. Greg and I argued that it proved we had, in fact, discussed the provision—otherwise he would not have written notes correctly describing it. Bewildered, Greg and I left the room. Latham did not raise objections to the policy again until he later wrote in *The Latham Diaries* that we were trying to empower big unions to intimidate milk bars in Campbelltown into signing collective agreements.

SENIOR SHADOW MINISTERS were obliged to argue their policies at ALP national conferences, such that they were rarely free of controversy. Julia and I created our own obstacles the night before she was to sponsor her health policy at the 2004 conference in Sydney. Staying at a hotel near the Convention Centre at Darling Harbour, we retired for the night, with Julia's last words before falling asleep being: 'Emmo, I forgot to bring my contact lens case, so I've put them in a glass of solution in the bathroom. Don't drink it, will you?'

'Of course not', I said, slightly indignantly.

Who would be stupid enough to drink contact lens solution? I asked myself.

Julia would jokingly say to me from time to time: 'Emmo, you're smarter than you look' and 'Emmo, you're not as dumb as you look.' And now she was questioning whether I was dumb enough to drink a glass of saline solution containing contact lenses.

She was soon to find out.

It is said that you can't buy beer — you can only rent it. In the middle of the night, the rent on the four beers I had drunk that evening fell due. I stumbled into the bathroom without turning on the light, completed my ablutions, and noticed the outline of a glass of water on the shelf above the sink. Without a moment's hesitation, I consumed the contents and plonked the glass back onto the shelf.

The clatter of the glass bottom hitting the shelf woke Julia with a start.

'Emmo! You didn't …?'

Before she had finished the sentence, a rush of adrenaline told me I was in terrible trouble.

'Oh no! I did. They're gone.'

'Emmo!'

I offered various proposals for retrieving the contact lenses, none of them attractive to either of us.

'I've got to present the health-policy platform in the morning. I can't see anything without my contact lenses', she lamented.

'But you can't be both short-sighted and long-sighted, can you?' I inquired hopefully.

She was.

The next morning, Julia toiled her way through the health-policy presentation, blind to both her notes and the assembled conference delegates. I thought she did a good job, but decided it was best not to praise her lest I stray within punching distance.

I thought there might be a joke in there, somewhere, starting: 'With the benefit of hindsight …' But again I decided on balance that Julia might not be in the mood for jokes.

THE ALP CONFERENCE was the time and place for the Labor tribe to put on the war paint for the coming election. In the lead-up to Howard calling the election, and recalling my assembly of the anti-Howard *Quotable Quotes* material while working for Bob Hawke, I began compiling a list of Howard's broken promises. Based on the Children Overboard scandal, I named the document *Truth Overboard*. Before long, it was a very substantial document. After I handed it over to Latham's office, junior staff there embellished it to the point where some of the allegations against Howard could not withstand scrutiny. When Latham's office released *Truth Overboard*, Howard was incensed. From television footage, I could see him clutching a rolled-up copy of the document as he walked into radio and television studios to defend his integrity. He called an election, which he announced would be based on trust. This was one angry man.

Late in an erratic campaign, I watched the evening news bulletins in horror at my electorate office as they showed footage of Latham in an intimidating pose with Howard, a virtual head-butt that reminded viewers of an incident when Latham broke a taxi driver's arm before entering parliament. I turned to Jennilyn Mann, head of my office and a rock of stability since the 1998 election, and said: 'We're in big trouble here in Rankin.'

That night, I wrote a final letter to voters in an effort to insulate myself from the anger they would inevitably feel about Latham's treatment of Howard. We printed as many as we could through the night, enveloped them, and rushed them to the post office for immediate dispatch. They arrived just before polling day.

As the counting of votes began on Saturday evening, I positioned myself alone, in front of a computer screen in my office, away from the open areas where my staff sat, and logged onto the Australian Electoral Commission's website. Soon the first count for Rankin trickled in, less than 1,000 votes. I was behind. Although it was a bad start, it was only the beginning of the count. But by 7.00pm a meaningful number of votes had been counted. I was still behind. Jennilyn came into my office to ask how it was going.

'I'm worried', I said, 'but our big Labor booths might not have come in yet.'

Jennilyn closed the door to my office to prevent other staff members wandering in. Half an hour later, she returned. She told me I looked white. Solemnly, I told her: 'A quarter of the votes are counted, and we're on 47-and-a-half per cent. We can't win.'

When Jennilyn returned to the open office area to let the rest of our staff know, they began crying.

Then, bizarrely, I began making a comeback. As I watched the screen, the vote shifted before my eyes: now I was on 52 per cent, with more than half the vote counted. We were going to win!

Only later did I learn what had triggered this extraordinary turnaround. Former ALP state secretary Mike Kaiser had noticed the anomalous Rankin figures coming in, and rang the Electoral Commission for an explanation. Upon conducting a quick investigation, the commission discovered that its staff had been loading the results from individual booths into the wrong columns — the Labor votes into the Liberal column, and vice versa. I had, in fact, been ahead throughout the count.

A number of good friends who had voted for Latham against Beazley were not so fortunate, losing their seats in a national anti-Labor swing. Out of guilt for my role in Latham's ascension, I decided to move to the backbench. I told Julia of my decision, but within days I learned it was redundant; the decision had already been made for me. Joseph Ludwig, very reasonably, put up his hand for a frontbench position. My Queensland right-wing colleagues would support Joseph against me, and I did not nominate. The next evening, on ABC's *Lateline*, this time with my mobile phone switched off, I defended Joseph's right to nominate and his credentials for a frontbench position, wishing the leader and the freshly elected shadow ministry well. After six years in parliament, I was back where I started, on the backbench.

In the days following the appointment of the new shadow ministry, the chairs of caucus committees were being determined. Since I had been appointed chair of the caucus economics committee as a fresh-faced backbencher back in 1998, I realised I would need at least to regain that position six years later if I were to avoid sinking without a trace. Surely Latham and his supporters would back me, I reassured myself. Heartened when Latham told me in response to my phone call that 'You will get support for the caucus committee chair's position', I began phoning friends and colleagues.

The other candidate was a newcomer, Chris Bowen, who was later appointed treasurer in the second Rudd government. Bowen was phoning around, too. I was happy with the response I was receiving, and, confident that I had majority support, I wanted to proceed to a ballot. But factional convenor Robert Ray rang to ask whether the matter could be settled without a divisive internal ballot so soon after the election rout. Bowen and I met, and agreed to share the positions of chair of the caucus economics committee and chair of the House of Representatives economics committee that, from time to time, held hearings with the governor of the Reserve Bank. We would chair one committee each, and swap mid-term.

At the same time as my professional life was falling apart, so was my romantic relationship with Julia. We mutually agreed to end it. As many of my colleagues across the political divide also found, political life can place great stresses on personal relationships. With Julia and me both in politics, the pressure proved too great. Much was lost. But I had the delight of three wonderful children to sustain me.

34

Survival

Uppermost in my mind during my exile to the backbench was political survival. A number of highly trained economists had won seats in the Australian parliament over the years, but the likes of Professor Harry Edwards, who had been described as a great economist but a poor politician, failed to make the transition to the ministry. Would I suffer the same fate? Would my colleagues consider me a quaint technician who could not behave like a good politician and go where the numbers dictated? Despite the many allegations of disloyalty against me, I had always supported the incumbent leader. No one in parliament lacks ambition. Now that I was on the backbench, colleagues from my own political generation, along with a generation of newcomers, could readily overtake me.

I sought advice from an ex-staffer colleague from the Hawke era, Peter Barron, who remained influential in the New South Wales branch of the Labor Party and whose judgement I respected. We met over a cup of tea at Sydney's Wentworth Hotel. I had informed Peter by phone of the purpose of the meeting, and as we settled in, Peter said he had given my situation some thought. My contemporaries, he pointed out, were Wayne Swan, Stephen Smith, Kevin Rudd, and Julia Gillard. While I sat on the backbench, they would continue to move ahead of me to take on leadership positions. Peter's considered advice was that I should quit parliament.

I was devastated. My romantic life was a mess, and my professional life was definitely over if I took Peter's advice, and was probably finished even if I didn't. All the study, all the work, the struggle, the broken marriages—and now, at the age of 50, it was all for nothing.

As Peter left the hotel coffee shop, I reflected on what I had learned from my mother and my father. Mum's attitude was that if you wanted to get ahead, you needed to do what others did, behave as others behaved; otherwise they would trample over you, and you would be left behind. You had to get in for your chop, because no one would give you anything you didn't take. Dad's attitude was that you needed to be true to yourself and be honourable in your dealings with people. If you were, they might recognise it as a quality in you. If they didn't, at least you could live with yourself.

Well, here I was, living with myself all right. Alone, and, to all the world, a failure. At that moment, I resolved to prove Dad right. I recalled a wise old political saying: *There are two ways to get into the cabinet room—crawl in, or knock the door down.* I wasn't going to crawl. Another saying was from Martin Ferguson's father, Jack, who rose to the position of deputy premier in New South Wales. Jack told Martin that anyone who entered parliament with dignity and left with his or her dignity intact had done well. I decided I would try to stay alive politically by doing policy work on the backbench, writing a book, hoping to get my policy positions reported in the media, and then using my public profile to build external pressure on my senior colleagues to return me to the frontbench. I would not sink without a trace.

Most of the policy work I took on was in the portfolio areas for which shadow ministers Jenny Macklin and Penny Wong were responsible. Both were amazingly tolerant of me trampling through their portfolios, and I remain grateful for their forbearance.

Sustaining me through these difficult times was Greg Combet. On a warm autumn day, Greg and his wife, Petra, were travelling from Melbourne to Sydney while I was driving from Sydney to Canberra. We arranged by mobile phone to meet on the Hume Highway, where I handed Greg a compact disc titled *Full Metal Jacket*. It contained the best Vietnam War protest songs and other anti-establishment songs of the era. The raw sound of Steppenwolf belting out 'Born to Be Wild' as I stopped to greet Greg and Petra has never left me. Greg and I have sought each other's counsel ever since, on both personal and professional matters, as we have journeyed through our lives.

During my years of exile, Joe de Bruyn also provided constant support. He demanded nothing of me, but would have expected that I continue to support trade unionism, which I did. While Rudd and other ambitious Labor MPs wrote opinion pieces about the desirability of weakening the bonds between the ALP and the union movement, I never did. Sharing life in political exile with me were former frontbenchers Lindsay Tanner and Bob McMullan. Tanner had refused to serve on a Latham frontbench following the 2004 election debacle, and Latham had banished McMullan under suspicion that he had been leaking against him. The three of us set up a series called *Progressive Essays*, a vehicle for presenting fresh thinking on various policy challenges. It culminated with a dinner at the National Press Club featuring Greg Combet as guest of honour. It was a full house, including dozens of caucus members, Kim Beazley among them.

BY EARLY 2005, Latham's leadership was crumbling. He had failed to respond to the South-East Asian Boxing Day tsunami, and had developed pancreatitis. As it became clear that his leadership was terminal, I phoned Julia, who was holidaying in Vietnam. In my judgement, it was time to return to Kim Beazley for the leadership. Julia told me her supporters were urging her to run. Rudd, too, was sounding out caucus members for support. Following her hastened return to Australia, Julia stayed in touch with me, and, over the course of the following few days, decided it was best to let Beazley regain the leadership. During this period of Rudd's undeclared candidacy, I campaigned for Beazley, agreeing to do a stand-up media conference with him in Melbourne.

Lacking support, Rudd decided against nominating, and Beazley won the leadership uncontested.

Latham's resignation from the frontbench had opened up a vacancy, and Beazley selected Lindsay Tanner to fill it. When I learned of Beazley's decision, I sought a meeting with him in his office. While I fully supported Tanner for the vacancy, it would have been possible for Beazley to expand the size of his shadow ministry to include me. Disappointed that he was unwilling to do so, I asked Beazley what my prospects were under his revived leadership. He told me I would need Bill Ludwig's support if I were ever to return to the frontbench. I explained that such support would never be forthcoming. I was stuffed. Now my career was definitely over.

During this period of dark despair, the editor-in-chief of *The Australian* newspaper, Chris Mitchell, helped keep me afloat by publishing the results of research I did on education policy and on tax and welfare reform, serialising the book I had written — *Vital Signs, Vibrant Society* — and running front-page stories on my policy work. Mitchell liked my political philosophy of harnessing the power of the market to achieve economic growth, out of which social reforms could be pursued. Backbench colleagues remarked that I was getting more prominent news coverage than many frontbenchers. Singo helped fund the book's publication, and Kim Beazley and Bob Hawke attended the launch.

As I worked on tax-reform options, I was joined in the debate by one of the government's new backbenchers, Malcolm Turnbull. Our tax-reform packages had common features, but were different in important respects — most particularly, in our treatment of the highest marginal rate of personal income tax. Turnbull's plan reduced it, while mine did not. As we entered a television studio to spruik our proposals, I pointed out to Turnbull that he had under-estimated the cost of reducing the top marginal income-tax rate, since fringe-benefits tax was applied at the top rate and any reduction in that rate would also reduce fringe-benefits tax revenue. Turnbull looked mildly horrified, but delivered a polished television performance nevertheless.

A couple of weeks later, treasurer Peter Costello, enraged at Turnbull's meddling in his portfolio, briefed a Coalition backbench committee on Treasury costings of our two sets of tax-reform proposals. In a backhanded compliment, Costello stated that my costings were 'more accurate' than Turnbull's. Through this period, Turnbull and I developed a rapport as parliamentary colleagues, built no doubt on our close encounter as prospective business associates on my way out of Bob Hawke's office fifteen years earlier.

During 2005, I met Tracey Winters, an adviser to Martin Ferguson who not only knew where Baradine was, but also had a family connection to the Pilliga Scrub, and was happy to support my ultimately unsuccessful crusade to save Baradine's timber industry. At the National

Press Gallery's mid-winter ball, Tracey wore a satin green gown, and looked stunning. During the evening I had gotten sufficiently tired and emotional to value a lift home. Tracey drove me home and, before speeding off, agreed to dinner the following Saturday night. Thereafter, Martin Ferguson marvelled at the number of times I wandered into his office for a discussion on policy or politics. Tracey and I have supported each other ever since, through tumultuous times in Parliament House and in life beyond.

KIM BEAZLEY'S POPULARITY in the electorate began ebbing away and, as 2006 drew to a close, fresh leadership speculation started appearing in the media. Now Rudd was being touted as a possible challenger. To my horror, it had become evident that Julia and Rudd had entered into a political alliance. I phoned Julia, urging her to support Beazley. Howard had unleashed his draconian WorkChoices legislation upon the Australian people, making many workers worse off, and I argued that we would still win under Beazley. Julia judged that Beazley's position was irretrievable, but I could not believe that she and Rudd could form an alternative leadership team, given that she loathed him.

Beazley had approached me earlier in the week at a right-faction Christmas Party at Parliament House to inform me that he was supporting my elevation to the frontbench, together with that of my other dear friend from days of old, Peter Garrett. He had briefed *The Australian* newspaper accordingly, which had already phoned me to arrange a photograph for publication with the story. Chris Mitchell had been agitating for our promotion, and Beazley was responding positively.

At a dinner of right-faction members of the ALP in a Canberra restaurant, I sat with Joe de Bruyn and other union colleagues. We knew trouble was brewing, but I could not believe a leadership challenge would be launched. The next day, the challenge was declared. Beazley announced he was spilling not only the leadership, but also all frontbench positions. By that time I was in a car park outside a dental surgery in Logan City, where I had radical tooth surgery in preparation for a crown. As the temporary tooth fell into pieces in my mouth, Joseph Ludwig phoned to advise me of the frontbench spill, and pledged his personal support for me. Beazley followed, urging me to hit the phones to secure a shadow ministry position if he survived the spill.

I made numerous phone calls, to a reasonably positive reception, but the responses of the Rudd–Gillard supporters ranged from circumspect to downright hostile. I stayed in regular contact with Beazley, seeking to persuade my closer colleagues to support him, and later walked into his office, where he was in a closed-door discussion with Arch Bevis, to accompany him to the caucus meeting that would decide his fate. As we walked together to the caucus room, I asked Beazley how his meeting with Bevis had gone. 'Oh, Arch is all right', he replied glumly, conveying to me in his demeanour that he considered himself to be doomed.

Upon entering the room, I approached Julia and asked for her assessment. 'We have a margin of ten votes', she confidently advised me. She was exactly right. Rudd was the new leader, and Julia was his deputy. There was to be no ballot for any other frontbench positions. Angrily, I approached Julia again, complaining about a lack of opportunity to return to the frontbench. 'You are pushing against an open door', she said, indicating that it had already been agreed with Rudd that I would be returned to the frontbench.

Rudd gave me the title of shadow minister for small business, independent contractors, and the service economy. At a shadow ministry meeting in Adelaide to announce a Green Car Fund, Rudd informed us of the membership of a strategy group. It was, effectively, a shadow cabinet, and I was not on the list. Still, where our policy work intersected, Rudd and I got on well; there was no obvious animosity. He even publicly praised me at a Parliament House luncheon for my proposals to remove unwarranted business regulations.

In my capacity as shadow small-business minister, I worked with Julia as shadow minister for workplace relations, and with business groups and unions, to develop a simple fair-dismissal code that, if followed, would allow small-business employers to dismiss staff without facing legal claims. The unfair-dismissal regime that had been introduced by Labor in the mid-1990s had tied up small businesses in red tape, and had been repeatedly used by the Coalition over the ensuing years as evidence of Labor being hostile to small business. Following the implementation of our fair-dismissal code once we were back in government, nothing adverse was again heard about the unfair-dismissal system for small businesses—we ended 20 years of divisiveness with that policy.

In the lead-up to the federal election, Howard and Costello had not released a tax policy. Wayne Swan judged that they would not release one during the campaign, and preferred not to develop a tax policy of his own. As it turned out, though, one of the government's first election-policy releases was a fully detailed, fully funded tax policy, complete with tax scales and the income levels at which they applied. A week passed. Labor had no response, and the media attacked Labor for its tardiness in releasing an alternative policy.

Rudd phoned me and asked me to begin work on a tax policy, but to restrict knowledge of it to him and his then acting chief of staff, Alister Jordan, his lead economic adviser, Pradeep Philip, and another economic adviser working at campaign headquarters, Rod Glover. He made it clear to me that I was not to tell his shadow treasurer, Wayne Swan.

Based on the modelling work I had done in competition with Malcolm Turnbull and the policy outlined in my book, I prepared a tax package for Rudd's consideration. He made some minor variations, using some of the funds I had devoted to tax cuts to create an education-tax refund and apply a more generous child-care rebate. Both these variations were guided by private polling, which revealed the popularity in middle Australia of a tax refund for education expenses, and the desire of higher-income mothers returning to work for extra assistance with child-care costs.

Having made these variations, I told Rudd the policy was finished. He asked me to his hotel room in Sydney to take him through it. Rudd was happy with the policy, and asked me to brief *The Australian*'s Chris Mitchell about it the next day. Mitchell liked it, and gave it strong positive coverage. Rudd's office was delighted, too, with the front-page coverage of Melbourne's *Herald-Sun*, as well as the favourable reporting of it on the evening news bulletins. We had countered the Howard government's main claim for re-election.

Encouraged by this success, Rudd asked me to work with his advisers on other policies, including drought-proofing cities that were suffering acute water shortages, and a deregulation agenda for an incoming Rudd government. Labor also released a policy on renewable energy, which Howard said he would take his time in responding to.

I phoned a senior journalist at *The Australian* newspaper, Dennis Shanahan, for his opinion on whether Howard would campaign against the policy, with the aim of preparing Rudd's advisers for any likely criticism of what inevitably would be a controversial policy. It was, I thought, a well-motivated conversation. I reported it to Rudd's advisers, and thought nothing more of it. Late in the campaign, I again phoned Shanahan to see if he had received any feedback from the Liberals on the final published opinion poll of the campaign, which showed the long-standing gap in Labor's favour suddenly narrowing. Again, I thought this was a harmless conversation. It wasn't.

35

Revival

Labor won the election in a landslide on 24 November 2007. Following the victory, shadow ministers waited for Rudd's office to contact them for meetings with the new prime minister, where they would be told of their portfolios. I had become apprehensive; though Rudd and I had been texting each other through most of the campaign, he had stopped responding in the final week or so. Now, after winning government, there was total silence from him. *He's just busy*, I tried to reassure myself.

Through the day and into the evening ahead of the next day's caucus meeting to formalise the first Rudd ministry, my colleagues were called in, one by one. Rudd swore them to secrecy about the portfolios he had given them. By 10.00pm, most had been told, but a few had not. I was one of the few. At my request, close colleagues sent me text messages once they had had their meetings with Rudd. One message came in at 2.00am. Still, I had not been called. I lay awake through the night, finally receiving a call to be at Rudd's office at 7.45am, before the caucus meeting. Now I feared the worst.

Upon entering Rudd's office, I was met not only by him but also by senators Robert Ray and John Faulkner, and Rudd's chief of staff, David Epstein. Rudd sat behind his desk, facing me, arms folded tightly across his chest. He launched into a tirade of abuse towards me.

'I stuck my neck out and put you back in the ministry', he started, 'but you've shown me nothing but disloyalty. You briefed senior journos against me in the first half of the year. Then you told newspaper editorial staff during the campaign that Labor couldn't win and that Labor's campaign was no good.'

He went on to claim I had been disloyal over a period of 15 years 'to me, who brought you to Queensland, to Wayne Goss, to Bill Ludwig, and to Bob Hawke when you worked for him'. Never had I shown a skerrick of disloyalty towards Bob Hawke. Rudd was a Queensland opposition staffer at the time, living in Brisbane. How would he know one way or the other? But that didn't stop him. 'None of your colleagues like you; none of them want you on the frontbench', he continued. 'Everyone knows what you are up to. I want a pledge of loyalty from you in front of these witnesses.'

This was a critical moment. Would I plead guilty of systematic disloyalty as charged, in exchange for a ministry position? Or would I tell Rudd what I thought about his ignorant, outrageous allegations of my disloyalty to Bob Hawke? Would I point out that my alleged act of disloyalty to Bill Ludwig was my support for Labor leader Simon Crean, whom Rudd had ungratefully and disloyally undermined from the outset in pursuit of his own ambitions? I chose a middle path.

'It would be easier for me to accept all of this, but I won't', I said. 'I did have a conversation with Chris Mitchell on the tax policy you and I worked on.'

'That was authorised', Rudd interrupted.

'Yes, it was', I said. 'I don't think I had a further conversation with Chris during the campaign. I spoke to Shanahan on the night of the final Newspoll. I said I thought the election would be tight. I haven't spoken to Shanahan more than twice in the last six months. I spoke to Chris some months ago, after he'd met with Murdoch. Chris said Murdoch was unlikely to direct editors on which party to support. Chris asked me whether it would be a good government. I said that yes, it would.'

Robert Ray said I should never deal with Shanahan. Rudd added: 'The only time he ever supports us is when it's for a prospective new leader against an existing one.'

Then Rudd issued his warning: 'If ever there's a repeat of you briefing Shanahan or leaking, I will reconvene this gathering and fucking punt you.'

I said I was happy to pledge loyalty but, drawing on the experience of my phone conversation with the presiding commissioner at the foxtail palm inquiry 13 years earlier, I added: 'I'm not going to be fitted up with talking to Shanahan when I haven't done so, just so that you can sack me whenever you want to.'

John Faulkner reassured me: 'That's why we're here. You won't get fitted up.'

Rudd wound up the meeting: 'You're a very talented guy. There's no reason why you won't progress.' He reached for a piece of paper that David Epstein had placed in front of him. 'I'm giving you your existing portfolio, plus assisting Lindsay Tanner on business deregulation. If you do business deregulation well, you can progress.'

It turned out I was not the last shadow minister to meet with Rudd. As I departed, shaken and angry but relieved to be a minister, Bob McMullan entered. He was told he was not to be appointed to the ministry, but would be given a parliamentary secretary's position. Several other shadow ministers missed out altogether. John Faulkner, Robert Ray, David Epstein, and Julia Gillard took responsibility for meeting them and offering what comfort they could.

In the afternoon after the caucus meeting to rubber-stamp the ministry, Chris Mitchell phoned to warn me that Rudd had quizzed him about me leaking to *The Australian* during the election campaign. Mitchell had assured Rudd that I had not done so; that I had briefed him on Labor's tax policy, but at Rudd's instigation. I told Mitchell that Rudd had already accused me of leaking to senior News Limited executives and to Dennis Shanahan, and that I was to have nothing further to do with Shanahan, or else I would be dumped from the ministry.

Mitchell found this curious, since Rudd had asked Shanahan to lead his prime ministerial media office. Shanahan had been interested in Rudd's offer, but Mitchell improved his remuneration package with a car, and persuaded Shanahan that it was in his long-term interests to stay at *The Australian*. Rudd told others I had been leaking to senior management at Fairfax, which would have been difficult since I did not know them. It seemed to be a case of tailoring the crime to fit the guilty.

WITHIN WEEKS OF MY MINISTERIAL APPOINTMENT, the opposition accused me of having cheated taxpayers by spending an inordinate amount of time in Melbourne with Julia during the period 2003–2007. The accusation was in the form of a document handed to *The Sunday Telegraph* journalist Glenn Milne, listing the total number of days I had spent in Melbourne in that period, and itemising a number of the visits.

Luckily, the highly professional Jennilyn Mann in my office had assiduously kept a detailed electronic diary of every event I had attended in the electorate, my parliamentary commitments in Canberra, and every day I had spent elsewhere around Australia. Within two days we were able to demonstrate that the allegations in the document were false and that, on average, I had spent less than two days a month in Melbourne. Since most unions and business organisations were headquartered in Melbourne, this was a very small amount of time for a shadow minister for industry and workplace relations to spend there. Milne decided against running a story.

I went on to work closely with the finance minister, Lindsay Tanner, on 27 areas of regulatory reform that I identified by taking a marking pen to every report on deregulation that had been prepared over the preceding decade. Lindsay, justifiably confident in his own abilities, gave me free rein, but attended key meetings with the states. We made good progress. Rudd acknowledged my role at meetings of the Council of Australian Governments in front of state and territory leaders.

Apart from my policy roles, I happily took on responsibility, offered by my friend and the leader of the House, Anthony 'Albo' Albanese, for using humour against the opposition in Question Time to maintain morale among the troops. After asking one question early in the life of the new parliament, my portfolio counterpart and friend, Gold Coast Liberal MP Steven Ciobo, either did not seek or was not granted by the Coalition tactics committee the opportunity to ask me further questions in the parliament. As the months turned into years, Steve's silence became a matter of mirth in the chamber.

When I was allocated a question from the government side, none being forthcoming from the opposition, I researched the number of days without a question from Steve, and compared it with a notable world event such as Captain Cook's voyage of discovery from the Motherland to Australia and the Siege of Leningrad. As luck would have it, the day I was given a question ostensibly about small business, the Toy Story character, Buzz Lightyear, had been orbiting the earth in the International Space Station for 467 days, 'exactly the number of days since the Shadow Minister for Small Business last asked me a question'. Buzz Lightyear had been immortalised in the Australian parliament.

These Question Time performances, designed mainly to amuse and lift the spirits of the Labor backbench, weren't always easy to carry off. They required a lot of concentration, particularly as Coalition MPs routinely took points of order with the Speaker — mostly, understandably, about the relevance of my answer to the question I had been asked — in order to disrupt my flow. Usually I catnapped for half an hour on the couch in my ministerial office before Question Time to freshen my mind. Seated next to me for much of my frontbench career was Chris Bowen. Each time as I was about to rise to my feet to respond to a question from a Labor backbencher, Chris would say: 'Emmo, don't fuck it up.' Of course, I returned serve wherever Chris was readying to answer a question from our side.

From time to time, as we were leaving Question Time, an affable member of the Opposition would express frustration that I never let them throw me off course when giving my answers. 'Emmo', one said, 'how come you can just plough on when we're all interjecting and carrying on as if we weren't there?' I didn't tell him that mostly I didn't wear my glasses during Question Time and I was half deaf, so I could neither see nor hear them.

My approach to Question Time so amused the independent member for New England, Tony Windsor, that he had scorecards made up, and distributed them to parliamentary colleagues seated near him. For the Buzz Lightyear comparison, I scored a respectable average of five out of 10. Fellow independent Rob Oakeshott was reasonably generous in his subsequent scoring, but Tony Windsor was more severe than a Russian judge scoring US gymnastic performances at the Olympics during the height of the Cold War. I counted my blessings if Windsor gave me a four.

By this time, Malcolm Turnbull had defeated Brendan Nelson to take on the role of leader of the opposition. Turnbull and I remained friends, but in various contributions during Question Time I had reason to compare him to David Bowie's Major Tom from the Ziggy Stardust album, and to Doctor Zachary Smith from *Lost in Space*, for being isolated and out of touch. In the aftermath of my later adaptation of Skyhooks's 'Horror Movie' to 'No Whyalla wipeout there on my TV', and the associated near-universal condemnation of my singing ability, I reflected on the failure of all my friends and colleagues, including Tony Windsor, to warn me during these Question Time performances that I could not sing. I hold them totally responsible for their negligence.

When the defence minister, Joel Fitzgibbon, was obliged to resign, a cabinet vacancy opened up. Being in the outer ministry was satisfying, and I enjoyed my portfolio work, but the big decisions affecting the country are made by the cabinet and its committees. I sought to make an appointment with Rudd to press my case for promotion. Instead, he telephoned me to advise that he intended to appoint Chris Bowen to cabinet, but that he was adding competition policy and consumer affairs to my portfolio responsibilities in the outer ministry.

I asked Rudd what I needed to do to get into cabinet. He told me that if I thought he and I had had our problems over the years, they were nothing compared with Wayne Swan's animosity towards me, and that if I were ever to get into cabinet, I would need Swan's agreement. At that moment, I knew I would never be a member of a Rudd cabinet—not because I believed Swan would go out of his way to block me, but because Rudd always had a reason ready to keep me out.

36

Turmoil

After Rudd's decision to abandon a carbon emissions trading scheme in April 2010, his electoral popularity faltered. It was not catastrophic, and Labor still led the Coalition in published opinion polls. But, behind the scenes, Rudd used his position as prime minister to abuse, embarrass, and even humiliate his Labor parliamentary colleagues in front of their peers. Although I had read media reports of this indulgent behaviour, I had had no further personal experience of it following his tirade the morning he appointed me to the ministry in late 2007. Nevertheless, a small group of colleagues, including New South Wales senator Steve Hutchins, South Australian senator Don Farrell, and Western Australian minister Gary Gray, began meeting to discuss a post-election leadership transition from Rudd to Gillard. This, Steve explained to me, would happen within a year of a 2010 election victory.

The group, which eventually involved Bill Shorten, had begun discussing possible candidates for deputy prime minister. It had been agreed that this position would be filled from the party's right, and that it should be someone who had been in parliament for a long time to provide stability in the leadership team through a left-right balance, and who could be moved on after some time in the position. Wayne Swan was mentioned in discussions, and so was I, though my time as Julia's partner had created reservations within the group about my viability. After several meetings I was invited to attend, which I did before rushing to catch a plane. It was clear to me that we were discussing a post-election scenario.

Soon a report appeared in a weekend newspaper that moves were afoot to remove Rudd from the prime ministership. I didn't place a lot of weight on it, since I knew from the meetings that no early leadership change was being discussed. On Sunday 20 June, I received a phone call from Don Farrell. He asked me what I made of the story. I said that changing leaders would be ridiculous, and that Queensland voters in particular would go nuts. Don agreed, telling me he had been asked to support a move against premier Mike Rann in his home state of South Australia and that he had opposed the idea.

That was the last I thought about it until the next Wednesday. At two minutes before the ABC television 7.00pm news bulletin, I received a text message from television host Tony Jones inviting me to appear on *Lateline* that evening. The Victorian left, Jones' message said, had moved against Rudd, and a challenge was imminent. I watched the news story in my office with incredulity, and immediately walked next door into Martin Ferguson's office. Since Martin was of the Victorian left, I reasoned he would know of any coup. 'It's bullshit, mate', he said.

Within minutes, my mobile phone began ringing. The first caller was Steve Hutchins. 'There's a move on against Rudd', he informed me. 'Will you come on board? Julia's got the numbers.' I told him I didn't think it was a good idea, but that I'd get back to him. I rang Joe de Bruyn and said I didn't want to support a change of leader. Joe told me he had assured Rudd about six weeks earlier of his continuing support, and would not go back on his word. Next to call me was Don Farrell. He asked whether I was with them. I told him I needed time to think about it. He gave me five minutes. I left another message for Joe, advising him that I would be supporting Rudd. While I was talking with others on the phone, Joe left a voice message saying I was doing the right thing.

I told my staff I was supporting Rudd, and went downstairs to see Albo, who was already phoning colleagues for Rudd. I visited Rudd's office, and told them I was supporting him. Through the night, it became clear to me that Rudd was struggling for support. His chief media adviser, Lachlan Harris, asked whether I would be willing to appear on the morning television bulletins to advocate for Rudd. I readily agreed. At 2.00am, I left Parliament House for home, texting Rudd that he had to stand and fight.

From around 6.00am, before the caucus ballot, I did television and radio interviews in the press gallery. By just before 9.00am, I had appeared on every radio and television station that wanted me, explaining why I was supporting Rudd. But when I rushed to the caucus meeting, I was told that Rudd had decided not to contest the ballot. No one from Rudd's office had thought to tell me of his decision. Maybe they didn't know. Julia had the numbers.

As Rudd received an ovation from caucus for his declaration that he was stepping down and for his service as prime minister, he remained standing, his entire body shaking. I walked up to him and shook his hand. After the meeting, I joined Rudd, his family, and several colleagues in his office as he began preparing for a press conference. It was a terribly sad and painful time for him.

In sticking with Rudd, I had been conscious of the potential damage it could do to my prospects of Julia elevating me to the cabinet. Some journalists speculated that I had ruined my chances. If I had done so, I considered it a price I was willing to pay for supporting the leader against a challenger. But I also sensed that Julia would understand, based on our experiences together in supporting Crean as leader against the challenge from Beazley. We established and maintained a dialogue through the ensuing weeks.

Having battled through an election campaign marred by damaging internal leaks against her, and after weeks of negotiations with the Greens and independents to form a government, Julia turned her attention to the composition of her cabinet. We met in her office, just the two of us. I had gotten into my head a belief that she was not going to promote me into cabinet—not out of vengeance for my having backed Rudd against her, but because she had too many supporters to accommodate. If I were to be passed over again, I knew there would be no chance of moving into cabinet in the future.

Julia spoke frankly. She wanted me in cabinet, but the right would be over-represented if I were promoted, and the left would have to give up a position. She needed time to work that through with the left to see whether it could be achieved. We arranged to meet again on the coming Friday.

Around noon on Friday, as I was standing in the hallway of the house that Julia and I had bought seven years before, my mobile phone rang.

It was Julia. 'I am putting you in cabinet as trade minister', she said. My first reaction was one of shock and incredulity. Having not served a day on Kim Beazley's front bench despite our closeness, and having been barred from cabinet by Rudd, the woman and former partner whose elevation to the leadership I had opposed was telling me she not only wanted me in her cabinet, but that she had insisted on making a place for me. My legs began shaking. This was the moment for which every parliamentarian yearns and, yet one that, for me, over the previous six years of demotions and setbacks, had seemed so improbable.

Suddenly, my sheer delight about entering the cabinet was followed by a sense of anxiety that the trade portfolio would mean a lot of time away from my children.

'Thank you so much, Julia', I replied. 'Would you consider putting me in as climate change minister?'

'No', she said, 'There's an opening for trade minister, and I'm giving you that.'

I thanked her profusely, and wobbled out to the granny flat where my son Ben had been living. I slid open the screen door and said: 'Ben, I'm going to be Australia's minister for trade', and began crying. They were tears of relief and tears of hope that Ben, Tom, and Laura would be proud of their dad being picked to represent Australia.

Much earlier, I had taken Ben through my thoughts about Mum and Dad's attitudes to life. Now, Ben remembered this.

'You proved your mum wrong', he said.

'No, I've proved Dad right', I said, hoping he and his siblings would be encouraged to stay true to themselves throughout their lives—just as my father, with his shy and quiet demeanour, had encouraged me to do.

37

Playing for Australia

If I were to represent my country to the best of my ability, I would need to be as physically fit as possible. In a crazy decision back in 2003, I had accepted the challenge, at the age of 48, of playing in the parliamentary Rugby World Cup, which immediately preceded the real World Cup tournament held in Australia. After somehow surviving matches against France and England, watching a Frenchman cough up blood after being smashed by a former Wallaby playing for us, our team had made it to the final against New Zealand. A sensationally good tackle by a Kiwi opponent tore all the ligaments in my right shoulder, but we won it with a little help from half a dozen ex-Wallabies. Julia and I missed the post-match celebrations, waiting in the emergency department of Canberra Hospital as more serious and urgent cases were treated into the night.

Having achieved a reasonable level of fitness while training for this madness, I then resolved to maintain it, playing several more games over the years for the parliamentary team and for the ACT Veterans. My greatest fear was not of torn ligaments or being whacked in the head, but of suffocating at the bottom of a ruck beneath a pile of exhausted, grossly overweight, and horribly smelly veterans.

Now, as trade minister, I developed a strict regime of exercise when I arrived at an overseas destination. After chasing squirrels around Washington monuments, and meeting formally with the irascible US trade representative, Ron Kirk—a black Democrat and former mayor of Dallas—my next assignment was a meeting of the trade ministers and foreign ministers of the 21 APEC economies in the Japanese port city of Yokohama.

Security would be tight for the leaders' meeting the following week, and the Japanese security contingent used us ministers as practice. Arriving at Tokyo's Narita Airport late at night, my superb chief of staff, Lynne 'Lynnie Wynnie Woo Woo' Ashpole, and I were ushered into vehicles escorted by an astoundingly large number of police cars. Sirens blaring, the police directed the freeway traffic to the sides of the road as we sped past. Or at least that was the plan. Motorists simply ignored the police vehicles, including officers sitting on the car windowsills waving them down with long metal flashlights. So exasperated did the police become that they began smashing the headlights of disobedient motorists.

When I inquired at the hotel about access to the gymnasium, I was told it did not open until 10.00am the next day. Our first meeting was an informal breakfast of ministers. Determined to jog a few kilometres ahead of that early-morning meeting, I headed out after daybreak. Apparently, local security policy dictated that I be joined by five security agents in swanky suits and polished black shoes. I tried to convince them that I would be safe running around the waterfront, but they insisted on accompanying me. It was quite a sight for passers-by; a foreigner in running gear surrounded by Japanese men in suits, their coats concealing their weapons but making them perspire all the more profusely. Only later did I learn that my five companions had no place to shower and no other clothes to change into, ensuring that they remained, let's say, in poor odour for the rest of the day.

At the breakfast meeting, our Japanese host opened with his country's aspirations for the outcome of the leaders' meeting. Upon completing his presentation, he asked for responses. No one at these meetings, it seems, ever wants to go first, so, as the new kid on the block, I did. Then other countries chimed in, supporting Australia's call for a revival of the stalled global trade negotiations. This was to be a lesson to me; Australia often was expected to take a leading, or at least a facilitating, role at international trade talks. Although we were not one of the largest economies represented at the negotiating table, we were respected for our historical commitment to open trade.

My return to Davos after more than two decades, this time as trade minister, reinforced these perceptions. A dinner was organised at a restaurant atop a snow-covered mountain outside of Davos for the trade ministers of the countries considered pivotal to re-starting the global trade talks that began in 2001 but had stalled since a breakdown in negotiations in 2008. There were just seven of us, from the United States, the European Union, China, India, Brazil, Japan, and Australia. A cable car took us most of the way up the darkened mountain, but we were to walk the last couple of hundred metres in snow boots handed to us as we alighted. It was an easy walk crunching through the fresh snow, joking and laughing as we made our way to the mountaintop.

Gathered inside a private room warmed by a hearty open fire, we drank beer and wine, waiting for the final guest. More than half an hour later, our colleague from India joined us, having refused to walk and instead having been hauled the final distance by sled. It would be a sign of the times. India was to play a blocking role at every meeting I attended as trade minister. Over dinner we had a convivial discussion about the future of the talks, but, as we readied to leave our lofty retreat, I asked America's Ron Kirk what he thought of the meeting. 'It was just like déjà vu all over again, my friend', he said, signalling that he had sat through several equally friendly meetings that had also produced no result.

As we met with trade ministers from 22 countries the next day, many excitedly asked me how the greatly anticipated dinner had gone and who had said what to whom. I realised that not only was Australia privileged to be invited to such exclusive meetings, but we were all just ordinary people, like eager kids in a schoolyard trying to pick up the latest gossip.

The Americans wanted China to offer more by way of reductions in its trade barriers, since China's low-cost manufactured exports were inflicting heavy damage on US manufacturers. China refused to agree to American demands that it further open up its markets. Observing this impasse, most countries were ready to abandon this so-called Doha round of multilateral trade negotiations.

Our journey to the restaurant at the mountaintop in Davos had been unsuccessful, but the imagery stayed with me. I recalled a time when, as teenagers, musing in the bough of a Moreton Bay fig tree in Sydney's Moore Park, my dear friend Bluey Godsell told me that

Martin Luther King had said in a speech that there were many paths to the mountaintop. Based on our evening ensconced in the fig tree, I reasoned that the pathway that had been mapped out for the Doha round was blocked. Never mind, I thought, Martin Luther King said there were *many* paths. I conceived the notion of new pathways towards completing the negotiations, which Julia embraced and we advocated subsequently at meetings of the Commonwealth Heads of government, the G20, APEC, and the East Asia Summit.

ON THE WAY from Canberra to the Commonwealth Heads of Government meeting in Perth in late October 2011, I diverted to Baradine, where I had been invited to open the nuns' residence at St John's Convent School that had been fully renovated from funds paid out of the Labor government's Building the Education Revolution program. The place of my early education was in such a poor state of repair, and the nuns so long gone, that it would have needed to be demolished if not for that funding.

My kindergarten mate Tony Purdy persuaded my childhood sweetheart, Anne Tassell, to return to Baradine to attend the ceremony. I officially opened the renovations, professed my love for Anne, and walked hand in hand with her to the little church where I had for so long been an altar boy, reliving an important part of my childhood now as a minister in an Australian government.

Just over a month later, as I addressed the 155 members of the World Trade Organisation (WTO), I spoke of our new pathway, which would involve reaching agreement on some of the issues being negotiated instead of waiting for a grand bargain to descend from the sky. I argued that the developed world owed it to poor countries to assist them in facilitating trade by helping to improve customs procedures at their wharves and airports. That way, equipment could be brought in to build roads to connect poor people to world markets, giving them the opportunity to earn an income from their primary produce.

Following my speech, the chairman of a group comprising the world's least-developed countries sought me out and told me how much he appreciated my motivation to help the poor. It was, for me, a very proud moment. I had found a way, through my university education and political training, to realise the ideals that the nuns at St John's Convent School, Baradine, had instilled in me.

In December 2013, five months after I stepped down from the ministry when Kevin Rudd successfully challenged Julia for the prime ministership, the WTO reached agreement on my new-pathways proposal to facilitate trade with poor countries, together with some modest agricultural-trade improvements. To its great credit, the US used its weight and influence to prevail over India and achieve this agreement.

While working on these global trade negotiations, I also sought to complete trade deals with single countries and smaller groups of countries. My first assignment from Julia when she appointed me trade minister had been to complete the long-running negotiations for a Korea–Australia free-trade agreement. We had high hopes of finalising a deal, but hit a hurdle when the Koreans insisted on their corporations being able to sue Australian governments for regulations that adversely affected their profitability.

Called 'investor-state dispute settlement', this requirement could have impinged upon the sovereign right of Australian federal and state governments to make laws and regulations affecting health, workers' pay and conditions, and the environment. While the Koreans offered comforting language in the agreement that these areas of public policy wouldn't be affected, they also insisted on including a caveat that such action would not be taken against Australian governments 'except in rare circumstances'. Since I felt it was likely that each corporation seeking to sue Australia would claim it was a rare circumstance, I was coming to the view that the comforting language was of no value to us at all. My anxieties were confirmed when I was walking out of a meeting with the third Korean trade minister with whom I had been negotiating. As just the two of us walked along a corridor, he said: 'We want the clause so we can take action against the New South Wales government for using environmental regulations to block a Korean coal-mining proposal.'

With these words ringing in my ears, I arranged a meeting with Julia, Wayne Swan, Joseph Ludwig as agriculture minister, and attorney-general Nicola Roxon. It didn't last long. I explained the impasse. Swan said if we agreed to the Korean demand for investor-state dispute settlement, we would have to agree to the same demand by the United States in negotiations for the 12-country Trans-Pacific Partnership. As health minister before she was appointed attorney-general, Nicola had introduced a law requiring cigarettes to be sold in plain packaging, which was being challenged by American tobacco giant Phillip Morris, using the same provisions in an old investment agreement between Australia and Hong Kong. Julia wrapped up the short meeting by saying: 'I think Craig was coming to the view that we say "No" to the Koreans.' I was.

The Americans didn't believe me when I said Julia would not agree to investor-state dispute settlement in the Trans-Pacific Partnership. No doubt they assessed that she would fold under pressure from the president. To dissuade them of this view, Julia replied to a letter from the US Chamber of Commerce confirming that she would not allow their members to sue our governments. For good measure, Julia replied in similar terms to a letter from the Australian Council of Trade Unions urging us not to fold. I know, because I drafted both of them. The Americans told me they would accept the Australian government's position and would insert a footnote into the Trans-Pacific Partnership agreement exempting Australia from investor-state dispute-settlement provisions. This might come at some cost in terms of concessions the US would offer Australia, they warned, but they would accept our decision. Since the US negotiators were not offering Australia much anyway, any such cost would be small.

While I was negotiating with Korea, I was also seeking to finalise a free-trade agreement with Japan. The Japanese were not insisting on investor-state dispute settlement. If we could close that deal, it might put pressure on the Koreans to drop their demand. We had all but reached agreement with Japan, awaiting only its offer to reduce tariffs on Australian beef. This was related to its application for membership of the Trans-Pacific Partnership, which all eleven existing members had to agree to. At an April 2013 meeting on the sidelines of the APEC trade ministers' meeting in Surabaya, Indonesia, trade ministers from the Trans-Pacific Partnership countries, one by one, agreed to allow Japan to enter into negotiations for the agreement. I was the party pooper, as we had still not received the offer on tariff reductions from the Japanese.

Ministers from some countries threatened to hold media conferences announcing they had agreed to Japan's entry, but that it was being vetoed by Australia. Others showed more solidarity, assuring me that if Australia did not agree, then they did not either. I asked that the meeting re-convene the next morning after I had told the Japanese of the group's position. The Japanese ministers were distressed. They agreed to hasten the beef offer, and I agreed to Japan's entry into the Trans-Pacific Partnership. As it happened, the Japanese beef offer arrived after I had resigned as trade minister and the Labor government had been defeated. We had been within a couple of paragraphs of finalising the free-trade agreement with Japan, but the incoming Abbott government took the credit for it — though its new trade minister, Andrew Robb, acknowledged my contribution.

If brinkmanship with Japan was nerve-wracking, threatening to veto Russia's entry into the WTO was traumatising. All the other 154 members of the WTO had agreed to allow Russia to join. But Russia would not agree to treat imports of Australian beef on the same terms as it had offered the Americans. Consequently, Australian beef producers would face higher Russian trade barriers than their American competitors.

Meeting me in Honolulu during the APEC trade ministers' meeting in November 2011, Russia's trade minister, Elvira Nabiullina, a slight, articulate young woman, was most anxious about the prospect of an Australian veto. Russia had been seeking entry into the WTO for years, and now Australia was potentially blocking it. Nabiullina was asking me to be reasonable. We agreed to draft a letter of assurance from Russia that it would treat Australian beef the same as American beef. Drafts with track changes flew across the continents. Unfortunately, the Americans forgot to remove their identifying marks on their tracked changes, making it obvious that we were, in reality, negotiating not only with Russia but with the United States as well. After several more exchanges of draft letters, I reached agreement with Nabiullina, and Russia joined the WTO. I later met again with Nabiullina when, as his sole adviser, she sat on one side of Vladimir Putin, and me on the other, at the meeting of APEC leaders at Vladivostok in September 2012.

BEEF OCCUPIED MUCH OF MY TIME as trade minister. Through my adult life, I have become increasingly distressed about the way humans treat animals. When the ABC's *Four Corners* program screened footage of appalling treatment of cattle in an Indonesian abattoir, I could barely bring myself to watch it. Middle Australia was appalled—not just greenies and lefties, as the Coalition was claiming.

The cabinet discussion was not very contentious. Julia was deeply concerned that we could not assure ourselves that the incidents shown on *Four Corners* were isolated and unlikely to be repeated. Nor could the Australian live-export industry provide any such assurance. In those circumstances, several colleagues and I argued that the only viable option was to suspend the trade to Indonesia and enter into discussions about how to improve the system, such that slaughter would take place only in abattoirs that met the relevant international standards.

Cabinet instructed me to phone my counterpart, Indonesia's trade minister, Mari Pangestu, who had gained her Master's degree from the Australian National University just a few years after I had completed my PhD. Mari and I had become good friends and, after attending a meeting of APEC trade ministers at Blue Sky, Montana, in the Rocky Mountains, we had spent a Saturday afternoon together visiting Yellowstone National Park. When I phoned Mari, she was very understanding. We resolved to work together and with the agriculture ministries in both countries to identify abattoirs that could meet international animal-welfare standards, so we could resume the trade as soon as possible.

Indonesia's agriculture minister, Suswono, was less understanding. He was committed to self-sufficiency in beef for Indonesia, and took the opportunity to argue against any resumption of live-cattle imports from Australia. Following the identification of a number of compliant abattoirs, Mari and I quietly worked behind the scenes on the resumption. Mari was able to inform me how events that would lead to Indonesia's announcement of the resumption were likely to unfold and when we could expect it. Joseph Ludwig, our agriculture minister, received most of the criticism for the suspension, which he did not deserve. He did not have the relationship with Suswono that I had with Pangestu. Nor could he have been expected to have a close relationship with a minister whose preference was to stop the trade altogether.

Claims that the suspension permanently damaged the relationship between Julia Gillard and Indonesian president Susilo Bambang Yudhoyono are false. At the recommendation of Mari's successor, Gita Wirjawan, I suggested to Julia that she nominate president Yudhoyono for the Nobel Peace Prize for his work not only in entrenching democracy in Indonesia, but also in encouraging the military leadership in Myanmar to make the transition to democracy. As a former army general, Yudhoyono had great credibility in assuring his counterparts in Myanmar that such a transition could be undertaken successfully. President Yudhoyono had told me of his letter to the president of Myanmar, Thein Sein, as we chatted ahead of lunch in Davos, Switzerland.

While we were unwilling to conclude trade deals that we assessed were not in Australia's national interest, Malaysia was keen to finalise a promising deal with us. This would build on the ASEAN-Australia-New Zealand Free Trade Agreement negotiated by my predecessor, trade minister Simon Crean. Julia had met the Malaysian prime minister, Najib Razak, in her office before inviting him into the cabinet room for a further meeting with relevant cabinet ministers. The two of them asked me to join them in a corner for a private chat.

They advised me that they wanted to announce a deadline of twelve months for signing an agreement, and asked me if I considered this feasible. I said it was, if prime minister Najib revamped his negotiating team of officials. He did so, and I worked closely with his trade minister, Mustapa Mohamed, who had studied at the University of Melbourne and was very fond of Australia from his happy experiences here. We signed the Malaysia-Australia Free Trade Agreement with one day to spare.

In all these endeavours I was strongly supported by top-flight negotiators from the Department of Foreign Affairs and Trade, literally too many to mention by name. They were decent, dedicated, and eternally patient professionals of immaculate reputation and international standing, to whom their country owes a great deal. While the formal negotiations involving large numbers of officials from both sides were mostly characterised by the pronouncement of fixed positions, much of the real work was conducted in private over dinners. One quietly spoken female official told me that, when her lead counterpart put to her an unreasonable demand on behalf of his government, she told him to 'Fuck off.' The next day he came to the table with a more realistic proposition.

FROM TIME TO TIME, I filled in as acting minister for foreign affairs. One such time was in early 2012, when Rudd announced he would challenge Julia for the leadership. Ahead of that challenge, he resigned as foreign minister. Julia asked me to step into the position while she decided who would take on the role permanently. Rudd had been instrumental in the international agreement to establish a no-fly zone over Libya, preventing Muammar Gaddafi's air force from striking rebel forces. When the rebels defeated Gaddafi, a meeting of the Friends of Libya grouping of countries was called for Paris. I said to Julia I should attend. 'Bless you', she replied. My itinerary involved flying for 24 hours to Paris, arriving at my hotel at 10.00am, going for a five-kilometre run through the Trocadero and under the Eiffel Tower, and attending the meeting from 2.00pm before flying back home.

World leaders began streaming into the Elysée Palace. As Australia's acting minister for foreign affairs, I was well down the pecking order; presidents or prime ministers represented most other countries. Nevertheless, I chatted to Greece's prime minister, George Papandreou, Germany's chancellor, Angela Merkel, and the European Union's foreign minister, Catherine Ashton. Most leaders wanted to speak to Hillary Clinton, so I said a quick hello and stepped away from the stampede. By the time the meeting started, diligent Australian officials had managed to get me placed close to the top of the speaking list. But each time my turn approached, another president or prime minister pulled rank on me, and I continually slipped down the list.

As the meeting moved into the evening, Sarkozy announced: 'Okay, okay, we have heard everyone pledge their support to Libya. Those of you who have not spoken can have your speeches incorporated into the official record. Unless anyone has something different to say, I am going to close the meeting.' I had arrived in Paris that morning, and was booked on an 11.00pm flight back to Australia. I had no intention of travelling halfway around the world and back just to make up the numbers, so I turned my Australia nameplate end-up to signify I wanted to talk. Sarkozy looked annoyed, but was obliged to invite me to speak.

I spoke for two minutes, reminding the meeting of Australia's role in establishing the Libyan Contact Group, and pledging that the Australian government would financially assist Libyan students studying in Australia. Sarkozy closed the meeting, and I was even able to report my cameo speech to Australian audiences through an interview with the ABC's Emma Alberici outside the palace. I boarded the night flight to Sydney, and arrived back in Canberra totally wrecked, having not stayed even one night in Paris.

After first having met Hillary Clinton at a garden party in Honolulu ahead of the APEC leaders' meeting in late 2011, and again at Vladivostok, we had become quite chatty. By the time we met again, in Phnom Penh towards the end of 2012, I grabbed her by the arm as we left an official banquet and said: 'Hillary, you guys have got to win the presidential election.' She reassured me: 'Craig, we're trying.' I thought as much, but I just wanted to double check.

Following the election, a victorious President Obama hosted a meeting of the parties to the Trans-Pacific Partnership, to which leaders and their trade ministers were invited. After explaining his desire for a high-quality agreement, Obama came over to meet us. Julia introduced me, and I said: 'You sure kicked Republican butt, Mr President.' Perhaps this wasn't out of the diplomatic copybook, but Julia laughed and the president grinned. President Obama spoke with the confidence that goes with the job, and the cheeky smile that goes with the man.

AS TRADE MINISTER, I invested a great deal of time and effort in strengthening Australia's ties with China. My mentor, Bob Hawke, had built the relationship on the back of Gough Whitlam's visionary recognition of the People's Republic of China as one of his first acts as prime minister. Inexplicably, only two countries accepted China's invitation to speak at a conference on the role of services in its 12th Five Year Plan. Australia was one of them. My Chinese counterpart, commerce minister Chen Deming, a grandfatherly figure and a thoughtful and gentle man, became a good friend and confidant. We sought each other out at international meetings and sat together at official banquets, chatting privately in English as guests moved around toasting each other in accordance with Chinese tradition.

At one such dinner in Beijing, I asked minister Chen whether China would be interested in cooperating with Australia in agriculture to help meet the rising demand for safe, premium-quality food amongst its rising middle class. Chen was pleasantly surprised about my approach. 'I didn't think you'd be interested', he said. 'We have been to Africa and South America looking at their agricultural potential, but we thought Australia would not welcome Chinese investment in your agriculture.' I agreed it would be controversial, but explained that it would, at the same time, revive Australia's declining towns and regional cities.

I suggested the two of us oversee a joint Australia–China food study. Chen readily agreed, and proposed we include the agriculture ministers of the two countries. I released the report, *Feeding the Future*, just before Christmas 2012. It helped set off a wave of interest in Chinese investment in Australian agriculture and in Chinese purchases of our premium produce.

So familiar did I become with minister Chen that we began discussing our families. As I relaxed in my plush seat at the dinner table, I asked Chen possibly the dumbest question of my life: 'How many children do you have?'

Without missing a beat, Chen replied: 'One. He's a boy. He's grown up now. He has one child, too.' It was impossible to determine whether minister Chen assumed I was the only Australian government minister who had never heard of China's One Child Policy, or if he figured that, in the lateness of the evening, I had had a momentary lapse, but he cheerily went on to tell me all about his son's family.

Shadow minister Barnaby Joyce had been running around the country campaigning against Chinese investment in Australian agriculture, falsely accusing me of being in cahoots with Bob Hawke in orchestrating the West Australian Liberal government's decision to award to a Chinese company the rights to develop a further stage of the Ord River Scheme. Tony Abbott supported Joyce's anti-China campaign. To their credit, shadow treasurer Joe Hockey and shadow finance minister Andrew Robb did not, speaking out against him. Disgracefully, during the 2013 election campaign, Kevin Rudd positioned himself and the Labor Party to the right of Abbott, asserting in a televised debate that Abbott wasn't going hard enough on the issue.

Cabinet discussion about how to deal with Abbott's anti-China position on the purchase of Australian farmland was robust. Some ministers argued for a tightening of the foreign-investment screening processes for Chinese investment in Australian agriculture. That was until Julia made her position clear: 'We are not going to try to position ourselves to the right of Tony Abbott on this', she declared. It was one more reason why I supported Julia so strongly when she was being destabilised by Rudd and his supporters. Another was her acknowledgement in the parliament, when under pressure from the Coalition about putting a price on carbon, of the courage that Hawke and Keating showed in pressing ahead with tariff reductions when the economy was heading into the 1991 recession. Hawke and Keating, she told parliament, did not flinch when tariff reform was necessary, and she would not flinch when carbon pricing was necessary.

38

Triumph and tragedy in Vladivostok

Wanting to build on Bob Hawke's legacy, I suggested to Julia that we prepare a white paper on Australia's place in the Asian century. She promised me she would do it, as soon as she and Greg Combet had bedded down the emissions trading scheme. Julia was true to her word. We set up a task force headed by former Treasury secretary Ken Henry, together with a cabinet committee that included leading academics and business representatives. While travelling around the world as trade minister, I drafted and redrafted sections of the document, which, when released in late 2012, was well received. China was especially pleased, noting that Australia was the first developed country to prepare a plan for its engagement with the region. To ensure proper implementation of the plan, Julia appointed me minister assisting the prime minister on Asian Century policy. I was collecting titles and portfolios, and this was not to be my last.

Personal credibility and trust were to count again during crucial negotiations ahead of the APEC leaders' meeting in Vladivostok in September 2012. Two years prior, the United States had proposed an agreement among APEC members to limit tariff rates on imported goods used in the preservation of the environment, such as water-purification equipment, photovoltaic cells, and wind turbines. China had argued at the 2011 APEC trade ministers' meeting in Big Sky, Montana, that APEC was not a negotiating forum for reducing trade barriers. At the request of the United States, I spoke after a coffee break, reminding ministers that APEC had agreed in 1994 to a goal of free trade in goods by 2020.

We were not seeking a legally binding agreement but a voluntary one, for the sake of the environment. China remained at the table, but was never keen on the American proposal.

It all came to a head at Vladivostok, when China announced it was willing to consider including no more than 20 environmental goods in the recommended statement for leaders to adopt. I argued that this would be an embarrassingly small list of goods, especially as the original American list ran to more than 300 items. As host, Russia could not have cared less, its trade minister indicating he would be happy with an agreed list of 20 goods. I re-joined the debate, advising that Australia would not sign such a pathetic declaration, preferring instead to announce failure. I encouraged other countries to join the boycott. Several, including the United States, Canada, and New Zealand, made it clear that they, too, would refuse to sign. I asked for the meeting's agreement to Australia developing an alternative list overnight in consultation with key countries. Permission was granted, and, after toiling all night, our officials came up with a much more respectable list of 60 goods.

A handful of middle-sized countries had problems with some items on the list. Mexico's brief from its government, for instance, was to refuse to agree to a couple of goods, but its trade minister, Bruno Ferrari, was a friend. His party had recently been defeated at a general election, so this was to be his last APEC trade ministers' meeting. He told me that despite the position held back in his home capital, he was signing up to my list.

Now it was up to China. I walked over to its delegation for a private discussion. They told me that as long as LED lights were on the list, they would sign. I informed the American delegation that had worked so long and hard on this exercise. They were ecstatic; we had achieved agreement. Or so we thought. When I advised our Russian hosts that we had an agreement, they insisted they would not agree to the inclusion of LED lights, since Russia was intending to become a major producer of these energy-saving lights, and wanted its industry protected from imports. Again, Russia was indicating it did not care if the agreement collapsed.

Dismayed, I walked over to the Chinese to alert them to the Russian position. The Chinese said they had to have LED lights included, since they were a major producer. At that point, I told them to go and sort it out with the Russians. A scrum of around 40 Russian and Chinese officials and their ministers quickly formed around the Russian delegation's place at the front of the table. Fascinated, I looked on with the Americans. After around 20 minutes, the scrum broke up. A terribly disappointed China had agreed to exclude LED lights, but to sign the agreement.

Julia arrived, and I was able to tell her the good news. But terrible news was to follow. Her father had died suddenly. John Gillard was a humble, gentle man whose quiet dedication to the care of others had been an inspiration for Julia's entry into public life. When Julia's adviser informed me of the tragedy, I made my way to a holding room next to the formal meeting rooms at the APEC venue on Russky Island. Julia's long-time electorate officer and friend, Michelle Fitzgerald, arrived at the same time. Julia was grief-stricken. The three of us hugged and cried. Julia asked whether I might be able to stand in for her at the leaders' meeting. I said of course I would, and that she should return to Australia to be with her mother and family.

Vladimir Putin, as host, had been advised of Julia's bereavement, and tried phoning her. Our officials informed the Russian hosts that I would be representing Julia. That night, Julia left for Australia, which seemed so far away. My main concern was not my ability to represent Australia at the meeting of world leaders, but that there might be a misunderstanding, and that I would walk through the wrong door the next morning, or be denied entry by uninformed security officials. My fears were unfounded. I was transported to the meeting venue in the official vehicle the organisers had allocated to the Australian prime minister. Putin had been greeting leaders as they arrived, one by one, according to predetermined protocol. He was expecting me, we shook hands, and he said in perfect English how sad he was that Julia had lost her dad. He said he had tried to ring her to offer his condolences. I assured him that Julia was grateful for the calls. It was a very human moment.

Inside the venue that had been restricted to leaders, I walked up to Hillary Clinton, who was also very sad for Julia. They had become very close. We discussed the grief of losing fathers and mothers, just as each of us had done. We were, when it was all said and done, just ordinary people with feelings of sadness and sympathy for those we knew who had suffered the loss of a family member.

At the formal session, we took our assigned seats, with Australia being seated next to the host, Russia. A leader of one of the APEC countries opened the discussion at each session. Australia had been nominated to lead the discussion on food security, about which I was able to speak with some confidence since I had been writing and speaking on the subject for two years. I contributed to the other discussions as well, briefing the leaders on the agreement to limit tariffs on environmental goods.

At lunch, our guest speaker was the International Monetary Fund's chief, Christine Lagarde. Several leaders came up to me to say how interesting they found my views on food security and the challenge of feeding a global population that would exceed nine billion people by 2050.

If this was the proudest moment of my career, I was also about to see the most touching display of compassion from any journalist in my life. Following the leaders' meeting, I met the travelling Australian media to brief them on the agreements that had been reached. When they asked after Julia, I cried, saying that of course she was upset about losing her father. Before leaving Vladivostok for Australia, Julia had written her own statement explaining why she could not attend the APEC meeting. Hugh Riminton, the chief reporter for the Ten Network, told viewers back home of Julia's loss, and said of her statement to the media: 'It read more like a love letter from a daughter to her father.' What a thoroughly decent, caring man.

As APEC wrapped up, leaders prepared to leave Vladivostok. My plan had been to join Julia aboard the Air Force flight home, but she had already departed. In the ANZAC tradition, the Kiwis helped out the Aussies: I thumbed a lift to Tokyo with New Zealand's prime minister, John Key. We yacked most of the way, already knowing each other from a leadership dialogue dinner for the two countries where I had lamented that New Zealand had beaten Australia that year in every imaginable sport, from rugby to netball, and even marbles. I told the dinner audience that we had arranged a water polo match, but it had to be cancelled when all the horses drowned.

39

No Whyalla wipeout

Although I had not been heavily involved in the design of the Gillard government's carbon emissions trading scheme, I was asked to help sell it to a wary public. Tony Abbott and his shadow ministers had taken their campaign against carbon pricing to hysterical heights, warning of 'unimaginable' price increases and that it would swing 'like a wrecking ball through the economy', wiping industrial cities such as Whyalla off the map.

On the last parliamentary sitting day before the date of the scheme's introduction, Julia, Albo, Greg Combet, and I had arranged a question from our side to enable me to ridicule Abbott's claims about Whyalla's destruction. I had crammed into my suit pockets a tape measure and a swimming-pool temperature gauge, which I passed off as a light meter. Mine was the tenth and final question from the government side. We were well into Question Time when Abbott, as he had done so nauseatingly often, moved a suspension of standing orders to trigger a debate on carbon pricing. This disruptive technique took us past the allocated time for questions, making it usual for the prime minister to call an end to Question Time as soon as the debate on the suspension of standing orders was finished.

As we voted on the Abbott motion, we huddled in a crisis meeting. What to do? Albo proposed that, in violation of the parliamentary procedures agreed with the Coalition, Julia refrain from calling an end to Question Time, enabling a Labor backbencher to ask me about Whyalla. Julia agreed, but I knew I needed to keep my answer tight or face numerous disruptive points of order. I mentally gave myself two minutes. When the Speaker announced the result of the vote on the Abbott motion, a Labor MP rose, to the opposition's surprise, and asked me a question. The manager of opposition business, Christopher Pyne, objected, but Albo countered with a fabricated argument that the duration of Question Time was entirely at the prime minister's discretion. I held my breath, Pyne relented, and I was on.

I announced I was going to Whyalla on the coming Sunday, 1 July 2012. Brandishing the tape measure, which I described as my 'sky-height measuring device', I argued that if Abbott, as a modern-day Chicken Little, was correct about the sky falling in, I would be able to reach up and measure it. And if the sky was indeed falling in, Whyalla should become darker during the day, which I would be able to test with my trusty light meter. My answer went to plan, lasting just two minutes, and the government side left the chamber in good cheer.

On the weekend, I did indeed travel to Whyalla, with my chief media adviser, Mark 'Mulliguts' Mulligan. Tweeting about 'carbon zombies' and 'Carbongeddon', we arrived just before midnight. The city centre was almost deserted, and it was dark, cloudy, and raining. Perhaps Abbott was right? After a restless night, we woke to a brilliant sunny morning. The locals laid on a barbecue for us, and we made fun of Abbott's claims about the End of Days for Whyalla. A large media contingent joined us, including a television reporter who arrived from Adelaide by helicopter. The evening news featured me ridiculing Abbott's prophecy of a Whyalla wipeout.

Back in Canberra on Monday, Julia's media strategist, John McTernan, was keen to continue the mocking of Abbott's ludicrous claims about the effects of the carbon price. I had been in the press gallery on Friday ahead of my visit to Whyalla, and had dropped into the ABC bureau. Its chief political correspondent for the evening television news, Mark Simkin, had chatted to me at the time about my intentions in Whyalla. In response, I had jokingly sung a line that, impromptu, I had adapted from the Skyhooks' mid-1970s' hit, 'Horror Movie'. Simkin dared me to sing it for the ABC on Monday. I pointed out that in doing so I might breach copyright, but that was easily dealt with.

It just so happened that one of the Skyhooks' band members, Red

Symons, was an ABC radio presenter in Melbourne. Simkin took the precaution on Monday morning of checking with Symons, who assured him that my performance would be fine with band members. Mulliguts duly received a call from Simkin mid-morning on Monday, inviting me to sing my Skyhooks adaptation for the ABC cameras in the Senate courtyard.

My initial reaction was to decline the invitation, but I asked Mulliguts to check with McTernan before doing so. McTernan liked the idea, since it would serve the political purpose of demonstrating to the Australian public the absurdity of Abbott's apocalyptic claims about the impact of the carbon price. Mulliguts called up 'Horror Movie' on his iPad, we recorded me sort-of singing 'No Whyalla wipeout there on my TV, shocking me right out of my brain', and the rest, as they say, is history. All the four metropolitan television stations featured my tuneless performance on their nightly bulletins, and the video went global. My son Ben, who was studying in Berlin at the time, was shocked right out of his brain. I received messages from television viewers in Greece, and the story was covered on both British and American television news bulletins.

ABC radio's Triple J adopted 'No Whyalla wipeout' as its morning introduction melody, conservative radio hosts went nuts, and shadow treasurer Joe Hockey, who once dressed up as a fairy godmother, described me as a clown. Amid the furore, I flew to Darwin to join Julia for official talks with the president of Indonesia and his ministers. As we took our places at the table, Gita Wirjawan, himself a concert pianist, said, in front of the president, the prime minister, and assembled ministers from both countries: 'I enjoyed your singing on television last night, Craig.' Amid strained laughter, Julia welcomed the president, and we conducted the meeting.

After the joint media conference with the president, I explained to Julia that it was her media strategist's fault. She didn't buy it, and at the first available cabinet meeting, she banned all her ministers, other than Peter Garrett, from singing. As television journalists and commentators tut-tutted, an unexpected ally came to my defence. Red Symons appeared on ABC morning television to deliver his judgement: far from being gonged off the stage by him, as he had done innumerable times to amateur musical performers in a show called *Red Faces*, Symons defended my effort as respectable. Tens of thousands — perhaps millions — of Australians and overseas music-lovers disagreed.

In the lead-up to the 2013 election campaign, I was out jogging when I received a call on my mobile from a bloke purporting to be from *The Chaser*, the ABC's team renowned for its political satire. Although it was dusk, I looked around for cameras, suspecting I was about to be confronted with a 'gotcha' stunt. He invited me to join the team for *The Hamster Decides,* their pre-election series that would run for around six weeks. I was to introduce *The Chaser* team's special guest, adapting my adaptation of 'Horror Movie' in a tailor-made send-up. My instinct was to decline the invitation on the basis that I had already done enough damage to the international standing of the Australian music industry. But then again, I thought I might regret lacking the courage to appear on such a widely viewed program. I sought assurance from my *Chaser* caller. 'You wouldn't do anything to humiliate me, would you?' I asked, to which he replied: 'You've done a pretty good job of that yourself.' He had a point.

I checked with my children. None of them was keen, but they left it to me to decide. I accepted and, with a backing band, performed each week as 'Emmo and the Wipeouts' to audiences topping one million. Yet again, ABC morning television wanted me gonged off the stage, but Red Symons showed his true colours by coming to my defence once more. A song that had divided the nation lived on.

40

Subversion

During the entire period of Julia Gillard's time as prime minister, Kevin Rudd and his supporters were undermining her and destabilising the minority government from within. No useful purpose is served by recounting this all again. The ABC's three-part series *The Killing Season* has done that. I inadvertently gave the TV series its title by explaining to the interviewer, Sarah Ferguson, that I had earlier described the last sitting fortnight before going into an election year as the 'killing season'. This was a period during which MPs had their last realistic opportunity to change leaders. Simon Crean and Kim Beazley had lost their leadership at this time, and I asked rhetorically on ABC's *Lateline* on 20 November 2009, when the Coalition was in turmoil over the Turnbull opposition's negotiations with Labor to introduce an emissions trading scheme: 'Will the opportunists seize the day and use this as a leadership tilt in the killing season, or will common sense and the national interest prevail?' Eleven days later, Turnbull lost the leadership to Tony Abbott. I had adapted the term from *The Killing Fields*, the movie depicting the atrocities of Pol Pot's Khmer Rouge.

My attitude towards Julia's leadership was simple. While I had disagreed with the manner of her becoming leader, the caucus had elected her to the position, and the Australian people had confirmed her as Australia's first female prime minister. She worked her guts out for the disadvantaged. I was proud of her decency, courage, and determination.

For each of Rudd's challenges I kept, in liaison with Julia's office, a tally sheet of caucus members' voting intentions. In the first challenge, our tally was out by one vote. For the second challenge, called on Rudd's behalf by Simon Crean, we were well ahead. As we gathered in Julia's office for a final review of the numbers, the news came through that Rudd was not a candidate. In a display of terrible timing, a female senator rang Julia to explain how tortured she was to have decided to switch her allegiance to Rudd. Julia politely explained to her troubled colleague that she would not, in fact, be voting for Rudd, since he had just announced he would not be contesting the ballot.

Following that aborted ballot, a number of cabinet ministers, including Chris Bowen, stepped down. I wondered who would fill the position of minister for tertiary education, skills, science, and research that Bowen had vacated. I soon learned it was to be me. Julia trusted me, and asked me to take on the portfolio while retaining the portfolios of trade and competitiveness, and minister assisting the prime minister on Asian Century policy.

Julia and I, along with the foreign minister, Bob Carr, and the financial services minister, Bill Shorten, visited China in April 2013 to meet the new president, Xi Jinping, and the new premier, Li Keqiang, where we would formalise an annual leadership dialogue based on a strategic partnership with China. We met with president Xi at the Boao Forum on Hainan Island. Although he had notes, he spoke mainly impromptu, expressing his desire to complete negotiations for the free-trade agreement between our two countries.

In Beijing, it was the same story with premier Li. During a foreign ministers' signing ceremony officially witnessed by Julia, premier Li, and me, the premier asked Julia: 'Which one is the free-trade guy?' Julia pointed to me. Premier Li followed her lead and pointed, too. I responded: 'I'm the free-trade guy.' The moment was captured on camera, and it is among the more humorous of the official photographs of that historic visit.

Back in Australia, my office expanded with the additional responsibilities Julia had given me. I was shifted into the office that Paul Keating had occupied, which I had visited so often as a young adviser to Bob Hawke. Now I was on the other side of the desk, but the task was the same as Paul's: finding savings to reduce the budget deficit.

Before leaving for China, I had been working with the peak

organisation representing universities, Universities Australia, on slightly slowing down the growth in enrolments in order to ease the budgetary costs. When I returned to Australia, Julia rang to tell me that the budget review committee had, instead, decided to reduce the growth in university funding by 2 per cent in the coming year and by 1.5 per cent in the following year. Australia was approaching the end of the mining boom, and any new government spending needed to be accommodated by savings elsewhere. I planned to convert generous cash payments to students for books and other costs to repayable loans, and to remove the discount for paying university fees up front instead of taking out a loan. Universities Australia refused to accept this and went nuts, deliberately misrepresenting the plan as a cut to their funding. Despite the best efforts of my brilliant economic adviser, Hugh 'Rowdy' Hartigan, to produce statistics and charts showing no overall reduction in funding per student, Universities Australia ran an advertising campaign against Labor right up to the 2013 election.

On the night before the 2013 budget, the doorbell rang. My sons, Ben and Tom, had been at dinner at their mother's house, but they both had keys and never used the doorbell. I opened the door to two uniformed police officers. My heart sank. *Oh, no. Please, God, no.* In the darkness, I could see Ben approaching the house behind them. 'Ben', I trembled, 'where's Tom?'

'He's on his way', Ben assured me.

The police officers asked to come inside and for me to sit down. 'We have bad news for you, Dr Emerson. Your brother, Lance, passed away today.'

Lance had been becoming incapacitated by emphysema from heavy smoking, one consequence of his wretched childhood. An autopsy revealed he had chronic heart disease and that he could have died at any time. He had tried to walk from his terrace house in Newcastle to his vehicle to drive to a hospital, but collapsed into the passenger seat and died. My loving brother had asked me to provide from his estate for the payment of our three children's university fees, a gift inspired from our own parents' determination for us to have the opportunity of a good education.

AS WE HAD ALL YEAR, we continued to hear rumours of a Rudd challenge throughout the post-budget period. Stories to this effect appeared in newspapers, most particularly the Rudd supporters' favoured tabloid, *The Daily Telegraph*. In addition to my expanded portfolio responsibilities, I gladly took on the media role of defending Julia and her prime ministership.

To stay resilient and articulate, I stepped up my fitness regime, often going for a five-kilometre run when I got back from Parliament House around 10.30pm. The run made me physically tired, enabling me to get to sleep quickly after a shower and to remain asleep until 5.30am, when I would review the latest media speculation ahead of appearing on early-morning radio and television. As I walked each morning from my car to the elevator in the ministerial car park, I would gaze into the dark, narrow gap between the car-park floor and the elevator floor, and, as I stepped across it, I would say to myself, *Now you're entering the combat zone.* For me, that slender, black abyss symbolised the tiny distance between the relative sanity of life outside politics and the madness of a government tearing itself apart.

At the beginning of the final sitting fortnight before the winter recess and the federal election, Greg Combet and Gary Gray called on Rudd to challenge or desist from his destabilisation campaign. Two days before the first Rudd challenge in February 2012, Greg and I had arranged to have coffee in Cessnock, where we were to attend a New South Wales Labor Party conference.

We discussed a 'suicide bomber' scenario where Julia did not recover in the public opinion polls after defeating Rudd in the coming ballot, and Rudd made a second effort to defeat her. In those circumstances, we contemplated the idea of approaching Julia with the proposition that Greg and I run as an alternative leadership team, without deciding until then which of us would contest the leadership and who would nominate as deputy leader. We appreciated that a second challenge would be viable for Rudd only if caucus members were desperately worried about retaining their seats, in which case they would probably choose Rudd on the basis that he had led them to victory in 2007 and had proven campaign skills. Nevertheless, we would at least offer our colleagues a choice and, under our plan, Julia would urge her staunch supporters to vote for us.

Early in the last sitting fortnight, Greg again raised the 'suicide bomber' idea. I argued that caucus would either vote for Julia or Rudd, but not for either of us in sufficient numbers to defeat Rudd if Julia were to withdraw from the contest. Apparently, Julia had been separately talking to Greg about him running, but he had decided his health was not good enough to sustain the pressures of the top job.

As Julia reported Greg's decision to me in her office, she asked me for one final effort: 'Can you hold off the Rudd supporters until I can get the school-funding bill through the parliament?' At a time when her leadership was in peril, Julia's main concern was for the thousands of children in disadvantaged families whose life chances would be greatly improved with the passage of the needs-based school-funding legislation. I promised her I would. The bill passed the Senate in the afternoon of Wednesday 26 June. The leadership ballot was held at seven o'clock that evening.

A core group of Gillard supporters — comprising trusted friends Stephen Conroy, Don Farrell, Brendan O'Connor, Gary Gray, Chris Hayes, Warren Snowden, and me — had been meeting three times a day, counting numbers and urging waverers to stick with Julia. In the closing days of parliament, there were rumours that Rudd supporters were circulating a petition of caucus members calling for a leadership spill. Julia needed to decide whether to call a spill or wait for any such petition to emerge. My view was to oblige the necessary one-third of caucus members to write their names on the rumoured petition, but other influential supporters, including Paul Howes, a close mutual friend who had publicly backed Julia's challenge against Rudd in 2010, urged her to call a spill to resolve the matter once and for all. Julia again asked for my opinion.

'If you call a ballot, there's a good chance you'll lose', I advised her. But I also needed to make an assessment of whether or not the destabilisation would continue all the way to the election. 'My assessment is that there's a 30 per cent chance of Rudd and his supporters backing off if we get past these last two sitting days', I said. Her other supporters rated that chance at zero. 'Gee, Emmo, you're the most optimistic of all of us that Rudd will back off, and you put the chance at 30 per cent?' That was when Julia decided to announce a spill for that evening. For the sake of giving Labor some clear air to compete at the election, she added that if she lost the ballot she would leave parliament and that Rudd should make the same commitment.

As Julia listened to Tony Windsor giving his last speech in the chamber, I walked into her office and left on her desk a hand-written list of caucus waverers she should ring. As soon as Windsor finished his farewell speech, our group reconvened in her office. One by one, text messages arrived confirming that wavering supporters were switching to Rudd in an effort to save their seats. As one of our group reported on yet another such text that had just come in, I said to Julia: 'Now you can't win', causing an outbreak of groans and swearing, but not from her. 'It's okay, we're not going to drink the purple cordial', she said, a reference to Jonestown, Guyana where, in the late 1970s, more than 900 cult followers drank Kool-Aid laden with cyanide in a mass suicide.

As we accompanied Julia to the caucus room, we knew she would be defeated, but we wanted the opportunity to vote for her. I had returned briefly to my office to gather my staff together and advise them that Julia was about to lose the prime ministership, and that I would be resigning from the ministry after the caucus meeting. They were terribly sad, and they would be losing their jobs, but they were very understanding that I could not, in good conscience, work for Rudd. I drafted my resignation statement on my personal computer.

In the caucus room, Julia sat with Wayne Swan on the sofa facing caucus members, and I sat just a couple of metres away, facing Julia and Wayne. After Julia declared the leadership vacant, the chair of caucus called for nominations for eight scrutineer positions. The first few were all Rudd supporters. Julia nodded to me to nominate, which I did. As colleagues received their ballot papers in a room connected to the caucus room, voted, and filed past the ballot box, the mood was amiable enough. We scrutineers unfolded and counted the ballot papers, confirming what I already knew: Rudd had a majority.

As we re-entered the caucus room, I resumed my seat opposite Julia. She looked at me, inquisitively but not hopefully. With a motion that would have been perceptible only to the two of us, I gently turned my lips down. Julia had lost the prime ministership. The result was announced to polite applause, and Swan announced his resignation as deputy leader and treasurer. While New South Wales and Queensland television viewers tuned in for the State of Origin rugby league match, which had inconveniently clashed with the change of prime minister, a ballot for deputy prime minister of Australia would be needed. Simon Crean and Anthony Albanese nominated for the deputy's position. As I rose to resume my position as scrutineer, I took two steps towards Julia and Wayne, and discreetly asked which candidate I should advise any of our inquiring supporters to support. Before I could suggest Albo, they spontaneously answered in unison: 'Albo.' During the ballot, several colleagues quietly asked me for advice. I was happy to give it to them.

Albo won the ballot easily. Next, Stephen Conroy resigned as leader in the Senate, Penny Wong was elected uncontested to replace him, and Jacinta Collins was elected to fill the position of deputy leader in the Senate. Just when I thought it was all over, my friend and former flatmate, Joseph Ludwig, surprised everyone by rising from his seat to announce his resignation from the ministry. My intention had been to return to my office to issue my media release announcing my resignation, but Joseph's caucus announcement prompted me to do the same. I said something like: 'Kevin, congratulations on your victory. I wish you and the Labor team all the best for the coming election. But I can't … I can't …' I choked up and sat down. Tears welling in my eyes, I looked at Julia. She mouthed: 'Thank you.' It was done.

As Julia did her last media conference as prime minister and I issued my media release, word came from her office that we were invited to drinks at the Lodge. Tears were shed, but laughter was shared, too, as I used my iPad to video Julia's and Swan's speeches to friendly caucus colleagues and staff supporters.

From time to time during my parliamentary life, I had imagined what I would say in my valedictory speech. But now I was so upset that I knew I would not get far into it before crying, unable to regain my composure. By the morning, Greg Combet and Peter Garrett had also resigned from the ministry, as they told me they would. To avoid embarrassment, I made inquiries as to where we would be sitting as backbenchers during Question Time. Greg, Wayne, Julia, and I entered the chamber at around the same time, and guided each other to our seats.

After Question Time, I headed for the gymnasium, but noticed on an external television monitor that Peter Garrett was delivering his valedictory speech. I diverged to the chamber in my gym gear. *What is the worst that could happen to me?* I asked myself. *The Speaker might throw me out, one more time.* With some prompting from me by way of a mischievous interjection, Peter made a musical reference to me in his speech. I rose to my feet in my grey sweatshirt, and acknowledged the accolades for my performance of 'No Whyalla wipeout' from an imaginary admiring audience. As I reached the gym following Peter's speech, I reflected before stepping onto the treadmill. I had entered parliament with dignity, and I was leaving it with my dignity intact, passing Martin Ferguson's father's first test of a successful political career.

41

The Hawke and Gillard legacies

At its best, the Labor Party is a formidable agent of progress, reshaping our country in ways and directions so fulsomely embraced by the Australian people that they cannot be reversed. A perusal of the nation-changing advances of the post-war period through the Hawke–Keating era confirms a proud Labor legacy: the great post-war immigration program; the early recognition of the People's Republic of China; Medicare; a successful campaign against apartheid in South Africa; joining the World Heritage Convention and nominating eight of Australia's environmental icons to the World Heritage List; protecting Antarctica from mining; creating prosperity, economic resilience, and job opportunities by fashioning Australia's open, competitive economy; establishing a national superannuation scheme; and legislating native title for indigenous Australians.

Add to these the achievements of the Rudd Labor government: an apology to the Stolen Generation, successful navigation of the Australian economy through the Global Financial Crisis, and paid parental leave. As Rudd's deputy, Julia Gillard legislated a national, fair, and flexible industrial relations system and a national school curriculum, putting an end to a century of separate, inconsistent state-based systems for both. By uncapping the number of university places and creating special incentives to admit young people from disadvantaged backgrounds, Julia improved access to university education for the underprivileged — a goal that has eluded every Labor government since Whitlam's.

Among Liberal-National Coalition achievements, Malcolm Fraser's humane treatment of asylum-seekers from Vietnam helped define our nation, and John Howard's gun-control laws rank as a courageous and enduring gift to peace and civility. Unfortunately, more often than not, the Coalition has devoted its energies to trying to dismantle or undermine Labor reforms, including Medicare, superannuation for working people, and carbon emissions trading. Coalition governments have undertaken budget-repair work from time to time, but at other times have engaged in extravagant spending and fiscally irresponsible tax cuts. Labor governments have spent too much at times, but the Hawke and Gillard governments have also been responsible for the biggest cuts in government spending in Australia's post-war history.

Revisionist history credits the Howard-led Coalition with supporting the Hawke–Keating economic-reform program. At best, this is a half-truth. While Howard backed the tariff reductions and freeing up the financial system, he opposed Labor's 1985 fair and efficient tax-reform package, which introduced a capital-gains tax and a fringe-benefits tax. He opposed superannuation for working people. And he opposed the Petroleum Resource Rent Tax. Howard, too, opposed Medicare. Nevertheless, Howard was more supportive of the Hawke–Keating reform program than Labor in opposition ever was of the Howard government's more sensible reforms.

AS A POLICY ADVISER to Bob Hawke and a cabinet minister in the Gillard government, perhaps I am well placed to reflect on their legacies and on how the task of governing Australia has changed over the last several decades. Some commentators who lived through the Hawke–Keating era — and many who did not — look back on those times with misty-eyed sentimentality.

In truth, governing in the 1980s was hard, grinding work, a constant struggle against an often hostile media. Business organisations did not support tax reform. Opposition to tariff cuts from within the business community was strong. Some trade unions fought most of the reforms, but, under the strong leadership and advocacy of Bill Kelty, the union movement usually acquiesced in the end. The voting public was not on board for financial deregulation, tariff cuts, or privatisation. Within the caucus, much of the reform program was heavily contested, most particularly from the Socialist Left. Hawke, they complained, was too close to big business. Leading lights in the national left such as Bill Hartley, Norm Gallagher, and John Halfpenny despised Hawke. Much of the Socialist Left was opposed to the alliance with the United States.

Hawke's greatest strength was in dealing with these internal tensions and external opponents by running a strong cabinet government. As a young idealist, I was impatient about getting decisions made. After all, Bob was the prime minister, so I wondered why didn't he just tell his cabinet colleagues what he wanted, and expect them to fall into line. But he did the opposite. When an agenda item came up in cabinet, Bob usually expressed no view at the outset, instead inviting the relevant minister to speak to the submission. If colleagues did not agree with the recommendations, full and open debate ensued, arguments going back and forth, with the minister responding to concerns raised until the talking was done. In the course of the debate, ministers often referred to the coordination comments contained in the submissions prepared by their own departments, or even those of other departments. Public-service advice was taken very seriously.

It was not unusual for a cabinet debate to raise new issues or to lead to questions that remained unresolved. When this happened, Bob adjourned consideration of the contentious item, pending the commissioning of further work or analysis from the public service. Cabinet consideration of some of the most hotly contested issues, such as the environment and media ownership, ranged over several meetings.

A typical cabinet meeting lasted at least four hours, and many lasted much longer. And meetings of the Expenditure Review Committee of cabinet seemed endless. Pre-emptive leaks occurred from time to time, but rarely achieved their purpose. Through these exhaustive processes, a great deal of cabinet solidarity was achieved over most of the Hawke years. All cabinet ministers were encouraged to have their say, and, in a real sense, they owned the outcome, even if their view did not prevail.

Having praised the Hawke cabinet processes, I should acknowledge that there were several significant occasions on which they were not followed: Bob's announcement of a tax summit during the 1984 election campaign; his decision after the Tiananmen Square massacre that all Chinese students in Australia could stay; his Jervis Bay decision; his proposed compact with Indigenous Australians; and Australia's decision to join the first war with Iraq. As is inevitable, circumstances also arose from time to time requiring submissions to be prepared hastily and considered without full input from relevant departments. But, for the most part, proper cabinet processes were observed throughout Hawke's prime ministership.

Essentially, there was little difference between the Hawke and Gillard cabinet processes with regard to the preparation, lodgement, and consideration of submissions. The cabinet committee processes were also similar. They could last longer than the cabinet meetings. The productivity committee of cabinet, which I chaired towards the end of my time as a minister, did serious policy work, as did the special cabinet committee on the Asian Century White Paper, which brought together relevant ministers, officials, business leaders, and academics to oversee the document's preparation. Julia Gillard's cabinet meetings were, however, quite different from Hawke's. They didn't last as long; ministers spoke to their submissions; and colleagues stated their positions, where they had them, but there was not a lot of argument to and fro. Mostly the cabinet processes worked, in stark contrast to the shambolic Rudd processes. Julia restored proper cabinet processes that, like any other, were not perfect, but were generally effective.

As with the Hawke cabinets, on several occasions cabinet positions were determined by a small group of relevant ministers before the cabinet meeting, but some of these were overturned or modified by the full cabinet. Inadvertently, I triggered one such case. Ahead of a cabinet meeting, I had been walking from the office of one of my advisers to another when former foreign minister Gareth Evans strolled past the open doorway of my ministerial suite. I assume he had been to the office of the foreign minister, Bob Carr, which was about 40 metres along the corridor from mine. Gareth saw me through the doorway and asked if he could speak to me for a moment. We stood in my open office, where Gareth explained that the cabinet meeting that was about to start would determine Australia's position on a United Nations resolution involving Israel and the Palestinian people. The resolution was to grant observer status at the UN to the Palestinian people. The United States and Israel opposed it, and the Americans expected Australia would, too.

Gareth informed me that Julia would recommend Australia vote against the resolution, rather than simply abstaining from the vote.

While in Israel with Bob in 1987, I had viewed from a lookout the West Bank of the Jordan River on which the Israelis were building settlements, making peace harder to achieve. Now the Netanyahu government was stepping up the expansion of settlements. My view was that opposing the resolution would send a signal to Israel that Australia condoned the settlement policy at the expense of a lasting peace with the Palestinians.

The item had not been listed on the cabinet agenda, and there was no documentation. Julia introduced the item, advising cabinet that she had determined that the government would oppose the resolution outright rather than, as many other countries signalled they would do, abstain. As Julia finished her remarks, I recalled Paul Keating saying to me many years earlier that one of his cabinet colleagues had failed to discharge his responsibility to the portfolio to which he had been sworn. Keating's criticism of his colleague reminded me of the high office that I occupied and for which I was being well paid. I said to myself: *Craig, you've got a responsibility to speak up.*

I sought the call from Julia. I said it was the prerogative of the prime minister to make a call from time to time, that I accepted Julia's decision, and that I would advocate it publicly. But I added that, while the resolution had nothing to do with the West Bank, the decision would be interpreted as condoning the Israeli settlements.

I hadn't anticipated that other colleagues would follow. One after another, they spoke against opposing the resolution and in favour of abstaining. Only a couple spoke in support of Julia's position. Julia noted the view in the room, advising us that she would consider the matter overnight ahead of the next morning's caucus meeting. By morning, she had reversed her position, telling caucus that her recommendation was that Australia should abstain.

So how does the Gillard government compare with the Hawke government? Most historians and commentators would expect me to come down clearly in favour of the Hawke government—a great reforming government, and the best peacetime government Australia has ever had. I do. But the Hawke government ruled for almost nine years, with a healthy working majority in each of the four parliamentary terms it spanned. For most of those years, the government was free of internal destabilisation.

The Gillard government was in a minority in both houses, after Julia had been destabilised throughout the 2010 election campaign. This depressed the Labor vote, almost costing it government. Julia then worked hard and successfully to form a government with the support of the independents, Rob Oakeshott, Tony Windsor, and Andrew Wilkie. For most of its time in office, her government continued to be destabilised from within. As Julia and her colleagues dealt with internal instability, a thuggish Abbott-led opposition, and a hostile media, she met ahead of every parliamentary sitting week with Oakeshott and Windsor to negotiate the passage of legislation that inevitably would be opposed by Abbott's Coalition.

Yet, as prime minister for just three years, Julia successfully pursued an impressive suite of pioneering Labor policies. Through her negotiating skills—and those of Greg Combet—Julia achieved the passage through the parliament of a carbon emissions trading scheme. She also gained the passage of a National Disability Insurance Scheme developed by Bill Shorten and Jenny Macklin, this time with Coalition support. With Julia's full support, environment minister Tony Burke brokered the Murray-Darling Basin Plan designed to return the ecological system to health, 23 years after the launch of the Hawke government's environment statement on the banks of the Murray River. Julia established a royal commission into child sexual abuse. Her government's introduction of the plain packaging of tobacco products, led by health minister Nicola Roxon and now being replicated by countries such as Britain, France, and New Zealand, will be an enduring public-health reform. Julia commissioned a leading businessman, David Gonski, to develop a proposal to improve education opportunities for disadvantaged school students, securing its passage through the Senate just hours before she lost the leadership.

In the tradition of Whitlam and Hawke, Julia secured a strategic leadership partnership with China that very few Western nations have been able to achieve. The partnership provides for annual leaders' meetings between the two countries, supported by meetings of economic ministers. The relationship with China and the rest of the region was also strengthened by the White Paper on Australia in the Asian Century.

Add to these landmark achievements the national industrial

relations system and the national school curriculum that Julia achieved as deputy prime minister, and you have a list of progressive reforms that would make any Labor government proud and that are changing Australia for the better. Some of these — the emissions trading scheme, the needs-based school-funding system, and the Asian Century White Paper — have faced temporary reversals at the hands of subsequent Coalition governments. But sooner or later they will be revived, just as Labor policies on Medicare and compulsory superannuation were revived. It's hard to keep a good idea down.

Given only one-third of the time in office, the Gillard government was the equal of the Hawke government in implementing nation-defining policies. Governing in the modern era is hard, but the foes confronting the Gillard government were many and formidable. For her courage and determination to proceed with highly controversial progressive policies, Julia deserved support, not subversion. But that was not her fate, owing to the manner of her coming to the prime ministership, the challenge of minority government, and her pioneering role as Australia's first female prime minister. For me personally, it was a rare honour to serve as a cabinet minister and trusted member of her government.

When I asked Bob Hawke to review the manuscript for this book, he had no quibbles, telling me he enjoyed it. He asked for nothing to be removed. His final statement to me about my reflections in the manuscript was: 'History will treat Julia's prime ministership well.'

42

From both sides now

Since leaving politics, I have assembled a portfolio of activities: as the head of an economic-advisory business, an academic, a financial newspaper columnist, a television commentator, and as president of the Australia China Business Council of New South Wales. As managing director of Craig Emerson Economics Pty Ltd, I have been able to secure long-term engagements with a number of major businesses and with the global advisory firm KPMG. This has allowed me to continue a fabulous association and friendship with Jennilyn Mann, my tolerant and resilient executive assistant and personal life fixer-upperer of 18 years.

At the suggestion of the then editor-in-chief of *The Australian* newspaper, Chris Mitchell, I co-convened a National Reform Summit in August 2015, bringing together major business organisations, the trade union movement, and community service organisations in search of common ground on national economic and social policy. The summit was a reaction to the torpor in Canberra under Tony Abbott's prime ministership, the political well having been poisoned by years of partisan acrimony and bitterness.

While the Turnbull government initially showed a lot of interest in the national reform summit and the consensus model of government, the parliament has become even more rancorous, and the government and the trade union movement are at war. The Australian people are perplexed and dismayed at major parties seemingly preferring to fight each other instead of representing them and their interests.

Worse, the federal parliament has entered an era of transactional politics where political parties seek and gain the support of vested interests at the expense of the national interest. The mining industry wanted the removal of the Minerals Resource Rent Tax before the generous depreciation allowances that Labor had granted it had been exhausted, when they would have been liable for substantial amounts of tax. The Abbott government obliged.

While giving lip service to the need for Australia to reduce carbon emissions, business organisations wanted the Gillard government's emissions trading scheme scrapped. They succeeded. The Abbott government replaced it with an expensive system of subsidies to selected businesses to reduce their emissions, which the prime minister's chief scientist advised was incapable of achieving the emissions-reductions targets to which it had agreed at the Paris climate-change conference in 2015.

Succumbing to pressure from the hard right of his party, Prime Minister Malcolm Turnbull ruled out moving to a market-based system for emissions reductions, despite personally supporting it.

Australia's main business organisations gave, at best, lukewarm support to the needs-based school-funding system devised by David Gonski. They supported the Turnbull government's policy of cutting back on its funding to allow for a cut in the company tax rate for multinational corporations. In May 2017, the Turnbull government announced a revised needs-based funding model, involving less funding for disadvantaged students than the Gillard scheme, but at least taking money from the wealthiest non-government schools. Instead of voting in the revised scheme, so it could top up the funding in government, Labor opposed it.

The housing industry sought and obtained the Turnbull government's opposition to Labor's policy of limiting tax deductions for investments in rental accommodation, warning on its Liberal Party website that 'Labor's housing tax' would deliver 'lower home values'. Brazenly, after the 2016 election, the Turnbull government complained to the states that they were not doing enough to bring house prices down for first-home buyers.

Young people tell me that the system isn't working for them. They are right.

The Labor Party's challenge is to stick to its ideals and convert them into progressive policies while maintaining budgetary discipline. Allowing government debt to accumulate and expecting future generations to pay for today's living standards is no fairer than expecting the poor to bear the brunt of present-day spending cuts.

On the Coalition side, it is not immediately obvious what their ideals are. The Coalition presents itself as the party of low taxes and small government, yet the present government is the second-highest taxing government in Australia's history, trailing only the Howard government. The Coalition seems more energised about protecting the existing order, in which the wealthy prosper and the disadvantaged remain trapped in a cycle of despair and violence. One reason for this indifference appears to be that the most senior members of the parliamentary Liberal Party represent electorates whose residents are very wealthy. Neither their pre-parliamentary experiences nor their present representative work as local MPs have exposed them to the lives and localities of the underprivileged. Most of the Nationals, in contrast, represent constituencies in poor country towns. They have a better understanding of hardship than their Liberal partners.

In the middle of 2016, I travelled to the central coast of New South Wales to attend a farewell of one of my five classmates at St John's Convent School at Baradine, who was dying of leukaemia. I arranged with a fellow classmate, Tony Purdy, to pick me up at Hornsby, in Sydney's north, on his way up from Canberra. I made my way to Hornsby by train from Sydney's Central Station. As it happens, the three suburban stops before Hornsby all start with a 'W': Warrawee, Wahroonga, and Waitara. As the train passed through them, I was struck by the streets lined with trees, expensive houses, and parks. Socially, these seemed to be self-contained communities, worlds apart from Sydney's struggling outer-western suburbs.

It occurred to me that the children living in the three 'W' suburbs would rarely, if ever, come into contact with the children of western suburbs such as Auburn, Fairfield, Cabramatta, Mount Druitt, and Macquarie Fields. They would play sport against kids in other wealthy suburbs, and have no reason to travel to the west. Who could blame them for coming to develop a view as adults that their parents and they worked hard and took risks, only to be obliged to pay taxes to support whole communities of poorly motivated 'no-hopers' and 'bogans?' It's the only view they have ever had from the vantage point of their leafy suburbs. Expecting them to empathise with people they have never met, who live in places they have never visited, is fanciful. The three 'Ws' and other affluent suburbs are the breeding grounds of federal Liberal members of parliament, cocooned from the material hardship, dysfunction, and violence that afflict poor communities. It is understandable that their parliamentary representatives are likely to be motivated to preserve the status quo in their own communities.

Changing the worldview of the sons and daughters of the privileged is next to impossible. Perhaps the only way is to appeal to their self-interest. Continuing to deny disadvantaged children a quality education will only lead to more violence and more crime. The three 'Ws' and similar suburbs will become gated communities, divided by fences—physical and virtual—from poor localities. It is surprising that jihadists have not been more successful in radicalising teenage boys and young men living in poor Muslim communities in our country. Most of those who have come to the attention of the authorities are not immigrants; they were born in Australia. But the message they receive every day is that they are undervalued members of the Australian community, that they belong to a lower class, and that this is their destiny. Confronted with these judgements, it is not beyond comprehension that some of these young males would join street gangs where they are welcomed as equals and encouraged to participate in organised crime, coming to see the jihadists' calling as both credible and appealing.

Australia's security agencies clearly do a good job at identifying these breeding grounds and learning about young people who are targeted for radicalisation. The agencies also appear to advise politicians to refrain from provocative, divisive phrases such as 'Whose side are you on?'—especially when this appears to be done for political gain rather than for any legitimate, higher purpose. Effective investment in education and family support in disadvantaged communities is expensive, and it would require contributions to taxation revenue from successful people living in affluent communities across Australia. But if the assessment is made that this is too costly, we should anticipate more violence and more terrorist incidents in city centres and other public places.

Despite its faults, and notwithstanding my biases, Labor, among the mainstream political parties, has undoubtedly evolved further to meet the challenges of modern politics than have the Coalition parties. In most European countries, there are two mainstream political parties—a centre-left and a centre-right party—plus two alternatives—a hard-left and a hard-right party. Labor's hard left has peeled off to join the Australian Greens. In regional Australia, the Coalition is under siege from racist, bigoted nationalist parties such as One Nation and Rise Up Australia. The Coalition's own hard right has more in common with these splinter parties than with the traditional centrist Liberal and National Parties. Consider former Liberal Party leading lights such as John Howard and Peter Costello. In their heyday, they were members or supporters of the 'New Right', a group of economically dry, socially conservative Liberals. In the modern Liberal Party, Howard and Costello would be regarded as moderates, and its leader, Malcolm Turnbull, as a left-winger.

As nationalism continues to grow in the West in response to economic insecurity and Islamic terrorism, besieged Liberals and National MPs will be dragged further towards the hard right, just as inner-city Labor MPs are constantly under pressure from the hard left of the Australian Greens. It seems only a matter of time before the hard right of the Liberal and National Parties will split and join forces with nationalist right parties, especially while they are led by a prime minister whom they consider to be more Labor than Liberal.

Middle-grounders in the Australian community are searching for a leader of a stable, mainstream party who has a clear view of where to take the country. They want public safety, a strong economy, and a fair society with a sound social safety net, and an opportunity for all to have a go, work hard, and prosper. These voters do not seek to run the country; they reckon politicians are paid well enough to do that. Rather, they are happy to delegate the responsibility to a leader and a political party with the national interest at heart and a vision for the future. Consequently, they do not expect to agree with every government policy. They will tolerate policies that are against their own instincts—just as they tolerated the Hawke–Keating tariff reductions and financial-market deregulation—as long as their leaders are confident that those policies are right for the country.

43

Getting back to the garden

At this point in a book, you're supposed to reflect on your achievements and failings, nominating how you would behave differently if you had your time over. But in the words of a worldly philosopher: 'It is what it is.' That is not to say I have no regrets. I have many—all of them about how I have hurt beautiful women who loved me and placed their trust in me. But I won't be given my time again. My overwhelming sense of my life's journey is how amazingly fortunate I have been: how blessed to be the father of three fantastic young people, Ben, Tom, and Laura, who light up my life and Cathy's life every day.

We are all miracles, the recipients of the wondrous gift of life. Our chances of ever being born are minuscule, a percentage so small that our minds cannot imagine it. In my own case, I needed to rely on the rise of Adolf Hitler in Germany, the outbreak of World War II, my father being shot through the leg and taken as a prisoner of war from a hospital on Crete, Italy capitulating to the Allies, and this particular Australian prisoner being transferred to Germany and receiving a pen-pal letter from a Welsh nurse in a London hospital addressed simply 'Dear P.O.W.' I needed the war to end, the romance to flourish, the Welsh nurse to migrate to Australia and set up house in a small country town, and for her and her pen pal to have sex, where my chance of being born was one in many million.

During my career, I have personally known seven Australian prime ministers, one of them the godfather of our eldest child. I have met four American presidents and two Chinese presidents. I have conversed with other world leaders such as Rajiv Gandhi, Margaret Thatcher, Helmut Kohl before the Berlin Wall came down, and Angela Merkel after it did. And I have represented my country at a meeting of world leaders. If this account sounds like big-noting, it is. But its main purpose is to convey a message to young people who, like me, might have had a difficult childhood and grown up with low self-confidence as a result: you are at least as good as anyone else, and you are as capable as more privileged children of having an extraordinary life. You are talented. You are creative. You are one of nature's beautiful flowers who only needs nurturing through an inspiring parent, a teacher, or a friend.

If you are young, without a lot of self-confidence, and you are reading this, I want to share a story with you. As I was sending rough drafts of this book to my friend from the Hawke years, Geoff Walsh, he told me that when he was at school, he looked up to the really clever people making news, and thought he could never be as clever as they were. He graduated from school and went to university, where he expected to meet the really clever people. He met many fellow students, and befriended some of them. But they were just like he was. He talked about one day meeting the really clever people running big businesses and running the country. After graduating from university, he began meeting businesspeople and politicians. Still he looked forward to meeting the really clever people. Eventually, he met the best, the cleverest — people like Bob Hawke and Paul Keating. Yes, he thought, they were clever. But they weren't so much cleverer than he was. That was when he realised he must have been one of the really clever people, too — just a bloke from a humble background who studied hard, worked hard, and succeeded.

When Geoff told me this story, I was astonished, since my experience was exactly the same. When I left Baradine and enrolled at St Patrick's College, Strathfield, moving from a class of 14 to one of more than 100 raucous, self-confident city students, I wondered how I could possibly compete. Although I came dux at Baradine Central, I always thought my classmates were cleverer than me in so many ways. At St Pat's, I did well enough to gain entry to economics at Sydney University. There, in a class of 300 undergraduates, I met smart people from all around the state and beyond. To my great surprise, I was placed 30th at the end of my first year of Economics. My confidence began to grow. At the end of my second year, I was ranked sixth, and fourth after the third year. I couldn't believe it. The lecturers encouraged me to do Honours. My thirteen Honours-year classmates were seriously smart people. Again, I came fourth.

As a 23-year-old at the United Nations, I soon realised I was more highly trained than most of my much older colleagues. After two years in Bangkok, I was encouraged by two professors, Warren Hogan and Ross Garnaut, to do a doctorate. Then I was off to advise a cabinet minister on how the government could implement my PhD thesis, and then on to prime minister Bob Hawke's office as an economic and environmental adviser. Then came stints as the director-general of a state environment department, the CEO of a transit authority, and, finally, a member of parliament and a cabinet minister. All this came my way as a result of gaining a little extra confidence and a desire to achieve excellence. Like Geoff Walsh, I realised that I was now one of the so-called smart people, but in reality no smarter than the thousands of young people with whom I had shared classrooms when I was growing up.

Travelling along my pathway through life, I have never deviated far from the natural world I first experienced as a boy living in Baradine. When I go jogging, I say hello to the possums and lizards, and to the birds calling to each other in the trees. Animals make sounds beyond our audible range, and speak in languages we generally take no interest in understanding. Flowers flaunt their glorious colours, smells, and shapes in a display for the insects they hope to attract as carriers of their pollen for the great endeavour of propagation. As this grand symphony and brilliant display bursts around us, it invites us to join in: birds responding to our whistles and tweets, animals to our calls and embraces, plants and flowers to our tending and nurturing. If we hear and accept nature's invitation, we feel joy and find fulfilment, engendering a richer sense of sharing with the natural world and with each other.

Every day, humans admire their mastery of the natural world. Yet it is an illusion. Environmentalists warn that humankind will destroy the natural world if it does not change its ways. Their fears are unfounded. Through the ages, species have been destroyed, sea levels have risen and fallen many metres, deserts have replaced vegetation, and rainforests have grown in place of arid lands, but still the earth makes its way through the galaxy along the same trajectory. Humankind — not the planet — will be the victim of its own hostility towards nature, as settlements are displaced and the lands they once occupied are retaken by nature. Steel will rust, concrete skyscrapers will crumble and fall, and freeways will be broken up by the unyielding intrusion of weeds and vines. As human settlements move to more inhabitable regions, other species will be made extinct — an obnoxious imposition on nature. Though the natural world will survive, humankind, as we know it, might not. Only when we come to admire and respect the natural world will we be a truly high civilisation.

Progress in human society can be assessed by the way it treats other animals. A human who is cruel to animals cannot be compassionate to fellow humans. Cruelty is cruelty. We treat high-order animals such as pigs abominably, accepting their tissue as organs in our own bodies, but binding mothers into sow stalls where they can barely move. Cultured meat, grown from animal cells, could potentially replace living animals as meat sources, avoiding the ethical problems associated with the slaughter of animals for human consumption. It could also enormously reduce the amount of agricultural land needed to support the raising of domesticated animals and the growing of plant food for them, enabling much of that land to be returned to nature.

In a better, more beautiful world, we would feel empathy towards those who have suffered or fallen on hard times, and refrain from making judgements about their worth to society. It is not for us to judge, but to offer comfort and support. Throughout the course of civilisation, societies have developed class systems, with those at the top ruling over those at the bottom. Democratisation, often achieved through revolution, helped weaken the class structures, but did not remove them. Classless societies do not exist. In practice, communism created a new elite, while Western democracies involve systems of preferment in which wealth begets wealth, and welfare dependency is intergenerational. Elitists point to exceptions of young people who break out of the cycle of welfare dependency, as if to prove a false rule that anyone can succeed, and to brand those who do not break free from their misfortune in the lottery of birth as having freely chosen to remain a drag on society.

Education is the key that unlocks two doors: one to greater prosperity, and the other to a fairer society. But families who have been dependent on welfare payments for generations often lack confidence and self-esteem. Improving attitudes towards and access to quality education for the underprivileged is an enormous task—far too big for an unsympathetic elite. All the objective evidence points to there being no systematic difference in intelligence among infants of different ethnicities and socio-economic conditions, yet the children of the rich typically outperform disadvantaged children at school. Programs tailored to the circumstances of individual schools in disadvantaged communities and to the specific needs of individual students, while expensive, have proven effective. Dedicated funding, and the training of specialist teachers to improve the educational performance of disadvantaged children, are essential to achieving a compassionate society.

As a society, we remain disgracefully tolerant towards domestic violence and child abuse, as long as it goes on behind closed doors. Children in violent and abusive homes have no defence; they are totally at the mercy of their abusers. We can never call ourselves members of a civilised society while we show tolerance towards the abuse of children.

So, that's about it from me. I'm taking Joni Mitchell's advice: we are stardust, we are golden, billion-year-old carbon, and we've got to get ourselves back to the garden. I'd rather not degenerate into carbon just yet, but getting back to the garden has a lot of appeal.

The youngest of our children, Laura, saw the least of me as I tried to juggle my responsibilities as a local member of parliament and Australia's minister for trade. As a father, I was probably not there for Laura as she was growing up as much as I was for Ben and Tom. This is a matter of great guilt and sadness for me. I partially made amends through pledging to leave parliament at the 2013 election and spending a month with her travelling through the great cities of Europe. Laura and I are learning more about each other as she, while studying linguistics at the Australian National University, moves through her early twenties and I journey through my early sixties. Laura is displaying wonderful acting and, yes, singing ability in her performing and directing roles in various revues at the university. My gorgeous brown-eyed girl is a talented young woman, and will flourish in whatever she chooses to do.

Ben has gained a Bachelor of Philosophy degree with first-class honours from the Australian National University. Our second son, Tom, dux of his year at St Edmund's College, Canberra, has done the same. Both received their degrees from the university's chancellor, Gareth Evans—Australia's best foreign minister. Ben and Tom worked in my business while completing their studies, Tom providing technical support and editorial comments on the manuscript for this book, and Ben researching literature for consultancy reports, and developing a computer model of mining-taxation options in a report we prepared for the government of Papua New Guinea. They are carving out different and rewarding careers, living with their partners in my Canberra house.

Tom has a Kelpie named Billie. Every morning when Tom wakes up, he takes Billie for a walk. Every day, Billie behaves as if she is the luckiest dog on earth. I try to be like Billie. Every day is a gift to me, a winner in the lottery of life. In my most recent decade, I have had the love and joy of sharing my life with Tracey, a feisty, opinionated woman who wisely tolerates none of my obsessions—beyond barracking for the Mighty Bulldogs. As a bush girl, Tracey seems to understand that the sad little boy lives within me still and always will. Yet every day I look back with amazement at the rich life of a boy from Baradine who overcame adversity and, in his own way, made a difference. I could not have done this without the love and support of fine women—my first wife; Cathy; Julia; and Tracey—or of a struggling Welsh nurse and a timid Australian POW who sent her love letters from a hostile country. Thank you, and bless you, Mum and Dad.

Acknowledgements

As I first assembled a lifelong collection of notes into a rough draft of a coherent story, I received invaluable comments — and welcome encouragement — from Greg Combet, Geoff Walsh, Geoff Kitney, and Robert Hoge.

When the redrafting and reorganisation continued, Blanche D'Alpuget and Julia Gillard provided wise counsel.

Henry Rosenbloom delighted me with his verdict on the initial manuscript, assuring me that my story was worth telling, and that Scribe would publish it. He and his editorial team helped pull and push the manuscript into shape, and Laura Thomas designed the book's cover.

My son Tom read and edited so many drafts of the manuscript that I'm sure he feels he accompanied me on my life's journey well before he was born.

In an ex-politician's memoirs it is impossible to mention the contribution of numerous staff members spanning a long career. Here I take the opportunity to thank them all, including Kerri Alexander, Lynne Ashpole, Rachel Cameron, Ana Centilmen, Alexandra Craig, Stewart Dalley, Nikki Gordon-Smith, Patrick Hanlon, Hugh Hartigan, Julie Holden, Sarah Kleinschmidt, Teresa Lane, Matthew Lobb, Jennilyn Mann, Helen Marriott, Samantha Miles, Mark Mulligan, Alyssa Horgan, Simon Newnham, Hayley Pennock, Paul Scully, Tom Skladzien, Eve Smith, Mark Tavener, Kathy Temple, Elisa Thompson, Marcus Walsh, Chris Ward, and the late Don Wilkie.

Index